Light From the East

Authors and Themes in Orthodox Theology

Aidan Nichols, O.P.

Light From the East

Authors and Themes in Orthodox Theology

Sheed & Ward
London

Copyright © 1995 by Aidan Nichols. First published 1995, this edition 1999. ISBN 0 7220 5081 3. All rights reserved. Typeset by Waveney Typesetters, Norwich. Printed and bound in Great Britain for Sheed & Ward Ltd, 14 Coopers Row, London EC3N 2BH by Biddles Ltd, Guildford and King's Lynn.

Contents

		Page
	PREFACE	vi
I	Introduction	1
II	Vladimir Lossky and Apophaticism	21
III	John Meyendorff and neo-Palamism	41
IV	Sergei Bulgakov and Sophiology	57
V	John Romanides and neo-Photianism	74
VI	Panagiotis Trembelas and Orthodox Christology	91
VII	Nikolai Afanas'ev and Ecclesiology	114
VIII	George Florovsky and the Idea of Tradition	129
IX	Alexander Schmemann and Liturgical Theology	146
X	Panagiotis Nellas and Anthropology	170
XI	Christos Yannaras and Theological Ethics	181
XII	Paul Evdokimov and Eschatology	194
	CONCLUSION	205
	NOTES	206
	FURTHER READING	229
	INDEX	231

Preface

I have been greatly helped in my own Christian life, and reflection on that life, by the treasures to be found in the dogmatic theology of the Eastern Orthodox Church during the last hundred years.

It is in the hope of sharing those treasures more widely that I have written this book. Its title translates Abbot William of St Thierry's phrase *orientale lumen* as found in his *Golden Epistle*: its wider bearings are charted in P. McNulty and B. Hamilton, *Orientale lumen et magistra latinitas: Greek Influences on Western Monasticism, 900–1100* (Chevetogne 1963). The cover image is from a fresco of the Transfiguration of Christ (a favoured theme of modern Orthodox iconography and writing) in the Refectory of the Pontifical Russian College, Rome, to whom grateful acknowledgment is here made.

Blackfriars, Cambridge
Feast of St Catherine of Siena, 1994.

I
Introduction

My hope is that this book will achieve two things. In the first place, it will identify a variety of dogmatic issues, problems or ideas, raised or discussed by Eastern Orthodox theologians but of equal importance to Catholic theology as well. In other words, we shall be encountering dogmatic themes and ideas which *either* can be integrated into Catholic theology – to be, so to speak, 'repatriated' in the Catholic tradition, which is their proper home, *or* which, conversely, may stimulate from the Catholic side a critical response – a critical response that itself may help Catholic dogmatics to discover its own mind on various issues. In this sense, I am writing as a dogmatic theologian committed to the Catholic Church.

But in the second place, the aim of this book is to discover, through looking at the work of modern Orthodox dogmaticians, the character of the Eastern Orthodox tradition itself. And in this sense, as written by a Roman Catholic, this study is, rather, a contribution to ecumenics, the understanding, by a member of one confession, of the tradition of another.

In principle, an introduction to Eastern Orthodoxy might take any one of a number of forms. For instance, it could be an introduction to the *history* of the Eastern Orthodox Church. It might be argued that the present state of a community can only be explained by its past. To understand the Orthodox Church is to understand how it has become what it is. The religious awareness of the Orthodox is, certainly, very largely a matter of memory. In reading the New Testament, in reciting the Creed, they remember the story of their Church, the apostolic and patristic Church, the Church which never ceased to speak of Jesus Christ in the Greek language used by the Gospels themselves. In this way, Church history can be a privileged means of access to the inner truth of a Christian confession. As for an individual so for a Church, your history makes you what you are. An example of an introduction of this kind would be the late Alexander Schmemann's *The Historical Road of Eastern Orthodoxy*[1] – a book conceived precisely as an introduction to the Orthodox Church for the general reader, as its preface tells us.

This approach has definite strengths, some of which I have indicated; but it also has serious weaknesses. The Church historian is not in a good position to comment on the specifically theological dimension of a Church – the distinctive ideas or principles which govern its way of looking at the Christian faith. At best, the historian of doctrine may chronicle for us how and when specially Eastern Orthodox emphases in Christian thought came forward. But he is not well placed to evaluate their lasting significance. This, as he recognises, is the proper task of the theologian.

Let us turn then to a second possibility. This would be to concentrate on the lived experience of the Orthodox Church today as a believing community. The Orthodox Church as it appears on the ground, in its parishes, monasteries, dioceses. Here the aim would be to abstract both from history and from theology, and to concentrate instead on the human reality of the Church, in a quasi-sociological perspective. This is the approach found in Mario Rinvolucri's study, *Anatomy of a Church*.[2] Rinvolucri concentrates on the Church of Greece, but looks at it, in effect, as the classic example of Orthodoxy as a whole. The strength of this approach is the fact that it is highly concrete. It gives us a very good impression of what it feels like to live within the organisational and liturgical framework of the Orthodox Church. But can a Christian tradition be described without doing justice to the doctrinal vision that tradition has produced? To understand Orthodoxy we need to understand its dogmatic structure as that is reflected in the writings of its theologians.

A third possibility might be an amalgam of the approaches I have suggested so far. This would be a combination of the historical approach, as in Schmemann, with the sociological approach as in Rinvolucri, spiced with a dash of the theological approach, which is the perspective from which I have been criticising these two authors. An example of such an amalgam approach would be Timothy Ware's best-seller *The Orthodox Church*[3] or John Meyendorff's book, with the same title, published in translation at London the year before.[4]

With Ware, now Bishop Kallistos of Diokleia, we have a bit of everything and therefore, perhaps, the best of all possible worlds. His book is divided into two sections – an historical first half, and a second half consisting of a summary of present day Orthodox teaching along with thumb-nail sketches of the various local churches which make up the Orthodox family of communion. Since this is clearly the fullest approach, surely it is also the most satisfactory?

Probably it is. Nevertheless, I am not going to adopt it here. For one thing, if I did so, I would be in danger of simply reproducing Bishop Kallistos Ware's book. Certainly, I could not write a better one. For another thing, I would have to repeat too much of the material already offered in my earlier book, *Rome and the Eastern Churches*.[5] And thirdly, the approach I am proposing has the merit of being somewhat original in the sense, at least, that so far as I am aware, no alternative book (in English) is available which adopts it in a systematic way.[6]

The approach found here, then, is to concentrate on contemporary Eastern Orthodox theology, arranged in terms of major individual figures and the great themes with which they have been especially associated, and seen as a reflection of the distinctive mind of the Orthodox Church today. In this, I cannot altogether rule out references to Church history since Orthodoxy is a deeply traditional Church, for which continuity with tradition is supremely important. Nor can I rule out what might broadly be called sociological references, references to the way theological ideas are put into practice or not, in the Orthodox Church today.

Nevertheless, the centre of interest will be theological, and contemporary theological at that. 'Contemporary' here will mean, by and large, the theological writing of *twentieth century* Orthodox thinkers.

What is Orthodoxy?

My next task is to state what the Eastern Orthodox Church is. This may seem so obvious as not to be worth doing. However, any one who has ever looked at the origins of the Eastern schisms will be aware of a real problem of definition and demarcation. The historic Oriental churches fall into three groups of which the smallest is a group consisting of one: the Nestorian or Assyrian Church, which usually refers to itself as the Catholicate of the East. This is the body which broke away from the Great Church at the Council of Ephesus in 431. This book will not be concerned with the Nestorians, nor could it be, since they have produced no theology in this century or for several centuries. Secondly, there is the much more considerable group of churches formerly called Monophysite and now more courteously referred to as the Oriental Orthodox or, alternatively, the non-Chalcedonian Orthodox. As the latter title implies, these are the successor churches of the people who broke with the Great Church at the Council of Chalcedon in 451. This book will not be concerned with the Oriental Orthodox, though it could be, as several of these Churches have a vigorous theological life, notably the Syrian Orthodox in India and, at least until the revolution that overthrew the Abyssinian monarchy, the Church of Ethiopia. So the book will be concerned with everyone who is left after these two ecclesial families are eliminated. Basically, what this amounts to is the ancient patriarchate of Constantinople; the vestigial remains of the patriarchates of Alexandria, Antioch and Jerusalem in their Chalcedonian forms; the Church of Cyprus, which was carved out of Antioch in 431; and then a number of national Churches created either by the missionary efforts of Constantinople, or through emigration, or through taking the law into one's own hands. Thus, the Church of Russia was created by Byzantine missionary endeavour; the Church of Finland is based on Russian emigration during the period when Finland was governed as a grand duchy under the Tsar; and the Church of Greece declared itself self-governing after the Greek War of Independence in order not to have to rely on Constantinople which remained within the Ottoman Empire.

Two things should be noted straight away. First, the Orthodox Church is not a unitary Church, but a communion of sister Churches joined by sharing the same faith and sacraments. And a second point to be noted at the outset is that the position of the patriarch of Constantinople in Orthodoxy is not fully analogous with that of the Roman pope in Catholicism – despite the former's title of 'ecumenical' or universal patriarch. The Constantinopolitan patriarch was first called ecumenical by the Byzantine emperors for reasons of their own, connected with the desire to boost the prestige of their capital city. The only Church council to ratify the title was a local Constantinopolitan synod of 586. While subsequently all Orthodox Churches have in fact ratified it implicitly by their own practice or usage, the theological and canonical weight to be given it is very much in dispute among them. It is therefore not possible to define the Eastern Orthodox Church as all those in communion with Constantinople, in the way the Catholic Church may be defined as all those in communion with Rome. As far as the Orthodox are concerned, it is perfectly possible that the Church of Constantinople could lapse from Orthodox communion tomorrow. In that case, the Church of Alexandria would become the first see in the ecclesiastical *taxis*, being the next in honour after Constantinople itself.

From this there follows an important corollary. The fact that the Orthodox Church is not a unitary Church, and has no permanent centre of communion or authority means that it is open to enormous difficulties over jurisdiction. These jurisdictional disputes can lead, and have in fact led to ruptures in eucharistic communion. Thus for instance, at the present time, the Russian Church in Exile, which originated at the Karlovtsy Synod in Serbia in 1921, is not in communion with the patriarchate of Moscow. This means that in, for example, the United States and Canada are two sets of Orthodox living side-by-side but without inter-communion, namely, those who belong to the metropolia of the Russian Church in Exile, and those who belong to the so called Orthodox Church of America which was given self-government by the Moscow patriarchate in 1970. Nevertheless, both jurisdictions are to be found in the extremely useful *Orthodox Yearbook*, published annually (obviously!) at Munich by Alexander Proc Verlag in, for successive years of a three-year cycle, English, French and German; it offers a breakdown of the various Orthodox Church families throughout the world. Temporary or local schisms are regarded by most Orthodox as a regrettable but well-nigh inevitable fact of life, and something the Church can and must take in its stride. There is some truth in the suggestion that the Orthodox regard heresy as more serious than schism, while Catholics regard schism as more serious than heresy. For the student of Orthodoxy, however, the jurisdictional confusion often reigning among the Orthodox Churches can make life very difficult.

There are generally reckoned to be fifteen self-governing Churches within the Orthodox family. The technical word is 'auto-cephalous', which means able to provide themselves with their own head. Orthodox canonists accept that the term 'auto-cephaly' is not found in the ancient Church, but argue that the reality intended by the word was very well known in the patristic period. Early Councils often refer to groups of local Churches with the right to resolve internal problems on their own authority. These are, in effect, the Churches of a given civil diocese of the Roman Empire, the later patriarchates of the Pentarchy, the five great jurisdictions: Rome, Constantinople, Alexandria, Antioch, and Jerusalem. Conciliar references also support the right of such jurisdictions to appoint their own bishops, including the chief bishop of the region. However, the concept of autocephaly in the Orthodox Church today has gone well beyond the idea of the Pentarchy. Modern Orthodox canon law holds that if a region is located in the territory of a State which is not the State of the mother Church, then a daughter Church in that region has a right to ecclesiastical independence, provided it has enough bishops to provide for the apostolic succession – that is, according to the fourth canon of Nicaea, three bishops, and provided also that the daughter Church has originated in a canonically proper way from a mother Church which was itself autocephalous.

The difference between modern Orthodoxy and the ancient Church here is quite clear. Modern Orthodoxy has accepted, not without some misgivings, the idea of the national Church, whereas in the ancient Church, autocephaly was territorially-based but not nationally-based. Technically, the present constitution of Orthodoxy as a constellation of fifteen autocephalous Churches with a few planets, the so-called 'autonomous', but in fact dependent, Churches circling around them, turns on a misunderstanding of an early canon.[7]

According to this canon, 'The bishops of every nation, every *ethnos*, must acknowledge him who is first among them.' However, as the Orthodox canonist A. A. Bogolepov has pointed out,[8] the meaning of *ethnos* here is not 'nation' in the later – above all nineteenth century – meaning of that word. The Council of Antioch of 341, an important legislative council though not of strictly dogmatic significance, explained the term *ethnos* here as meaning a Roman imperial eparchy, or province: in other words, the main sub-division of the Roman civil diocese. By 'nation' is *not* meant, as we would mean today, a group of people bound together by blood, language and custom. However, this later sense of 'nation' crept in comparatively early in the affairs of the Eastern Churches, and already in the tenth century was infecting the attitudes of newly Christianised peoples like the Bulgarians and Serbs to the authority of the patriarch of Constantinople – even though it was not until the nineteenth century Romantic Movement, and the subsequent attempt to mobilise politically an inter-related population through mass literacy, that nationalism in the modern sense really arrived on the scene.

The Orthodox Church as we have it, then, is structured by a combination of the ancient pentarchy with the mediaeval and modern notion of a national Church. The first church to be permanently formed in this way was the Church of Russia which declared independence in 1448, using as pretext acceptance of the Council of Florence by the Greek Church in 1439. With the disintegration of the Ottoman Empire in the nineteenth century, the Churches of Greece, Serbia, Bulgaria and Rumania also left the Church of Constantinople, and became self-governing. After the First World War, further grants of autocephaly were made, mainly at the expense of the Church of Russia. However, sometimes this was not full autocephaly but only what was termed 'autonomy', or limited autocephaly, where the chief bishop of a Church must be confirmed by its former mother Church. Also, grants of autocephaly were on occasion contra-verted, so that a newly autocephalous Church was obliged to return to its mother Church. Needless to say, political considera-tions were extremely important here. Thus the government of the USSR forced the Church of Poland to accept re-incorporation in the Moscow patriarchate after the Second World War. Both world wars swelled the rate of emigration from traditionally Orthodox countries and led to a new complication, the problem of the Orthodox diaspora. This was especially acute in the United States where various (European and Asian) Orthodox churches had been establishing missions, parishes and dioceses without reference to each other since the end of the eighteenth century. The organisational chaos of the North American Ortho-dox led in 1970 to the formation of a new autocephalous church, the Orthodox Church of America, from which however, the Russian Church in Exile, as mentioned, held aloof, as did the Greek communities who remain under an exarch of the Ecumeni-cal patriarch.

To find out just how many different Orthodox Churches there are, therefore, one is advised to consult the *Orthodox Yearbook* for this year! To say that is perhaps cynical, but nevertheless, the *structure* of the Orthodox Church is the greatest problem facing the Orthodox today, and not just the greatest problem facing the outside student of Orthodoxy. Basically, we can say that if the rejection of the Council of Florence marks the definitive entry of the Eastern Church into schism, then from the beginning of its separate life until the nineteenth century its own vision of itself as a unity in plurality virtually disappeared in practice. Essentially, what we have between 1450 and 1800 are two mega-Churches, the Church of Russia, protected by the Tsardom, and the Church of Constantinople, to which the Ottoman Empire gave rights of governance over all other Orthodox Christians within the Turkish Empire. The Church of Russia dominated all the Orthodox that the Tsardom could swallow, and, notoriously, Tsarist Russia was an imperialist power, an expansionist power, from Peter the Great onwards. The Church of Constantinople dominated everyone else, and with the support of the Ottoman government made and unmade the patriarchs of the other ancient sees, Alexandria, Antioch and Jerusalem. Had this situation continued throughout the nineteenth and twentieth centuries – in other words, had the political history of Europe and the Near East been different – there would only be today *two* sorts of Orthodox theology. There would be Moscow patriarchate theology, and there would be Ecumenical patriarchate theology. However, what actually happened was that both of these two great churches used political events to break up the ecclesiastical empire of the other. To begin with, in the nineteenth century, this meant the Russian Church encouraging rebellion against Constantinople. Thus it was through Russian pressure on the Ottoman Porte that Alexandria, Antioch and Jerusalem regained their independence, Jerusalem in 1845 and the other two in 1899. Similarly, it was through Russian influence that the Greeks and the other Balkan peoples won their independence both political and ecclesiastical. Thus the Church of Greece became autocephalous in 1850; Bulgaria in 1870, Serbia and Rumania in 1879. In the twentieth century, the boot was on the other foot. The Church of Constantinople took advantage of the weakness of Russia after the Bolshevik Revolution and her international isolation to hive off huge chunks of the old patriarchate of Moscow, creating autocephalous Churches in Georgia, Poland and Czechoslovakia. As I mentioned, some of this has been undone by the emergence of the Soviet Union as a world power after the Second World War. Nevertheless, it is the rivalry of Constantinople and Moscow, the Second and Third Romes, which has produced the present multiplicity of Orthodox Churches and by the same token, what interests us more, the modest plurality of Orthodox theologies in the world today.

The Geography of Modern Orthodox Theology

Where are the principal centres of Orthodox theology in the present century to be located? By 'principal centre' I mean a school of Orthodox theology with a distinctive pattern or life of its own, and a school which has actually been productive, a school whose writings are available for us to read, insofar as we know the relevant languages, or the material has been translated into languages we do know.

THE CHURCH OF GREECE   First of all, then, the Church of Greece. It is hardly surprising that Greece produces a good deal of Orthodox theology, since Greece is the only country in the world where the Orthodox Church is the officially established Church of the nation. When Greece won independence in 1821 after four centuries of Ottoman domination, the Orthodox clergy played a major part in the political and military events that led to national liberation.[9] Since then, the Greek Church has seen itself as the soul of the Greek nation,[10] though not all Greeks have agreed, notably those under the influence of Socialism (whether in its Communist or non-Communist forms) or of secularism.[11] Whereas the practice of the Orthodox faith in Greece is essentially an affair of the small towns and villages, the two main centres of Greek theology are situated in the two largest cities, Athens and Thessalonica. Greek theology in the recent past has been split very sharply between Athenian theology and Thessalonian theology.[12]

Athenian theology may be described as a kind of Orthodox Scholasticism. It is formal and propositional, and devotes a great deal of space to laying out the evidence in the Fathers or later theologians for the dogmatic teachings of the Orthodox Church. Although the way the Athenian manuals are put together can sometimes suggest a genuine theological vision, even this aspect of their layout is often borrowed from Western manuals, either Roman Catholic or Lutheran. Sometimes an Athenian theologian will specifically say that Orthodox theology today cannot do without the help of Western dogmaticians, either Latin ones or those of conservative Lutheranism. Some Orthodox would say that Athenian theology is simply Western theology of a nineteenth century or early twentieth century sort, but with Orthodox dogmatic propositions replacing Catholic or Lutheran ones.

A typical example of Athenian theology, and probably the greatest, is Panagiotis Trembelas, whose massive study of Orthodox dogmatics[13] would compare in aim and structure with the German Catholic dogmatician Ludwig Ott's 'Fundamentals of Catholic Dogma'.[14] Starting with the nature of revelation, Trembelas considers in turn: God as one and three, creation and providence, and Christ. On Christ he treats Christology as the study of the person of the Redeemer, and soteriology as the study of his work. He then moves on to the incorporation of men into the Kingdom of God, realised by Christ. This brings him to grace, the Church and the sacraments. Finally, after a lengthy discussion of the 'principle of economy', whereby the Orthodox defend their recognition of the validity of schismatic sacraments, Trembelas closes his work with an account of eschatology, the study of the consummation of the Kingdom of God. It is noteworthy that the chapter on the Church deals with the Church first of all as a hierarchical society. In other words Trembelas's work, considered in its formal structure, would fit very well into the Roman Catholicism of the pontificates of the twentieth century 'Pian' popes. Trembelas, who was born in 1885 and died in 1977, stresses that the only sources of theology, properly so called, are the canon of Scripture and Church

tradition: he specifically rules out any rôle for Christian experience in theology's making. He insists that theology, while
ecclesial, is also scientific, and lays much weight on the certitude
of its conclusions, its use of a combination of empirical method
and direct reasoning, and the need to arrange its propositions in
a systematic whole. He justifies the separation of dogmatics from
moral theology and from bibical theology. He underlines the fact
that theology is in the service of the authority of the Church. As
he writes:

> To envisage a free exposition of Christian dogma by simply giving
> one's account a general Christian colouring, would only suit those
> who wish to shake ecclesiastical authority and the apostolic tradition
> unchangingly conserved in the Church.[15]

In other words, this is an anti-Modernist, neo-Scholastic theology which has taken over the characteristic anxieties – not
always, certainly, without foundation – of the Catholic Church
under the last three Piuses. On the other hand, Trembelas's use
of sources is excellent. His work can boast a wealth of patristic
citation, always relevant to his argument, though in part borrowed from two notable Western histories of dogma, that of
Joseph Tixeront (Catholic) and that of R. K. Hagenbach (Protestant). Among non-Scholastic authors, Trembelas has used the
Tübingen writer Johann Adam Möhler and the somewhat unpla-
ceable Rhineland theologian Matthias Joseph Scheeben. From his
study of Scripture and tradition, Trembelas is convinced that no
significant development of doctrine has taken place, and explicitly commits himself to expounding the Fathers on the basis of
the Vincentian canon: *ubique, semper et ab omnibus*: what in the
patristic age was taught by everybody, always, and everywhere.

The Thessalonian school presents a very different picture. It is
much more open, and some critics would say impressionistic
rather than clear-headed. The Thessalonian theologians have
been much influenced by modern German philosophy, especially
the later Heidegger, and also by the criticism of Scholastic

theology which has emanated from the Russian diaspora in Western Europe. A characteristic Thessalonian theologian, and the best known of the school, is Christos Yannaras. Born in 1935, a number of his writings have been translated into German, English, French and Italian; their titles speak eloquently of his difference from Trembelas. Thus, for instance, we find 'Heidegger and Denys the Areopagite. A theology of the Absence and Unknowability of God', or again, 'The Person and Eros. A Theological Essay in Ontology'.[16] Yannaras has also written, importantly for our purpose here, a study named 'Orthodoxy and the West',[17] the main argument of which is summarised in the foreword to his most acclaimed, and influential, work, *The Freedom of Morality*[18] – though this foreword has been unaccountably omitted in the English translation. Yannaras describes the schizophrenia he feels as a theologian writing in Greece today. On the one hand, the vital sap which feeds him theologically is Orthodoxy or, as he puts it, 'the theology and spirituality of the undivided Church and their historical continuation in the Eastern tradition'. On the other hand, he says that Western theology with all its concrete consequences, social, political and cultural, is what has shaped the manner of his life, whether he finds himself at home or abroad. He goes on to say that when, in his writing, he opposes Western theology the reader must not imagine that he thinks of Western theology as something existing outside of him. It is also inside him. As he puts it, 'I am both what is true and what is not true.' And he asserts that only the faith of the undivided Church of the first eight centuries can bring salvation to the Western world. This is a good reminder that the difference between Athenian and Thessalonian theology is not a matter of theological liberalism in the ordinary sense of the word. Both Trembelas and Yannaras are clear that Orthodoxy is the truth, and that the theology of the Western Churches is in various respects in error, sometimes with dramatic consequences wider afield. The difference between them is that, while Trembelas wants to use the methods of Western theology to convince Westerners that they are wrong on certain points of dogma, Yannaras regards the methods of Western theology as a very large part of what is wrong about Western theology, and part of the reason why it cannot bring a life-giving vision to Western society. So much at any rate for the Church of Greece. Before leaving the Greek scene, however, I should point out that theology in Greece is an almost entirely lay affair. Many seminary rectors are laymen also, as are nearly all seminary professors.

FRANCE   Next, I want to look at what is, to my mind, the second most important centre of theology in existence today, and that is France. Unlike Greece, France is not of course an Orthodox country. Her Orthodox population originated in the flight of anti-Bolshevik Russians – about one million all told – from the revolutionary turmoil of the years 1917 to 1921. A large proportion of those who fled Russia in this period belonged to the professional classes, and they included many members of the pre-First World War Russian intelligentsia. As luck would have it, in the years between 1900 and 1914 there had been something of a renaissance of the Orthodox Church in Russia, especially at the intellectual level.[19] Numerous figures in philosophy, economics and historical studies announced their conversion to Orthodoxy, sometimes from Marxism as with Sergei Bulgakov, who had been a Marxist professor of economics – and these were prominent among those who fled to the West. The Russian diaspora settled first in Serbia, next in Germany and finally in France, pushed westwards by the unstable political and economic conditions in eastern Central Europe after the First World War. The presence of all this talent, along with the need to train young priests for the Russian Orthodox in the West, prompted the founding of a Russian theological school in Paris, the Institut Saint-Serge, in 1926. The aim of the school was to keep alive the best of the pre-war Russian theological tradition and to build on it: in expectation that one day its leaders would be called back to Russia to help re-create the Russian Church from the ashes. Well into the 1920s it was confidently asserted in the West that the

Communist system in the USSR would collapse of its own internal problems within a few years: a prediction correct in substance, but not in time-scale.

The Institut Saint-Serge has been *the* outstanding centre of Orthodox theology in this century.[20] The Paris school, as we may call it, combines theological originality with respect for tradition. It puts together three things. First, a stress on the liturgical and mystical dimension of Orthodoxy. Orthodoxy is to a very high degree a liturgical church, just as it is also a mystically or contemplatively oriented church. The doctrinal richness of the Byzantine liturgy was to be regarded as itself a theological source; and so was the Orthodox spiritual tradition, summed up in the *Philokalia*, the standard anthology of all the best Oriental spiritual writers.[21] Secondly, there was in the Paris school a complete openness to Western scholarship. Its members used Protestant, Anglican and Catholic scholarship in biblical and patristic studies with no sense that in so doing they might be endangering their faith. Finally, the Paris school had a very strong speculative bent. It wanted to make an original contribution to Orthodox dogmatics. To some extent other Orthodox found it *too* speculative, and it was criticised from the Athenian side in particular. For many Orthodox the elaborate 'sophiology' or theology of the divine Wisdom, worked out by Bulgakov, is in the full sense an heretical element in the Saint-Serge tradition. On the other hand, a larger number would regard the masterwork of another Parisian theologian, one who, however, for jurisdictional reasons remained detached from Saint-Serge – namely, Vladimir Lossky – as the classic statement of Orthodox theology in our time.

What we have in the Paris school is an attempt to combine two traditions from the pre-revolutionary Russian Church. On the one hand, there was a tradition stemming from the four pre-Revolution Academies, those of Moscow, St Petersburg, Kiev and Kazan. In the later nineteenth century these Academies had witnessed an attempt to go back, behind the heavily Catholicised or Lutheranised Russian theology of the seventeenth and eighteenth centuries, to something more distinctively Orthodox. This element survived at Saint-Serge and accounts for the importance there of patristics, liturgical studies and Church history. On the other hand, there was another tradition stemming from the lay circles which returned to Orthodoxy on the eve of the Revolution. Here the interest was in the philosophy of religion, and philosophical theology. This element also survived at Saint-Serge and accounts for the importance there of speculative dogmatics. In dogma, the Russian Church had utilised for many years a manual written by Makarii Bulgakov, not to be confused with Sergei, the earlier Bulgakov having been Metropolitan of Moscow in the 1880s and 1890s. Both the traditionalists and the liberals at Saint-Serge agreed that Makarii's manual was lifeless and often inconsistent. But they could not agree on what should replace it. The traditionalists wanted a new dogmatic theology founded on the Fathers, the liturgy and the spiritual experience of the Church. The liberals believed that philosophical thought had moved on beyond the stage which the Fathers knew, and that a new Orthodox dogmatics must be a fresh synthesis of ancient theology and contemporary concepts.

The main representative of the 'liberal' element was Sergei Bulgakov. His new dogmatics was to turn on the idea of the divine Wisdom, a concept introduced into Russian religious thought by the pre-Revolution philosopher Vladimir Solov'ev. Bulgakov identified the Wisdom of God with the divine *ousia*, the being common to the three persons, and he held that the world had eternally pre-existed in this *ousia*, just as, indeed, according to his way of thinking, the missions of the Son and the Spirit in salvation history had been eternally anticipated in God. On the basis of these affirmations, Bulgakov worked out an entire theological system, deposited in a huge corpus of writing, much of it still untranslated from the Russian.

The main representative of the traditionalist current, George Florovsky, who died in 1979, has been called the most Orthodox of all contemporary Orthodox. His genius lay in re-creating the thought of the Fathers, especially the Cappadocians, Maximus the Confessor, and Gregory Palamas, and in showing how lively and inspirational it could be when presented in a modern idiom. Florovsky broke with the school of Saint-Serge just after the Second World War, owing to his bitter opposition to the sophiological theology of Sergei Bulgakov, just mentioned, and retired to the United States where he became a professor first at Harvard and then at Princeton.[22]

The two remaining principal Orthodox centres of theology today are those of the Rumanian Church on the one hand, and on the other, of Orthodoxy in the United States. We look at each in turn.

RUMANIA The Rumanian school is the only major school to survive life under a Communist government. Whereas, in the Ceaucescu era, Rumania possessed the most liberal foreign policy of any Eastern bloc country, internally it was, and to some degree remains, extremely repressive – probably more so than any other Warsaw Pact country. What, nonetheless, gained the Rumanian Orthodox Church a measure of State support was its special position as bearer of the Rumanian national culture. Under Turkish or Hungarian government, the Rumanian Church – Orthodox or Uniate, respectively, kept the Rumanian spirit alive. The Uniate Church was forcibly incorporated into Orthodoxy in 1948, and is only now, with considerable difficulty, re-emerging, to the fury of the Orthodox hierarchy. There are two institutes of theology, one at Bucharest, and the other at Sibiu in Transylvania, the former Hapsburg Rumania, where the Orthodox metropolitan is himself an Eastern-rite Catholic by baptism.[23] The outstanding theological figure is, however, at Bucharest: Dimitru Staniloae, a description of whose achievement forms part-and-parcel of a commemorative volume on the state of Rumanian Orthodoxy today, under the sub-title 'Orthodox Theology in Rumania from the Origins to Our Own Time'.[24] There three characteristics of Staniloae's theology are singled out. First, he wishes to re-unite dogma to spirituality. This is a theme which has many echoes in modern Catholic theology, but among the Orthodox is especially characteristic of the more conservative element at Saint-Serge. Secondly, Staniloae stresses the openness of the Church to the world. This is not at all characteristic of Orthodox theology anywhere else, and probably derives from the need to make some kind of response to the Marxist society in which Rumanian Orthodoxy was set. Thirdly and lastly, Staniloae is concerned to write a theology of Orthodox ecumenism. In this he is related to the liberal wing of the Paris school who took a major part in the Ecumenical Movement in the 1920s and after.[25] It is worth noting that Rumanian theology has gained considerable spiritual depth from its association with the monastic revival, which has been a major feature of the Rumanian Church since the Second World War. The Jesuit student of Orthodoxy, Michael Fahey, has opined that, thanks to its theological vitality, Rumania 'might be considered from that point of view the dominant Orthodox country today'.[26]

UNITED STATES   Finally we have the Orthodox in the United States. Although not much Orthodox theology has been written in that country by American-born Orthodox, it is likely that we will hear a good deal more from them in the future. For, first, some of the finest European Orthodox scholars and thinkers have migrated to America for professional reasons, and must surely have some influence on those they have taught: not only Florovsky, but also the (quite recently deceased) dogmatician and Church historian John Meyendorff and the liturgiologist and sacramental theologian Alexander Schmemann, both of the St Vladimir's Seminary in Westchester, New York. Secondly, there is a good chance that American Orthodoxy may be able to put together the best elements from the different traditions already mentioned, and notably from the Russian and the Greek, since it has inherited both. Thirdly, the American Orthodox have the advantage, shared with the French, that they can draw on Catholic and Protestant scholarship in a language which is their mother-tongue. However, they are still hampered by jurisdictional problems, in particular the refusal of the Greek metropolia, which are under an exarch of the Patriarch of Constantinople, to join in with the new church. The Greeks retain their own theological school, Holy Cross, at Brookline, Massachusetts.[27]

OTHERS   Before leaving this whistle-stop tour of twentieth century Orthodox theology, I ought to note the obvious absences from the scene. The most remarkable is of course the Church of Russia with an estimated 50 million practising members, that is, some 25 per cent of the Soviet population. After the Second World War, two of the pre-war theological academies were reopened, Moscow's at the monastery of the Holy Trinity, Zagorsk, and Leningrad, the former Petrograd or St Petersburg. However, no significant work of a theological nature was published in the Soviet Union in the entire period between the Revolution and the advent of Mikhail Gorbachev. Throughout that period, the only publications permitted to the Russian Church were calendars and other para-liturgical literature, together with pro-government propaganda, such as the *Journal of the Moscow Patriarchate* and occasional collections of pro-Soviet sermons by selected bishops. Limited numbers of Bibles and liturgical books could be imported from Cyrillic-alphabet presses, mostly situated in Czechoslovakia. The seminary manuals were simply typewritten.[28] We can expect, however, that with the passing of the Leninist State, the Russian Orthodox Church will rapidly expand its activities and influence, as indeed it is already beginning to do, and that this expansion will include the revival of theological culture.

Secondly, we should note the silence of the four great historic patriarchates, Constantinople, Alexandria, Antioch and Jerusalem. The theological silence of Constantinople is imposed by the Turkish government which because of its anti-Greek feeling has closed down the patriarchal college on the Turkish Aegean island of Halki, and refuses to allow more than a skeleton staff at the patriarchal headquarters in Istanbul, the Phanar. More recently, however, in an attempt to improve its international image as part of a political campaign to become a member state of the

European Community, the Turkish government announced that
it will permit the patriarchal theological academy to re-open.
Unfortunately, before this plan could be realised, the explosion of
civil war in the former Yugoslavia, and notably the threat to the
Bosnian Muslim population as well as the Greek refusal to
recognise Macedonia, plunged Turkish-Greek relations into a
new crisis.

In addition, the Ecumenical patriarch has charge of two centres
abroad, one in Greece and the other on the French shore of Lake
Geneva. The first is essentially a patristic institute, the second an
ecumenical institute. Alexandria and Jerusalem are too tiny to
support much theological life. Antioch is more numerous and has
produced a certain amount of pastoral theology, whose aim is the
revival of the Orthodox Church in the Middle East in a truly
Arab, that is non-Greek, form. Finally, in the other autocephalous churches, such as those of Serbia or Cyprus, while there are
theological books and journals being published, their contents
are very largely derived from the four schools I have touched on
in this introduction.[29]

II
Vladimir Lossky and Apophatic Theology

Vladimir Lossky was born in 1903, not in Russia but in the German Empire, at Göttingen, where his father, a professional philosopher, was currently staying with his family for reasons connected with his university career. However, Lossky *was* brought up in Russia itself, at St Petersburg. From 1920 to 1922 he studied at the University of St Petersburg where he was much influenced by the historian of ideas L. P. Karsavin. Karsavin encouraged him to study the Fathers of the Church, though the young Lossky's interests also wandered farther afield, to take in the history of the mediaeval West – mediaeval history was, in fact, the official title of Karsavin's chair. While Lossky's family were deeply opposed to the Revolution of October 1917, they refused to join the flight of the emigrés from Russia during and immediately after the Civil War, eventually won as that was by Trotsky's impressively efficient 'Red Army'. Nonetheless, in 1923, the Soviet government expelled them, whereupon Lossky settled at Prague, where a Russian academy in exile had been established, supplementing the activities of the Charles IV University, the oldest in German-speaking Europe. But in 1924 he moved again, this time definitively, to Paris.

At the Sorbonne, Lossky enrolled as a student of mediaeval history, and at once encountered Étienne Gilson who was making his own name and career as an interpreter of the history of philosophy – above all, that of the mediaeval Scholastics. In 1925, Lossky joined the newly founded Confrèrie de Saint

Photius (Confraternity of St Photius), whose aims were to encourage among Orthodox in the West a lively sense of the distinctive Orthodox confessional identity, and yet at the same time to make them look outwards in a missionary spirit, to testify to the universal relevance of Orthodoxy. In 1927, Lossky began research into the fourteenth century Dominican mystical theologian Meister Eckhart.[1] This led him back, through St Thomas, to Denys the Areopagite, the sixth-century Syrian author who wrote under the pseudonym of a pupil of St Paul, and on whose most important theological work, the *De divinis nominibus*, Thomas had commented. It was Denys who would be the subject of Lossky's first scholarly article.[2] More importantly, Denys, and his idea of negative or mystical theology, would become, as we shall see, not simply one of Lossky's chief theological themes but also, in a sense, the foundation of his theology as a whole.

In 1931 Lossky became somewhat estranged from the greater part of the Russian Orthodox community in France, owing to his refusal to withdraw from canonical allegiance to the Moscow patriarchate. This was at a time when the majority of the Franco-Russian community broke off ties with Moscow, on the grounds that the patriarchate had become the tool of the Soviet government, and placed themselves instead under an exarch of the patriarch of Constantinople. Lossky took the view that this was not only canonically improper but tended to undermine the Church's mission. The Church in Russia had to do the best it could, within the limited room for manoeuvre permitted it by the Soviet authorities. Orthodox in the West, he felt, should show it sympathy and solidarity, not break off brotherly relations.

The tension created by this decision was aggravated during the years 1935–36 when Lossky was involved in a serious doctrinal debate within Orthodoxy: the sophiological controversy, or debate about the wisdom of God, aroused by the writings of Sergei Bulgakov. Lossky, as he explained in his first book *Spor o Sofii* ('The Question about Wisdom'),[3] published in 1936, regarded Bulgakov's thought as an illicit attempt to marry Christianity with pantheism.

Rowan Williams, the principal living authority on Lossky's work, describes the book in these terms:

> Essentially, it is a protest against what Lossky sees as Bulgakov's divorcing of theology from the canonically regulated life of the Church and the subordination of theology to speculative metaphysics. In Lossky's eyes, Bulgakov, in common with most of the Russian intelligentsia, does not experience ecclesiastical tradition as a living reality, but has a merely antiquarian interest in it as 'a monument to ecclesiastical culture'. *Spor o Sofii* crystallises very sharply what it was that distinguished Lossky from the older generation of Russian religious thinkers; it reveals the strength of his commitment to the visible, concrete ecclesiastical institution and his suspicion of any hints of Gnostic mystagogy.[4]

Accordingly, Lossky – or rather the confraternity, at the request of the Russian metropolitan in Paris – delated Bulgakov to the authorities of the Moscow patriarchate. Some short while later, the latter proceeded to condemn Bulgakov's theological system as heretical. But Lossky recognised that the question Bulgakov had raised, through the idea of *Sofia*, namely: 'How should the God-world relationship be understood in the light of Christian revelation?' was a vital question, which could not be answered by ecclesiastical prohibitions. The anonymous author of the short biography of Lossky contained in the memorial edition of the French Orthodox review *Contacts* believed, indeed, that Bulgakov's thought had an ultimately positive effect on Lossky's theology:

> The whole theology of Vladimir Lossky, centred as that is on uncreated Grace, on the Palamite conception of the divine Energy, will try to express Father Bulgakov's fundamental intuition in a traditional and rigorously orthodox manner.[5]

The sophiological affair also had a second important consequence, in that it would lead to a friendship between Lossky and the *locum tenens* of the patriarchal throne, a bishop who, after the Second World War, was allowed by Stalin to take on the title and office of patriarch. Later, the friendship enabled Lossky to make a lecture tour of Russia in 1956, and made possible the publication of some of his work in the government-controlled *Journal of the Moscow Patriarchate*.

During that war, the German army had soon reached Paris. From 1940 to 1944 Lossky played a courageous part in the French resistance, by now fully identified, as he was, with his adopted motherland. At the same time, he was giving quasi-public lectures on Orthodoxy – addresses at a private household to an inter-confessional group of theologians and philosophers, and published while the German occupation was still in force. This study, with its identification of an existentialist and personalist slant to the patristic dogmatics of, especially, Gregory of Nyssa and Maximus Confessor, soon acquired the status of a classic.[6]

In 1945, in the more spacious liberty provided by the ending of the war, Lossky helped to launch the ecumenical series *Dieu vivant* whose statement of intent spoke eloquently of his own priorities. Emphasising the eschatological aspect of Christian faith – but not in opposition to the incarnational, for the two are connected by the doctrine of the resurrection of the body – the contributors to this library of Francophone theology would remain open to contemporary thought and historical milieu while prescinding from social and political questions, the Christian understanding of which must develop, so they considered, from a re-discovery of eschatology and grace in their full dimensions.

During the academic year 1945–46, Lossky lectured at the newly founded Institut Saint-Denis, a centre for French-speaking, Western-rite Orthodoxy. As Williams has pointed out, Lossky's commitment to his adopted *patrie* has been intensified by the experience of the Second World War – and is attested in his private journal, now in the possession of the Orthodox lay theologian Oliver Clément.[7] A factor in Lossky's choice of platform was the ill-feeling between himself and the professors of the distinguished Institut Saint-Serge: the latter shared the anger of most of the Russian diaspora in France at the collaboration of the

Moscow patriarchate with the Bolshevist State and, accordingly, had transferred themselves *en bloc* to the jurisdiction of Constantinople.

Unfortunately the 'Western Orthodox' experiment, a kind of Uniate Church in reverse, proved no viable alternative. After 1953, with the loss to the staunchly ethnic and anti-Bolshevik 'Russian Church in Exile' of the Westerners' leader, Father Evgraphy Kovalesky, it entered rapid decline. At the Institut Saint-Denis, while it lasted, Lossky's subject, closely relevant to the negative or mystical theology which he had studied in Denys and Eckhart, was the eschatological vision of God, and the apparently divergent traditions of East and West on that issue.[8]

In 1947, Lossky began to play a major part in the Ecumenical Movement: first, at a conference at High Leigh, Hertfordshire, of the Fellowship of St Alban and St Sergius, a body formed so as to foster mutual understanding between Orthodox and Anglicans, and subsequently, later that same year, at a second conference in Oxford, which also included Catholics, on the ecumenical importance of the *Filioque*. In 1952, Lossky wrote an important essay on the nature of tradition, published as a lengthy introduction to a book by the iconographer Leonid Ouspensky on the meaning of icons.[9] In 1954, he contributed to the international congress of Augustinian studies held at Paris in commemoration of the sixteenth centenary of Augustine's birth. In 1955, he returned to Oxford, for the second of the patristic congresses organised by the Anglican patrologist Canon F. L. Cross. Here Lossky put into more scholarly form the ideas on the vision of God in the Byzantine tradition which he had expounded in his lectures of 1944–45 on the same subject.

Lossky died in February 1958.[10] His work was published in a variety of forms, both during his lifetime and posthumously.[11] Yet, apart from the massive study of Eckhart, Lossky's is a comparatively slender *oeuvre*. The same favoured Fathers of the Church recur constantly, and most of his themes are treated in much the same way throughout his life.

What, then, does Lossky have to say about Christian theology, and, notably, about the motif of apophaticism or negative theology which is certainly the heart of his work – bearing in mind Lossky's own warning that the use of apophasis in the history of Christian thought is very varied, so that, in each case, the student should try to ascertain the end or goal into whose service, at the hands of a given writer, it is pressed. I divide an answer to this question into two parts. First, there is apophaticism as the key to Lossky's view of what *all* theology should be like, even when not specifically concerned with the apophatic idea as part of its own content, and secondly, apophaticism as a specific topic or theme within dogmatics.

Theology as Apophasis: Lossky's Manifesto

First, therefore, let us look at apophaticism as a condition of all theologising, as Lossky saw it. The primary feature distinguishing Lossky's theology is his insistence that Christian mysticism must play an all-pervasive part in the theological enterprise. When he entitled his chief work *Essai sur la théologie mystique de l'Église d'Orient*, Lossky meant to say that, in the Eastern Church, all theology is, or is meant to be, mystical.[12] The intimate connexion of mysticism with apophasis was already made clear in Lossky's study of the sophiological crisis, where he wrote:

> It [apophasis] is not a branch of theology but an attitude which should undergird all theological discourse, and lead it towards the silence of contemplation and communion.[13]

As Williams comments:

> The source and end of apophatic theology for Lossky is ... a fully conscious though non-intellectual relationship of personal confrontation between man and God in love.[14]

In this stress on the fundamentally mystical finality and character of all theology, Lossky's work stands in sharp contrast to the mainstream of Latin Catholic theology since the late sixteenth century. Within that Latin mainstream, mystical theology has been thought of as a department, or division, within theology, rather than as a feature of all theology. In the West, at least in recent centuries, mystical theology has been a subject-matter. The term stands for one limited area of theological investigation, call it 'mystical experience', 'mystical phenomena', or, more soberly, 'the spiritual life', 'the life of prayer', or – even more generously, this time – the Christian life, Christian existence *tout court*. In the East, however, or so Lossky wished to maintain, mystical theology is not a subject-matter at all. Rather is it a mode of doing all theology: indeed, it is *the* mode *par excellence* of theological practice, the *unum necessarium* of theological existence. As he wrote in *La théologie mystique de l'Église d'Orient*::

> The Eastern tradition has never clearly distinguished between mysticism and theology, between a personal experience of the divine mysteries and the dogmas declared by the Church... The dogma which expresses a revealed truth and appears to us like an unfathomable mystery, must be lived in such a way that, instead of assimilating the mystery to our manner of understanding it, we must, on the contrary, strive to bring about a profound change, an inner transformation of the soul, so that we will be more receptive toward the mystical experience.[15]

And Lossky concluded:

> Far from being opposed to each other, theology and mysticism mutually support and supplement each other. One is impossible without the other. If mysticism is the application by the individual of the content of the common faith to his own experience, theology is the expression of that which can be experienced by each one for the good of all.[16]

In this statement Lossky is challenging at the same time a number of different streams within Christian thinking.

First, and most often noted, there is an implicit attack on Latin Scholasticism, as that had developed or, perhaps, had undergone re-invention around the turn of this century. The original Scholastic movement had not made the sharp distinction between personal experience and dogmatic theology which Lossky attacks. St Thomas specifically says that the same understanding which the theologian gains by reflecting on *sacra doctrina* exists in a non-theologian through the 'connaturality' or sympathy with God which charity brings about. In other words, an experimental intimacy with God, on the part of the saint or the lover of God, leads to an intuitive grasp of what the theologian comes to understand in a more roundabout way. In the *Secunda Pars* of the *Summa Theologiae*, Thomas's account of the theological virtues and of the Gifts of the Holy Spirit sets out to show in some detail how this can be so. Furthermore, the whole character of theology as a science in St Thomas is linked to the notion that by faith we have a share in the absolutely certain and manifest knowledge which God has of himself and which the blessed have of him by participation. However, a good deal of later Scholasticism, without necessarily denying *ex professo* these convictions of St Thomas, was cast in a strict deductive mould, dependent on a somewhat narrow propositionalist view of faith, differing markedly from Aquinas' own. A certain kind of neo-Scholasticism, accordingly, had difficulty coping with the contemplative, and subjectively engaged, aspect of historic Thomism. In brief, a breach had opened between theology and Christian experience. This breach was widened by the Modernist movement. In trying to redress the balance between formal theologising and religious experience – in itself an entirely proper and laudable objective – Modernism finished by subverting confidence in the Christian access to a supernatural revealed content of truth, given in history and now available through doctrinal tradition. As an error in fundamental theology, perhaps the first that the Church had encountered since the Gnostic crisis of the early centuries, Modernism threatened to undermine all doctrines rather than, as more customary with heresies, the occasional one or two – thus earning from Pope Pius X, in his encyclical *Pascendi*, the sobriquet 'heresy of heresies'. The effect on the Catholic Church of both Modernism and its mirror-image, 'integralist' anti-Modernism, was to make the word 'experience' taboo for decades. Only in the later 1940s did the Abbé Jean Mouroux of the Institut Catholique in Paris succeed in retrieving the word 'experience' in the context of Catholic theology in his book, *L'Expérience chrétienne*.[17]

Also relevant to Lossky's case here was the controversy concerning the restrictedness or otherwise of contemplation – a debate of the later 1920s and 1930s, largely conducted between Jesuits and Dominicans, where the former were found arguing that there is no universal call to contemplation in the Church. Clearly, if contemplative experience is *not* a natural development of baptismal grace, then it is pointless to ask all theologians to be contemplatives in the way that Lossky was doing. This, then, is the most obvious context of Lossky's remarks, and it is here that he stakes out a claim for Eastern Orthodox thought as an alternative to the – as he perceived it (for many strands of Catholic theology are omitted in this selective summation) – rationalising reflection of the later Latin West.

But this is not the only way in which to see Lossky's manifesto of a new-style Orthodox theology which according to him is also absolutely traditional and old-style. He was also taking on, secondly, an aspect of an earlier generation of Eastern – and especially Russian – Orthodox theology, namely, Idealism, in the philosophical or, at least, philosophy-of-religion sense of that word. The insistence that dogma is an unfathomable mystery which cannot be assimilated to our manner of understanding is an attack on an element in Russian theology stretching from the mid-nineteenth century right up to the inter-war period. Writers from Vladimir Solov'ev in Tsarist Russia through to Nikolai Berdyaev in the post-revolutionary period do tend to identify faith with rational understanding, though, for this to be possible, one must, of course, entertain a very exalted picture of what rational understanding is.[18] The writers I have mentioned possess a philosophical doctrine of man, and especially of the human mind, according to which faith is really the fullest development of our natural powers of knowing God. This element in Russian theology derives from the deep influence which the German Idealists – and notably Hegel and Schelling – brought to bear, through their disciples, on early and mid-nineteenth century Russian culture. For both Hegel and Schelling, in their different ways, wished to achieve the full reconciliation of reason with faith. To Lossky's mind such a project was chimerical. It overlooked the fact that our share in, and knowledge of, the divine life is entirely gracious, the free gift of God, and so could never be postulated from the side of nature *a priori*, nor thought through, *a posteriori*, in rational terms. Lossky's treatise is also, accordingly, a broadside against the invasion of the Russian Orthodox tradition by philosophical Idealism.

Thirdly, Lossky's insistence that it is we who must be assimilated to the Christian mystery, and not the other way round, can be taken as a challenge to theological liberalism wherever it may be found. It is characteristic of liberalism that it wants to cut the suit of Christian teaching according to the cloth of what is thought important, or relevant, or credible, or imaginatively acceptable, in any given age. As Newman saw, liberalism is essentially a surrender to the spirit of the age, a loss of nerve before the contemporary. The Losskian insistence that theology is intrinsically bound up with Christian mysticism is one way of saving theology from corrosion by liberalism. This it does by underlining the fact that theology's epistemological status is quite different from that of any other kind of knowledge – for which reason theology possesses a certain autonomy, which it should guard with jealousy, *vis-à-vis* the changing intellectual fashions of the day. Of all the great Christian traditions in the world today, Eastern Orthodoxy is the least affected by theological liberalism: this is due in no small part to Lossky's work.

In coming to terms with Lossky's account of the nature of theology, it is important to note the relation he sets up between the individual and the community in the theological task. To cite once again a crucial passage from the opening chapter of the *Essai*:

If mysticism is the application by the individual of the content of the common faith to his own experience, theology is the expression of that which can be experienced by each one for the good of all.[19]

Here the individual is thought of as the concentration or the typical manifestation of the community, and the community is the inter-relation of individuals. Lossky's schema here is much indebted to the Slavophile picture of the Church, the work of a group of mid-nineteenth century Russian writers of whom the best known is Alexei Khomiakov. For the Slavophiles, the community of individuals, the *sobornost'*, is the essential guide to faith. The role of texts, like the Scriptures, and of officers, like the bishops, is downplayed in comparison with the community itself. Later Orthodox theologians have corrected Lossky's account by pointing out that mysticism and theology are both indebted to an objective content found in Scripture and the teaching of the episcopate. The more conservative Greek theologians are particularly supportive of the objectivity of the rule of faith; theologians in the Russian tradition, whether in France, the United States, or elsewhere, stress rather that, while the process of the reception of revelation is, as Lossky said, the work of the whole body of the Church, within this body Church officers play a crucial part – for example, through the ecumenical councils. Both schools, then, correct Lossky at this point, one more sharply than the other.

What then are we to make of Lossky's manifesto which has set its mark on nearly all present-day Orthodox writing to a greater or lesser extent? There are difficulties in Lossky's view that theology and spirituality should coincide. For instance, to what extent can the reality expressed by the doctrine of the Virgin Birth be experienced by us today? One might argue that the deepest implications of that doctrine have to do with the novelty and unexpectedness of God's gift of himself in Christ, and that this is something which all Christians should be able to experience in their lives. However, this would be a matter of the further implications of the doctrine, and not of the doctrine itself. It is hard to see how the content of the doctrine could be experienced by anyone other than Mary of Nazareth, Joseph and God, and in the case of God the word 'experience' is hardly appropriate. The fact is that a large part of the Christian faith depends on the transmission of claims about what happened in history. And this historical dimension is only partially open to confirmation by faith experience. Lossky's dictum that all theology must be mystical theology has given a certain anti-historical bent to contemporary Orthodox writing, and partly accounts for its comparative indifference towards the field of biblical studies, that is, the study of the historical origins of the Christian faith.[20]

The criticism I have ventured here of Lossky, and so of the most distinctive dominant trend in Orthodox writing, is perhaps a criticism of what could be called 'vulgarised Losskianism' in the Orthodox Church. Lossky himself was careful to qualify some- what the thesis that theology and mysticism are co-terminous. First, although his use of the word 'mysticism' fluctuates a good deal, the closest he comes to a definition appeals to the idea of our final union with God by grace. On this definition, a doctrine is mystical if it can be shown to have a bearing on our deification. Thus, for instance, the Nicene doctrine of the Son's consubstan- tiality with the Father can be called mystical since unless the Son were really God our union with him would not be a union with God. But this sense of 'mystical' co-exists in Lossky with a more usual sense, in which mysticism involves personal experience. According to *this* meaning of the word, theology is the expression of Christian experience at its most profound. Also, while Lossky sometimes implies that all theological themes are mystical, that is *either* related to our final deification, *or* the articulation of mystical experience, at other times he is much more modest and says: not *all* theological themes but only *some* of them. Thus he speaks of 'the dogmas which constitute the foundation of mysticism' as being something less than 'theological doctrines as such'.[21] In other words the doctrines relevant to his study are simply part of a greater whole, which is the faith of the Church. However, vulgarised Losskianism has been more influential among many

Orthodox than the historical Lossky who was a good deal more subtle than many of his admirers. It is often the fate of great theological minds to suffer this kind of simplification at the hands of disciples.

Apophaticism as Doctrine: God Known as Unknown

Turning now from apophaticism as a general characteristic of Lossky's theology to his more specific treatment of the apophatic theme in the context of the doctrine of God, we find that he gives great emphasis to the patristic language of the 'divine darkness'. Lossky, stimulated by certain of the Greek Fathers, and especially, in this context, by the Cappadocians, embraced, in other words, a radically apophatic doctrine of God. According to Lossky, God is truly known only when he is known as unknown.

It is important at the outset to distinguish this position from that of agnosticism. We can usefully identify two kinds of agnosticism. First, agnosticism may consist in a hesitation as to whether there is a God at all. In this sense, Lossky's apophaticism is clearly not agnostic. Whether we think of his favourite ancient authors like the fourth century Gregory of Nyssa, or of his own profound commitment to Christ and the Church, we are hardly dealing with thinkers who failed to make up their minds about God's existence. But secondly, another form of agnosticism agrees with theism that there is a God, that a divine realm exists, but differs from theism in arguing that nothing substantial can be said about the character of God, or the divine. At first sight, this stance may seem to be identical with that of radical apophaticism. Lossky held that, since God is transcendent, he lies beyond any knowledge that we may claim of him. God's transcendence does not consist merely in his lying beyond the natural order. All theists would agree that God *does* lie beyond the world, over against pantheists who identify the being of God with the world's own being. According to Lossky, however, God also, and to the same degree, transcends the human mind, and the chief instrument of that mind, language. Just as the world is not identical with God, for God is greater than the world, so too the human mind and human language are incommensurate with the divine reality. God escapes all our concepts and images, and thus all our words. But, we might ask, in what way does this differ from the second kind of agnosticism described above?

To throw light on the nature of Lossky's apophaticism it may be useful, indeed, to compare his doctrine with that of what may be termed 'moderate agnosticism'. At least three differences separate Lossky's apophaticism from such moderate agnosticism. First, Lossky's insistence that we must go beyond all positive, or cataphatic, description of God into the divine darkness is not mainly a philosophical position. Frequently, it is not a philosophical position at all. Principally, and sometimes exclusively, it is a practical or spiritual position. Lossky believed that, by purifying our minds of the idolatrous notion that they can capture the essence of God, Christians are actually brought closer to real union with God. This union, of which intellectual humility is a necessary condition, takes place, after all, not by way of rational theology, but through mystical or contemplative encounter with the Trinitarian persons.

Secondly, Lossky does not deny a limited validity to the positive or cataphatic account of God. In the divine act of creating, as also in God's inspiring of Holy Scripture, the deity has disclosed what patristic and mediaeval tradition calls the 'divine Names'. He has manifested himself within his own work, thus giving us a certain amount of positive knowledge of what he is like. Lossky maintains that these divine Names are best found in certain images which fit the mind for contemplation of the Mystery which passes all understanding. Scripture speaks of God as, for instance, the 'Rock' or, again as a 'refining fire'. The created images thus invoked are like steps which we can use so as to mount up into the divine darkness. However, having reached the top of the ladder, the ladder becomes useless and can be kicked away. The true knowledge of God is an experience beyond understanding. If any single source underlies this kind of theology, it is certainly Denys. Both the stress on the divine darkness, and the belief that images are vastly superior to concepts in mediating a knowledge of God, come straight from him. It is an odd fact of theological history that, whereas in the Middle Ages, the influence of Denys was far stronger in the West than in the East, the rôles today are exactly reversed. Lossky played a major part in the revival of Eastern Orthodox interest in the work of the Areopagite.

A final reason for distinguishing Lossky's apophaticism from agnosticism is that it is, in fact, simply the essential background for a doctrine of the divine economy. As Lossky wrote in his essay 'L'apophase et la Théologie trinitaire' apophasis is

> implied in the paradox of Christian revelation: the transcendent God becomes immanent to the world; but in the very immanence of his economy ... he reveals himself as transcendent.[22]

The shared life of the divine persons manifests itself in history, above all in the Incarnation of the Word, as a gracious condescension on the part of the naturally unknowable God, through which we know him whom otherwise, naturally, we could not know. Yet as the passage just cited brings home, the historic revelation – and climactically, crucially, the Incarnation – does not rob God of his mystery. Lossky's Christology takes as its focus, in fact, the episode of the Transfiguration of Jesus on Mount Thabor, and the reason for this interpretative choice is surely connected with his apophaticism. God's darkness may be regarded as the effect on us of the super-abundance of his radiance, his light. The moment *par excellence* in the life of Jesus Christ where we can appreciate this must be the Transfiguration. Here the apophatic dimension breaks through the cataphatic structure of the words and gestures of Jesus. Overwhelmed by it, the disciples are bewildered and at a loss, and in traditional Byzantine iconography they shield their faces from the divine Glory. The mystery of the Transfiguration, as Lossky interprets it, confirms that radical apophaticism also applies to the life of Jesus.

More generally, Lossky argues that, whereas the *essence* of the Holy Trinity is not revealed in the saving economy, the common *energies* of Father, Son and Spirit, *are* revealed. In other words, the *activity* which flows from the ever-hidden divine reality is made manifest to us in Scripture and in the life of the Church, and so one can speak of God's self-revelation even while insisting that his being (as it exists in and for itself) remains permanently beyond our knowledge. The divine *ousia* is in itself unknowable, even to the saints, but it can be known in its energies, which are communicated to us by the missions of the Son and the Spirit. Through grace we are raised up to know the Father, through the Son, in the Holy Spirit, those three who are, as Lossky puts it, 'absolutely different in their absolute identity', in a manner which exceeds all conceptualisation but is experienced by the saints in personal union with the personal 'Unitrinity', the triune God.[23]

What, then, are we to make of apophaticism as a specific theme in Lossky's dogmatic writing and above all in his doctrine of God? To arrive at a fair evaluation it may be helpful to place the theme within its wider context in the history of theology.

Lossky's apophatic doctrine of God forms part of what has been called the 'neo-Patristic revival' in Christian theology. This is a feature of early to mid-twentieth century theology across several confessions: apart from Orthodoxy, it was especially prominent in Anglicanism, where its roots lay in the mid-nineteenth century Oxford movement, and in Catholicism, notably in the so-called *Nouvelle Théologie* of the 1940s and 1950s. The neo-Patristic movement everywhere regarded the Fathers as the best guide to the interpretation of Christian revelation. The grounds for saying this were first, that their teaching was primitive, close to the apostles themselves; secondly, that their theology was used in the making of the classical creeds; and thirdly, that what they had to say was characterised by a balance and wholeness in expressing the Christian mystery not always found in theological history. One thing for which the Fathers were often congratulated by their admirers was their integration of theology and spirituality, and this if nothing else would have drawn to them the theologians of the Russian diaspora for whom the revolutionary upheaval entailed a crisis of the human, and Christian, spirit.

In point of fact, the Fathers did not really need to be discovered by the Orthodox. They were always massive presences in the Orthodox theological tradition. But what we find in this century is an attempt to recover the great perspectives in which the Fathers placed their teaching. Understandably enough, the Orthodox neo-Patristic revival set out to reconstruct theology on the basis of the *Greek* Fathers. Apart from some ritual genuflexions, the Latin Fathers rarely gain our attention in Lossky's work. The heroes are Athanasius, the Cappadocians, Denys the Areopagite and Maximus the Confessor. Although great chunks of Greek patristic citation loom large in Lossky's dogmatics, he did not consider his task, as a dogmatician, to be, in the main, one of historical reconstruction. His primary aim was not to make the Greek Fathers speak today in exactly the same way as they had spoken to their own contemporaries. Lossky's aim was, rather, to make the Fathers speak to *our* contemporaries in ways which the latter could hear, find credible, and so come to accept. Inevitably, this entailed, in some degree, the fastening on to the Fathers of categories and concepts not their own. In particular, Lossky's stressed what he called the 'existentialism' of the Greek Fathers, in rather the way that at about the same time Étienne Gilson was stressing the 'existentialism' of St Thomas.

What this meant in his case was an apophatic doctrine of the divine being. For Lossky, as we have seen, to practise apophasis is to go beyond any merely rational or conceptual approach to God; it is to transcend a purely mentalistic attitude to faith and the theological exploration of faith; it is to set out on a path which involves the whole person. At the goal of apophasis there lies a union with God which is beyond understanding, but which transforms one's whole existence at its deepest level. Apophasis is the perfect way: not because it is itself communion with God but because, in the words of Williams:

in its refusal to limit God with concepts it stands closer to and points more clearly towards the summit of theology.[24]

In his presentation of the patristic witness, Lossky had to pick his way with care if his concern for apophaticism was not to cancel out, rather than facilitate, his Trinitarian personalism. For there were patristic writers, such as Clement of Alexandria, whose apophaticism was deeply affected by the 'negative theology' of pagan Hellenism which found its culmination in Plotinus and Proclus. This pagan negative theology took its rise from the speculation on unity, or the relation of the One to the Many, in Plato's (very difficult) dialogue the *Parmenides*. Platonists argued that true transcendence must be a simplicity from which all differentiating qualities have been removed, and they tried to show by logic and metaphysics how God, the source of the world, must be conceived as *to hen*, the One, an ineffable reality beyond attributes and qualities, in other words beyond all description. 'Must be *conceived*': so this is an intellectualism, and one of a peculiarly sub-personal, even impersonal, kind. Lossky's concern, then, is to locate Fathers who, though not without indebtedness to the Middle-Platonist or neo-Platonist schools, practise an apophaticism of divine encounter, as a man with his Friend – a reference to the single most important locus for biblical apophasis, the meeting of Moses with the Lord in the 'thick darkness' of Mount Sinai, according to Exodus 20. At the same time, to do justice to the differentiated theological personalism of the New Testament (rather than the Old), these select Fathers must be figures who, through a decisive option against Arianism, direct their apophatic energies to the triune God of specifically Christian revelation. It is thanks to a sextet – the Cappadocians, with their predecessor Athanasius, and their successors Denys and Maximus – that Lossky's theological music is played. The personal God to whom Christian apophasis is directed must be, for Lossky, not the Father, but the Trinity: though whether this is the 'majority report' of the Greek and Byzantine tradition as a whole might be doubted.[25]

Two fundamental questions can be put to Lossky's apophatic divinity – the first, to be sure, less weighty than the second. In the first place, then, rejecting as it does the negative dialectics of ancient philosophy, does it not ignore natural theology at the Church's peril? For, whilst the Orthodox do not count as part and parcel of their doctrinal tradition the teaching on the natural knowability of God's existence of the First Vatican Council, they too must make their way, by defence of the faith, in a critical world.

Secondly, does apophaticism preserve the primary stress of Scripture which is, surely, on knowing rather than unknowing? God has opened himself to man in a covenant of life and knowledge, and wherever the language of covenant is found in Scripture a cataphatic theology is presupposed. In the course of the struggle of the Greek Fathers (and not least the Cappadocians) with the theological rationalism of Eunomius, and his successors, a peculiarly Oriental temptation arose.

> The emphasis on the Father having shown his face to us concretely in Jesus Christ was replaced by a radically negative theology of a Neoplatonic cast, in which greater stress was put on the incomprehensibility of God than on the truth that the Incomprehensible had, in an incomprehensible way, made itself comprehensible in Jesus Christ.[26]

These words of Bishop Walter Kasper do not apply in their full rigour to Lossky, yet they identify a danger by which his thought is ever waylaid. In the Western tradition, by contrast, where negative theology is seen as a corrective, or qualification, to cataphatic theology, a moderate apophaticism has been the order of the day. Such Latin theologians as Eckhart, responding to the siren voices of radical apophaticism,[27] have stood, as a consequence, in a not easily chartable relationship to the Church's rule of faith.

Yet, once again, Lossky's thought is too deeply Christian, and too subtle, to disappear into the *Ungrund* or to define itself against only one sin of theological living. Apophasis indeed, at the very moment of expressing its sense of the inadequacy of the language of knowledge, also, in Lossky's own words, 'at the same time, confesses its own'.[28] Not, then, the *identity* of mysticism and theology – that is an over-stated claim – but, rather, their mutual illumination: that is the truth, and the ideal for both spirituality and dogmatics today in East and in West, to which Vladimir Lossky's work is the eloquent witness. That it does not, however, monopolise the entire contemporary Orthodox doctrine of God should become clear if we turn, for our second 'author and theme' to John Meyendorff and neo-Palamism.

III
John Meyendorff and neo-Palamism

The protopresbyter John Meyendorff came from a family with a tradition of public service in Tsarist Russia. Born in 1918 at Neuilly-sur-Seine, near Paris, he was the last living representative of the emigré Russian Orthodox community in its theological aspect, a man who retained roots in, and a strong hold on, Russian culture in its pre-Revolution form. His father was the Baron Meyendorff, one of the last speakers of the Tsarist Duma. The young John – or, rather, Jean – trained for the Orthodox priesthood at the Institut Saint-Serge, where he graduated in 1949. His outstanding promise as an historical theologian already in evidence, he transferred to the Sorbonne, the première university of Paris from which he emerged covered in academic glory in 1958. His research concerned the fourteenth century Byzantine monk-theologian, later Archbishop of Thessalonica, Gregory Palamas, whose name is inseparably linked with that controversial doctrine of God and of the God-man relationship known (precisely) as 'Palamism'.

The year 1959 was Meyendorff's *annus mirabilis* when he published his edition of Palamas's main work, the 'Defence of the Holy Hesychasts';[1] his full length study of Palamas against the backcloth of his time entitled *Introduction à l'étude de saint Grégoire Palamas*, and the more popular *Saint Grégoire Palamas et la mystique orthodoxe*.[2] On the strength of these works, Meyendorff was made a professor at the Institut Saint-Serge, where he worked alongside Lossky.

Soon, however, Meyendorff was attracted by the United States, and by the growing reputation of the Moscow patriarchate seminary and theological school there: St Vladimir's, in New York State. His arrival at St Vladimir's to teach patristics and Church history was followed by a steady stream of books from his pen, all combining historical-theological and systematic interests, and typified by a remarkable power of synthesis. Characteristic of this period of Meyendorff's work would be: *Byzantine Theology*, sub-titled 'Historical Trends and Doctrinal Themes' and *Christ in Eastern Christian Thought*.[3]

The first of these books, *Byzantine Theology*, considers the progress of Byzantine theology 'after Chalcedon'. Its opening section investigates some major trends or historical developments in Byzantine thought, ranging from monastic spirituality, through Iconoclasm, to the emergence of the liturgical commentaries, and giving considerable attention to the question of the schism from the West. In the book's closing section, Meyendorff resumes the same material in terms of the main doctrinal principles of Christian believing, from the creation of the world and man, through Christological and Trinitarian confession, to the sacramental life, finishing with an account of 'the Church in the world'.

The second book, *Christ in Eastern Christian Thought*, is more straightforwardly historical: beginning with the situation of Christology in the century of Chalcedon, it charts the succeeding debate between Chalcedonians and Monophysites; the implications for Christology of the crisis over the more speculative aspects of Origen's system, condemned by Justinian's council of Constantinople in the 550s; the issue of Theopaschism raised by the famous formula of the patriarch Peter the Fuller, 'God has suffered in the flesh'; and the contribution of that other semi-Monophysite figure, Denys the Pseudo-Areopagite. Meyendorff then turns his attention to what the spiritual writers of the Byzantine East have to say of relevance to Christ; he looks at Maximus Confessor's work seen above all as a vindication of the *cosmic* dimension of Christ's work; the 'attempt at system' made by John Damascene, and, contemporary, in part, with Damascene, the controversy over the making and venerating of holy images, whose theology, both Iconophile and Iconoclast, had Christology at its centre. Finally, Meyendorff ends with a chapter on the mature Christology of the later Byzantine period, of which Gregory Palamas's work is presented as the culmination.

Subsequently, Meyendorff became Professor of Byzantine and Eastern European history at the Jesuit University in New York, Fordham, and a corresponding Fellow of the British Academy. In this phase of his life and work, Meyendorff's production centred on the writing of very detailed historical studies that are, however, extremely ambitious in their historical sweep. The first of these was *Byzantium and the Rise of Russia*,[4] an account of the Byzantine contribution to the making of Russian civilisation in the fourteenth century, the century of Palamas. Marshalling a number of under-utilised sources, Meyendorff considers the rôle played by Byzantium in the rise of Russia to be its chief bequest to modern European history. Thanks to its administrative activity in areas directly dependent upon the ecclesiastical jurisdiction of the Byzantine patriarchate, Byzantium exercised, in the framework of the 'commonwealth' of peoples and princes of which the Byzantine emperor was the symbolic head, 'the rôle of a universal centre, parallel to that of Rome in the Latin West'. The relevance to this of the movement of which Palamas formed part, Hesychasm, (as Meyendorff presents it) was that, despite the political weakness of the fourteenth century Byzantine Empire

the monastic revival in the Byzantine world and its impact upon the activities of the patriarchate contributed to this extraordinary new energy of the Byzantine church, which also communicated to the other centres of the 'Byzantine Commonwealth'.[5]

Meyendorff followed up this major historical monograph with a substantial, and richly documented, study of the development of Christian theology in the age of the seven ecumenical councils recognised by the Orthodox: *Imperial Unity and Christian Divisions*.[6]

He died in Montreal, Canada on 22 July 1992, the victim of a crushing workload as Dean of St Vladimir's, adviser to the Holy Synod of the Orthodox Church in America, editor of its newspaper, preacher and lecturer, and above all an indefatigable worker for the healing of its internal jurisidictional disputes and schisms, and its consequent emergence as an effective force in American life.

The Catholic student will be interested to note that Meyendorff was a committed ecumenist, but also a sharp critic of various post-conciliar developments in the Catholic Church of the West, and notably of what he considered the worrying inroads made there by secularism and theological liberalism.[7]

In this chapter, I consider Meyendorff's thought in relation to the Byzantine theologian he gave so much time to studying: Gregory Palamas. First, we must look at the historical origins of Palamism and its revival in modern Orthodoxy; secondly, attempt an outline of the Palamite position, with Meyendorff's aid, and thirdly, note some criticisms thereof, emanating chiefly from Catholic authors.

Palamas and his Re-discovery

First, then, the historical background to the present-day dominance of Palamism (thanks not least to Meyendorff's work) in Orthodox theology. The fourteenth century Byzantine Church was acquainted with three theological types: the humanists, a mixture of classical scholar and philosophical theologian; the Latinophrones, who wanted Byzantine theology to model itself on the theology of the West, and notably that of Thomism; and the monastic theologians, whose theology comprised a synthesis of patristic inspiration with their own contemplative experience or that of their fellows. Despite the circumstance that the controversially crucial terms 'essence' and 'energies', marking-posts of the distinction central to the Palamite doctrine of God, are philosophical terms, Gregory Palamas belongs very definitely to the third of these groups. He was not especially anti-

Unionist, hostile to the West, as were by and large the humanist theologians. Nor was he particularly Unionist, favourable to the West, as were the Latinophrones, though he was open to the possibility of reunion.[8] Above all, he was anxious that theology should be informed by Christian experience at its most profound – and this, in his age, at any rate, meant monastic experience. To defend the teaching of the Greek-speaking monastic Fathers of his day, Gregory used his own somewhat limited philosophical resources in order to produce a theological doctrine which, at three Byzantine councils of the mid-fourteenth century, was declared to be the authentic expression of the mind of the Church.

What, then, is the connexion between Palamism and monastic experience? In the Eastern Church, the monastic movement at large had accepted the possibility of a distinctively Christian direct experience of God. In some sense, grace can be perceived. Thus, for instance, in the fifth century 'Macarian Homilies' we read:

> In Christianity it is possible to taste the grace of God. 'Taste and see that the Lord is good.' This tasting is the fully active power of the Spirit manifesting himself in the heart.[9]

While the pseudo-Macarius, a Syrian monk of the patristic period, had spoken of grace as an experience of the Spirit's power in the heart, the Byzantine monks of the Middle Ages preferred a different symbolism, or terminology. In their approach to the spiritual life, the monks of Gregory's day belonged firmly to the tradition known as 'hesychasm' – a term which might be translated 'the pursuit of inner quiet', *hesychia*, were not this to make them sound like Quakers. The word 'hesychia' in Christian Greek possessed overtones of the biblical notion of rest, *shabbat*, that culminating enjoyment of the divine presence which is the keynote of the vision of God, the everlasting Sabbath day. Ascetically, the hesychast masters recommended specific physical postures, and the recitation of the 'Jesus Prayer', a repeated invocation of the name of Jesus as Saviour.[10] Their aim was the prayer of the heart, a condition where prayer goes on subconsciously throughout daily living: a literal fulfilment of the Pauline injunction to 'pray always'. In the case of those, at least, specially favoured by God's grace, this prayer will lead, even on earth, to a vision of the divine Light which the apostles saw in the Transfiguration of the Lord on Mount Thabor.[11] That Light, uncreated and so identical with God himself, becomes visible to man's physical eyes, though to receive it our senses must first be refined by grace and so able to bear that sight which, for many Old Testament people, was so overwhelming as to threaten life. The earth becomes hallowed by those who even now glimpse the uncreated Glory which all will contemplate in heaven. In this sense, the hesychast monks fulfilled a prophetic rôle in the Church, pointing forward to the second coming of Christ.

In the fourteenth century, hesychastic prayer was a speciality of Mount Athos, the peninsula, jutting out into the Aegean Sea, which monks had colonised some four hundred years earlier. There Palamas discovered this spiritual way on entering the religious life in 1318 when he was twenty-two. The Athonite monastic settlements were often difficult of access, so it might be thought that their spirituality would remain a private affair. But monasticism had made a sustained impact on Byzantine society, not least in the later Middle Ages. (Palamas's own family were aristocrats, and included an imperial senator.) The teaching on the uncreated Light was virtually bound to become widely known, and it soon aroused theological opposition, chiefly from the humanist theologians.

The humanist objection was twofold. First: by claiming to see God himself by way of our physical organs, the hesychasts were talking theological nonsense. Secondly, in this the monks were departing from the radical apophaticism of the Greek patristic tradition. In their defence, Gregory Palamas came forward with his essence-energies distinction, and the theology that surrounds it, in order to show that those objections were insufficiently founded.

The ensuing controversy within the Byzantine Church was bitter, especially as it coincided with a civil war where one party was deeply committed to Palamism. But eventually the Greek Church swung round to the side of Palamas, and in three Constantinopolitan councils from 1341 to 1351 declared his teaching to represent the authentic Christian tradition. Palamas died in 1351 and was canonised by the Byzantine patriarchate. Although the councils mentioned here were only local synods, Palamas's doctrine was accepted with considerable enthusiasm in the Orthodox Churches at large over the succeeding century. While it was not regarded at the reunion council of Florence as an obstacle to the unmaking of the schism, nowadays most, perhaps all, Orthodox theologians would regard it as part of the assured dogma of the Church, since the particular councils which taught it have themselves been 'received' by the generality of the Orthodox.[12] Notable in this connexion is the inclusion of Palamite theses in praise of St Gregory in the Synodikon – a *vade mecum* of anathemas on the heresies read out in the Byzantine liturgy on the 'Sunday of Orthodoxy', the first Sunday of Lent.

And yet during the early modern period – the sixteenth to eighteenth centuries – Palamism was virtually forgotten in the Orthodox Church, at least as a theology.[13] Indeed, when in 1769 the Church of Russia revised the text of the Synodikon, it played down the Palamite elements to the point of near-obliteration. Even in the nineteenth century almost nothing was known about Palamism despite the rise of historical scholarship in the Ortho-dox academies of the Russian Empire. The reason for this ignorance must surely be sought in the domination of the Orthodox theological schools by Western, or Western-inspired, textbooks. Only around the turn of this century did the Orthodox re-discover the Byzantine doctor of grace. In part, this re-discovery was triggered by the attack on Palamism mounted by the Catholic Byzantinist Martin Jugie, an Augustinian of the Assumption.

The first truly systematic account of Palamism in a Western language, Jugie's article in the *Dictionnaire de Théologie catholique*, running to forty closely printed columns as this did, was published in 1922.[14] Jugie's view was baleful. He claimed that Palamism represented a distortion of the Greek patristic tradition, and involved a false idea of God's transcendence. To answer Jugie's attack on Palamite teaching, as well as to recover their own patrimony, Orthodox scholars returned to the Palamite sources and in so doing provided the broader context of John Meyendorff's work.

If we wish to understand Meyendorff's more personal motive for expending so much energy on retrieving the thought of this mediaeval Byzantine writer – and especially his view of the relation between man and God, we could do worse than follow up a clue offered in the introduction to his study *Byzantine Theology*. For there Meyendorff wrote:

> The central theme, or intuition, of Byzantine theology is that man's nature is not a static, 'closed', autonomous entity, but a dynamic reality, determined in its very existence by its relationship to God. This relationship is seen as a process of ascent and as communion – man, created in the image of God, is called to achieve freely a 'divine similitude'; his relationship to God is both a givenness and a task, an immediate experience and an expectation of even greater vision to be accomplished in a free effort of love. The dynamism of Byzantine anthropology can easily be contrasted with the static categories of 'nature' and 'grace' which dominated the thought of post-Augustinian Western Christianty; it can prove itself to be an essential frame of reference in the contemporary theological search for a new understanding of man.[15]

And if, then, in Meyendorff's view, Palamism is 'essential' for the reconstruction of the Church's anthropology, her doctrine of man, the same can be said for her soteriology, her doctrine of salvation.

> Whether one deals with Trinitarian or Christological dogma, or whether one examines ecclesiology and sacramental doctrine, the mainstream of Byzantine theology uncovers the same vision of man, called to 'know' God, to 'participate' in his life, to be 'saved', not

simply through an extrinsic action of God's, or through the rational cognition of propositional truths, but by 'becoming God'. And this *theosis* [divinisation] of man is radically different in Byzantine theology from the Neoplatonic return to an impersonal One: it is a new expression of the neo-testamental life 'in Christ' and in the 'communion of the Holy Spirit'.[16]

All these motifs are, as we shall see, the very ones Meyendorff picks out as characteristic of Gregory's work. A theology inspired by Palamas is thus to re-express the content of Orthodox Christianity in a way which will render its superiority to all rivals self-evident.

And as with the content of dogmatic theology, so also with its form. As Meyendorff writes in the same study:

> Because the concept of *theologia* in Byzantium as with the Cappadocian Fathers, was inseparable from *theôria* ['contemplation'], theology could not be – as it was in the West – a rational deduction from 'revealed' premises, i.e. from Scripture or from the statements of an ecclesiastical magisterium; rather, it was a vision experienced by the saints, whose authenticity was, of course, to be checked against the witness of Scripture and Tradition.[17]

And, underlining the primacy of a theology based on the experience of the saints to any mere conceptually coherent system, Meyendorff goes on:

> Not that a rational deductive process was completely elimated from theological thought; but it represented for the Byzantines the lowest and least reliable level of theology. The true theologian was one who saw and experienced the content of his theology; and this experience was considered to belong not to the intellect alone (although the intellect was not excluded from its perception), but to the 'eyes of the spirit', which place the whole man – intellect, emotions and even senses – in contact with divine existence.[18]

Meyendorff concludes with a statement which allows for no mistaking the relevance of such asseverations to Palamite claims:

This was the initial content of the debate between Gregory Palamas and Barlaam the Calabrian, which started the theological controversies of the fourteenth century.[19]

Indeed, in *A Study of Gregory Palamas*, Meyendorff sums up Palamas's theology of hesychasm in terms of integral personalism of a Christocentric kind: for the monks Palamas defended, the mind, while remaining turned towards God

> accomplishes afresh the function assigned to it by God, namely to lead the whole human organism, body and soul, towards its Creator

thanks to the grace found in Baptism and the Eucharist.[20]

The Palamite Doctrine

So much for the historical event of Palamism, and the historian of doctrine's assessment of its contemporary pertinence. But what then is Palamas saying, as Meyendorff interprets him, in the theology of God? Palamas believed that for the Greek Fathers we must distinguish between God's substance or essence, and his energies – as differentiated realities present in God from all eternity, and not simply by virtue of his saving action *ad extra*, much less as a merely 'formal' distinction, something demanded by the limited operating capacities of human minds. Palamas wished to argue that, first, God is in some sense unknowable – following here the traditional apophaticism of many of the Fathers, as studied in the last chapter of this book. But he also needed to affirm that God can genuinely be known by man – or else the mystical claims of the hesychasts as Christian disciples would fall to the ground. Gregory proposed, accordingly, that God is unknowable in his substance or essence, but knowable in his energies wherein we have communion with him, share in his life and become, as Peter puts it, 'partakers of the divine nature'.[21] Furthermore, since God is always the same God, whether before or after the start of his creative and saving work, the essence-energies distinction, if it truly be real, must also be everlasting. And so, for Palamas, the uncreated energies do not simply manifest the being of God to what is not God. They also mediate the relations of the divine persons one with another. And since the being of the divine persons *is* the divine essence – since, that is, God's *ousia* is that which is common to the persons, then the energies which express the mutual relationships of the persons are the very energies that have operated from all eternity *ad intra*, within the divine life, just as now in history they also operate *ad extra*, in relation to creatures, communicating the divine life to the world, to ourselves.

These uncreated energies are, in Palamas's term, 'enhypostatic' or *personalised*. They are never found save in personal form. Either, they are the activity of the *divine* persons, or they are received by *human* persons in the body of Christ. And so, in speaking of the energies, we are talking about our own salvation. For Palamas, the whole purpose of the Incarnation is the manifestation of the energies. Following the Christology of Chalcedon, and the two later Councils which confirmed and extended its teaching, Constantinople II and III, the pre-existent Word, now made flesh, has, in his two integral natures, everything, respectively, that God has and that we have. Because he was truly God, he became for us the source of those energies which communicate to created nature what in itself would belong to God alone: immortality, perfect happiness, a share in the common life of Father, Son and Holy Spirit. Because he was fully man, even Jesus Christ, considered as a creature, as one of us, could not share God's essence, or his humanity would literally have been deified. Yet that humanity could and did both share and pass on to others the real uncreated manifestations of that essence. In the Christian economy, therefore, God is known and loved not essentially but energetically.

The intention of Palamas's theology seems clear: it is to affirm the reality of Christian communion with God.[22] That covenant reality had been, it would appear, called into question by the humanist theologians, whose work showed tendencies towards theological rationalism and, even, what in the West would be called Nominalism.[23] They reduced the knowledge of God either to concepts of God, or to a quality of mind whereby the intellect becomes habitually receptive toward a divine truth it can never make its own. The fundamental intention of Palamism must be borne in mind in any critical evaluation of Gregory's teaching.

A Critical Evaluation

As already mentioned, when Palamism first became well known in the West, through the work of Jugie, little sympathy was shown it. Later, in the 1950s and 1960s, when Meyendorff at once replaced Gregory's work in the historical context of mediaeval Byzantine debate and brought out its pertinence to the twentieth century Church, this negative judgment changed its charge to positive. Palamas was acclaimed as a great realist of grace, and compared with St Thomas Aquinas in this regard though even then there were occasional voices counselling reserve, such as the Hungarian dogmatician and student of Christian Platonism, Endre von Ivanka.[24]

In more recent years, the Catholic response to Palamism has been a great deal more mixed. Writers like Juan-Miguel Garrigues (once a Dominican, now an 'apostolic monk' of a new Order based at Aix-en-Provence), the Dominican Marie-Jean Le Guillou and the Jesuit Bertrand de Margerie have revived in novel form the objections of Jugie, holding Palamism to be, in its characteristic 'distinction', not simply incompatible with Western Christian doctrine but essentially misguided. Others, like Yves Congar in the third volume of his pneumatology,[25] have been rather more hopeful about an eventual Catholic reception of Palamism, while the Franciscan André de Halleux of Louvain, at once a patrologist and an expert on Catholic-Orthodox relations, has vigorously opposed the fresh spate of Western onslaughts against Palamism, holding that the Latin and Byzantine traditions are, in this matter, simply two distinct conceptualisations of the same faith. While, as they stand, they cannot be combined as theologies, they can, he maintains, be shown to be identical at the level of confession, of dogma.

What are the difficulties which Western students have registered with Palamism, and not least with the neo-Palamism of which Meyendorff is the most outstanding exponent? The simplest to understand is the historical. Palamism is not, for some, an authentic re-statement of the teaching of the Greek Fathers, and notably of Athanasius, the Cappadocians and Maximus, but is a new theology, superimposed on these, and giving to terms used by the Fathers meanings they would never have recognised. Whereas de Halleux, and his older compatriot Gerard Philips considered that Palamism does represent authentically the mind of the Eastern Fathers at large,[26] Garrigues believes that Palamas's doctrine of the divine energies is not a legitimate continuation of the theology of Maximus Confessor,[27] while the Carmelite Jean-Paul Houdret, writing like Garrigues in the French Dominican journal for Eastern Christian Studies *Istina*, denies that Palamas really understood his Cappadocian sources.[28] Whereas certain turns of phrase in those fourth century writers are in themselves susceptible of a Palamite reading, once replaced in their contexts they have no specifically Palamite content. Indeed Houdret claims that the Cappadocian theology of the divine Names is fundamentally opposed to Palamas's doctrine, by placing the distinction between what is unknowable in God (his essence) and what his knowable (his attributes) in the order of our knowledge, rather than in that of God's being. Naturally, these points could not be adequately treated save by a full review of the numerous relevant patristic texts, seen in the light both of etymology and of the history of philosophy and theology. But many might concur in the judgment that, while the Greek Fathers often use the terms *ousia* and *energeia* in what is recognisably the Palamite sense, they can also deploy these terms without such a heavy theological load – using *energeia*, for instance, for whatever God causes to be in this world, the divine action producing some effect. Where Palamas's doctrine is more fully anticipated would be apparently the work of rather earlier mid-Byzantine theologians such as Gregory of Cyprus and Symeon the New Theologian,[29] – but these figures lived too late to be reckoned as 'Fathers' in the usual sense.

A more substantive criticism (though for those who regard patristic authority as vital *in divinis* the historical argument has itself, of course, a normative aspect) concerns the relation of ontology to epistemology. Does not the Palamite distinction turn something which is true of our knowledge into – illegitimately – something true of God's being in itself? Palamism rightly reminds us that in one sense we do not know God, but in another sense we do. In one sense we must be apophaticists; in another, we must be epistemological realists about God's salvation, which entails a covenant not of love only but of love-and-knowledge. But it cannot be proper to 'reify' or 'externalise' the limitations built into the Christian understanding of God, and re-locate them within the divine being itself. For some critics, however – such as Dom Illtyd Trethowan, a Catholic, and Bishop Rowan Williams, an Anglican – this is precisely what Palamas did.[30] To these strictures Bishop Kallistos Ware, for the Orthodox, has responded that the limit to our knowledge must itself be grounded somehow in reality, including the reality of God.[31]

And this brings us to a third objection which is the gravest of all. If we turn our experience of the God of salvation into statements about what God is like themselves controlled by the Palamite distinction, then we appear to be undermining the simplicity of God – the fact that everything God has by way of attribute, that he simply *is*. In the preferred vocabulary of the Byzantine churchmen, God is not *sunthetos*, made up of parts, as are creatures. How can there be an aspect of God not included in the divine essence? Are not *essentia* and *operatio* distinct in God only 'formally'? While Jugie highlighted the *prima facie* incompatibility here between Palamism and the Western tradition, not only theological, as with Thomas Aquinas, but doctrinal, as with the Fourth Lateran Council,[32] another writer of the 1930s, S. Guichardan, had pointed out that, in both Latin West and Greek East, fourteenth century theologians had difficulty with presenting the divine simplicity – not just Palamas, but also, for the Byzantines, Gennadios Scholarios, and, for the Latins, Duns Scotus.[33] For both Jugie and some later Catholic critics, the Palamite distinction is both paganising and heretical – reviving an impersonal neo-Platonist notion of participation in God, and the Christological heresy of Monoenergism to boot. The Anglican Williams holds that Palamas, who was not by Byzantine standards a trained philosopher, used the language of ancient philosophy poorly in his defence of the hesychasts. While his intention – to protect our participation in God through Christ by the Holy Spirit – was sound, the upshot was the restoration of a neo-Platonic view of God, in which the ultimate reality, the One, becomes participable through the mediation of quasi-divine emanations, the energies. For the Palamites, Meyendorff can reply that if the distinction between Father, Son and Holy Spirit does not overthrow the divine simplicity, why should that between God's essence and his energies do so?[34] And in any case, many Orthodox regard the notion of the divine simplicity as rather a philosophical theorem than a Christian doctrine.[35] They prefer to speak in this connexion of God's 'indivisibility'. The one God is indivisible, first, on the level of *ousia* – in his own total and unsharable self-possession. He is indivisible, secondly, on the level of the persons – in the unbreakable unity of their *perichôrêsis*, their common life. And similarly, he is also indivisible on the level of the energies, where there is a unified consistency in God's acts of self-expressive love.

Conclusion

These issues, raised by Meyendorff's work, are of some ecumenical significance. Following Meyendorff's lead, some Orthodox now believe that the non-reception of Palamism in the West is responsible for many of the ills of Latin Christendom, just as an earlier generation, that of Lossky, ascribed those troubles to the affirmation of the *Filioque*, seen as unbalancing the dogma of the Trinity, tending to suppress the person and work of the Holy

Spirit. For Yannaras, responding to Western critics of Palamism, the rejection of Palamite doctrine means the denial of any full-blooded teaching on grace as deification. In his catalogue of the evils anti-Palamism brings with it he includes

> the sharpest antithetical separation between the transcendent and the immanent, the 'banishment' of God into the realm of the empirically inaccessible; the schizophrenic divorce of faith from knowledge; the recessive waves of rebellion of Western man against the theological presuppositions of his own civilisation; the rapid fading away of religion in the West, and the appearance of nihilism and irrational-ism as fundamental existential categories of Western man.[36]

Not all Orthodox, surely, will find this sweeping statement plausible. What is feasible on the Catholic side is a recognition of, at any rate, the just intention of Palamism – to safeguard at once the real divinisation of man and the reality of the transcend-ence of God – though with an accompanying affirmation that the vocabulary of the energies is, as Palamas uses it, to be regarded as metaphorical – what he himself called 'by way of image and analogy', *paradeigmatikôs kai kata analogian.*

In any case, the response of the Catholic Church to Palamism as represented most authoritatively in the writings of John Meyendorff will not be just as a matter of theology – even in the sense of a theological doctrine of God. Meyendorff's work also raises issues of ecclesiology, or of foundational theology, and above all the extent to which regional councils of churches not in full communion with the Petrine see – like the Byzantine councils of the fourteenth century – could be validated retrospectively by Catholicism, through the process known as 're-reception': that is, the qualified acceptance of such conciliar teaching, modified by its placing in a new context of doctrinal thought which corrects or at least supplements any deficiencies it may possess. But thinking along these lines would take us into ecclesiology proper – and so too far from the doctrine of God in contemporary Orthodoxy that is our present concern.

IV
Sergei Bulgakov and Sophiology

Sergei Bulgakov was born into a priestly family in central Russia in 1871.[1] As he wrote: 'I was born into the family of a priest, and six generations of levitical blood flowed in my veins'.[2]

He grew up as a devout Orthodox child, and went to school in a minor seminary. This was quite common in the period even for boys who had shown no interest in the priesthood as a vocation. But the young Bulgakov was revolted by what he considered the subservient attitude of the seminarians to all forms of authority – religious, social and political. Thus, when he moved to a secular school and then to Moscow University he was already receptive to the ideas of the Russian intelligentsia, anti-monarchical and anti-Church in orientation as it had become.

Russian Marxism

The Russian intelligentsia amounted to almost a distinct 'estate' in Russian society. Belonging to no particular class, its most significant common denominator was the ideal of service to the people. Though on occasion this took a right-wing form, it more generally took a left-wing one. Bulgakov himself speedily embraced Marxism, which he regarded as a scientific instrument for analysing the conditions that produced the ills of the people, and so for predicting appropriate action to remedy those ills. However, it must be borne in mind that, until the advent of Lenin, Russian Marxism was far more open and pluralistic than it later became. In 1896, at the age of only twenty-five, Bulgakov's study of the working of the market in capitalist economies gained him the chair of political economy and statistics in the law faculty of Moscow University.[3] Soon after his marriage (1898), Bulgakov published an investigation into the relation of capitalism to the agrarian economy. This was a subject of great importance in Russia where the overwhelming majority of the population were peasants.

In the years between 1900 and 1903 Bulgakov became increasingly dissatisfied with what he saw as the ethical relativism of Marxism. He therefore tried to marry Marxist social analysis to the justification of rational ethics found in the neo-Kantian school of philosophy. In that Kantian tradition, Bulgakov sought what he called an 'absolute sanction' for the moral and social ideals of revolution. His aim was to justify radical intervention in the historical process in terms of the *a priori* and inalienable qualities of the human subject, to establish what Kantians would term a 'transcendental justification'. Bulgakov, that is, wished to preserve the socialist ideal of Marx, but to strip it of all suggestion of determinism. Man must not be seen as a passive object swept along by the forces of economic development, but as a creative agent in history, freely acting in pursuit of fundamental values.

In 1903, while lecturing at the University of Kiev, Bulgakov admitted that he could no longer stand the strain of combining Marxism with idealism, with a rational ethics based on the creativity of the personal subject. He therefore announced his conversion to idealism proper. This did not necessarily involve the shedding of all his earlier thought. As we shall see, his eventual theological activity as an Orthodox priest is at least partly to be explained on the basis of his Marxian inheritance.

Idealism and Sophia

What did conversion to idealism mean for Bulgakov? Russian idealism was essentially indebted to four people, two of them German, the other two indigenous. The Germans were Hegel and Schelling; the natives the lay religious philosopher Vladimir Solov'ev, and the eclectic, even syncretistic priest-theologian

Pavel Florensky. Hegel's influence on Bulgakov is important for his sophiology. For Bulgakov accepted Hegel's criticism of the usual Christian account of the God-world relationship, namely that the world, as generally presented in Christian theology, exists alongside God, or parallel to God. But in all other respects Bulgakov's debt to Schelling was by far the greater. Schelling's philosophy underlies Bulgakov's theology at many points, even in such comparatively non-philosophical areas as ecclesiology – so much so that Bulgakov can be called a Christian Schellengian.[4] Once again this is especially clear for his sophiology, where Bulgakov accepted Schelling's view that God, by the necessity of his love, undergoes a kenosis or self-emptying not only in the Incarnation. This kenosis is also present in the work of the Holy Spirit from Pentecost onwards; it is present in the very constituting of the Holy Trinity. The other two idealist influences on Bulgakov – Solov'ev and Florensky – contributed the crucial idea of divine Wisdom, Sophia. Without anticipating too much of what will follow, it may be noted at this point that the Old Testament uses the figure of divine Wisdom as a way of speaking about God's creative and self-communicative power at work in the world. At the same time, Old Testament writers also speak about a human wisdom, which comes from the divine Wisdom, and puts man in a state of harmony with that greater wisdom. In the Book of Wisdom itself, wisdom is presented as the very manifestation of God. Through her, God mediates the work of creation, providential guidance and revelation. She is the subtle power of the presence of God, permeating and enspiriting all things and bringing about God's immanent presence in the creation, in revelation, in redemption.

The New Testament has more than traces of a Wisdom Christology, which sees such wisdom fully incarnated in Jesus Christ. It has been argued by Louis Bouyer that there are Fathers of the Church, especially Athanasius in the East and Augustine in the West, who re-created the comprehensive Wisdom theology of the Old Testament but re-aligned on the new axis of Christ. Relying on such texts as Athanasius's Second Discourse against the Arians and Book XII of Augustine's *Confessions*, Bouyer goes so far as to ascribe to these Fathers a fully explicit Sophiology of their own, a vision of created wisdom as

> the final embodiment of the glorification of human nature in Christ, in his mystical body the Church, in the blessed Virgin Mary, first of all, and, finally, in the whole of creation, as an association of the whole of created reality, around man, with the life of God as it exists eternally in himself.[5]

Solov'ev and Florensky may be said to have such a biblico-patristic synthesis. But they also added to it a new dimension of their own. This was based, so it would seem, on their personal religious experience. In Solov'ev's case, the crucial experience involved a female stranger who saved him from a traffic accident. This was a sign, as he saw it, of the all-encompassing divine Wisdom. Solov'ev held that the human task consists in realising unity between this divine Wisdom and the created world. He referred to this as 'all unity' or 'Godmanhood'. Florensky accepted Solov'ev's account of Wisdom-Sophia and claimed to find her presence throughout Russian religious culture, notably in the icons of the holy Wisdom of the Iaroslavl' school. Both of these Russian thinkers may be called idealists insofar as they held the ultimate reality to be spirit, spirit understood as subjectivity, the power of being a subject endowed with knowledge and love.

Bulgakov never explained where he found the idea of Sophia. But we know that in the period of his break with Marxism he was reading Solov'ev. Furthermore, Florensky's influential *Stolp i utverzhdenie istiny*[6] was published in 1914, only three years before Bulgakov's first sophiological treatise, *Svet nevechernii* ('The Light Unchanging').[7] In his autobiography,[8] Bulgakov confines himself to describing three experiences of the reality to which the concept of Sophia applies: one of a landscape, one of a work of art, and one of an encounter with a starets in a monastery.

Having re-discovered the Orthodox Church of his childhood by way of the Russian Sophiologists and his own experience,

Bulgakov was back in Moscow, teaching in the university and active in that short-lived parliamentary experiment, the Duma. In the Duma, conscious as he was of the anti-Christian attitudes of the extreme left-wing parties, Bulgakov's became an increasingly conservative voice. In 1917, he published his first and fundamental theological work which gave his whole output its basic orientation. This was a reflection on Sophia.

Bulgakov was elected, in the same year, to the *sobor* or council of the Russian Church. It was at this time that he became a close adviser of the saintly Patriarch Tikhon (Belavin), the first Russian bishop to occupy the office of patriarch since the time of Peter the Great.

In 1918 Tikhon blessed the ordination of Bulgakov to the priesthood. In the turbulent times ahead, Tikhon was to be imprisoned (1923). That same year Bulgakov was to be expelled from his homeland as a reactionary and anti-Soviet element.

After brief sojourns in Instanbul and Prague he came to Paris, where he would spend the rest of his life, and where he died from cancer in 1944. For most of that period Bulgakov was dean of the newly-founded Institut Saint-Serge.

The Works of his Maturity

Bulgakov's great period as theologian was the 1920s and 1930s. It was then that he produced his two trilogies. The first, sometimes referred to as the 'little trilogy', was written in the 1920s, and inspired by the idea of the *deesis* or 'supplication' in Byzantine art: *deesis* is the name given to a group of figures in the middle of the icon-screen as found in a typical Orthodox church. Turned in supplication to Christ as divine-human mediator, the icons of the *deesis* show Our Lady, John the Baptist and the angels. These are, respectively, the subjects of Bulgakov's little trilogy.[9] The second trilogy, sometimes called, by contrast, the 'great trilogy', takes its point of departure from Solov'ev's term 'Godmanhood', and deals with the three main elements in the reunion of the divine wisdom with mankind. As Bulgakov saw it, these were the mission of the Son, the mission of the Holy Spirit, and the role of the Church.[10]

The Comforter

Uteshitel' ('The Comforter') may serve to give some idea of the ethos, problematic, and particular strengths or weaknesses of his theological approach. So far as theological method is concerned, Bulgakov's study of the Paraclete stresses the primacy of Scripture, berating participants in the *Filioque* controversy (whether Orthodox or Catholic) for appearing to place the Fathers on the same dizzy eminence. His appeal to the Bible incorporates some contemporary New Testament exegesis, just as his use of texts and materials from the Christian past generally involves a recognition of historical scholarship and recourse to the tool kit of the philologist. Still he is very free in his use of Scripture; in regard to the patristic witnesses he is not only free, but critical.

What is more specifying for Bulgakov's theological enterprise, however, is what we may term his theological and philosophical principles of order – the themes by whose instrumentality the contents of Scripture and Tradition at large are to be held up to intellectual light, there to be both analytically explored and synthetically displayed. So far as a theological principle of order is concerned, Bulgakov draws an all-pervasive analogy between nature and the structure of the inner-Trinitarian relationships. Thus for instance (in a way reminiscent of Augustine's comparison of the human mind to the Holy Trinity, yet also thoroughly different from his), Bulgakov compares the structure of the 'two-some' (*dvoitsa*) of Son and Spirit as revealers of the hypostasis of the Father to the structure of the mind of man as knower of truth. If the Word is the 'deep wisdom' (*premudrost'*) of Sophia, the divine all-unity, the Spirit is her 'glory' (*slava*). But man knows truth as both 'ideal' (in the form of the coherent intelligibleness of conceptual contents) and 'real' (as referred to the actual splendour of reality). Accordingly, the Word comes to him through Sophia as the content of revelation, while the Spirit he encounters, thanks to Sophia, as revelation's beauty or glory. Thus Bulgakov looked to the sophianic energies of the Holy Trinity to provide the transcendental conditions of possibility for human creativity: man is the image of the Sophianic creativity of God. The danger here lay in forgetting the sheer contingency of the creature, of natural reality.

Where a dominant *philosophical* problematic may be said to shape Bulgakov's selection and treatment of his materials, this must certainly be that of the God-world relationship. Just as the young Hegel had asked after a possible reconciliation of finite and infinite, taking as his inspiration the happy harmony of Greek religiosity (as seen by German students of his period), so Bulgakov manifests the self-same hostility to a distant God, likening Calvinism, in this respect, to Islam. For Bulgakov, there must be something mediate between the Uncreated and the created, the divine and the human, else neither creation nor Incarnation can be thought or realised. Sophia, not an hypostasis, but rather *hypostasia* or 'hypostaseity', makes possible, as an intermediate reality, immanent in both divine and human being, not only the Incarnation but also the action of the Holy Spirit in the world. It has been pointed out that Bulgakov threatens here the divine personalism of the New Testament, since he diverts attention to an impersonal cosmic Wisdom. Yet in other ways Bulgakov's thought is almost wildly personalistic, for instance in its rejection of the concept of causality as applied to the origin of the Trinitarian persons. For Bulgakov, the persons are not caused. Rather is each self-determined, self-qualified and 'self-produced'. This led him, in the course of *Uteshitel'*, to cry a plague on the houses of filioquists and monopatrists alike.

Father, Son and Spirit

What, then, of the substantive doctrine of Bulgakov's *Uteshitel'*? To grasp it – and especially its implications for the Sophia theme – we must cast an eye over the conclusions Bulgakov had already reached in his Christology, *Agnets Bozhii* ('The Lamb of God').[11] The *Father*, as the absolute Subject, chooses from all eternity to be self-knowing and self-revealed in the Son, who stands to the Father, accordingly, as the Father's 'not-I' – and in this sense as his nature. In this act, the Father is engaged in a self-sacrifice: he gives himself away, he 'annihilates' himself so that the Son may be begotten. This self-gift, though made in eternity, cannot, for Bulgakov, be sundered from the Son's mission to redeem the created universe. Thus, in the light of the cross as the high-point of the Son's redemptive work, the Father's begetting of the Son can be called by Bulgakov his 'self-negation'.

On the side of the *Son*, too, there is, from the beginning, sacrifice, and even – for Bulgakov – suffering, endured in the total surrender of his will to that of the Father, whether in the everlasting triune life, or in his earthly life as the incarnate. In the Holy Trinity, the Son allows himself to be begotten, that is, to be made the image of the begetter, the Father. To be the Father's image is a sacrificial condition, since it is to know and realise oneself only in him after whose image one is made. This 'self-exhaustion' of the Son in the Father is his eternal kenosis.[12]

Where, then, does the *Spirit* enter the play of the persons? The Holy Spirit, for Bulgakov, gives 'reality' to the union of the Father and the Son. He also 'consoles' them by contributing joy and bliss to the sacrificial suffering of their love. How does this come about? First, the Spirit renders the hypostases of Father and Son fully transparent to the divine *ousia*. Secondly, the Spirit overcomes the 'tragedy' in the love of Father and Son: in the moment of 'sending' the Spirit, the Father receives his love; and the Spirit, thus sent by the Father, 'reposes' at the same time on the Son. Yet the Spirit too, like Father and Son, suffers sacrificially: in his case, because his hypostasis is not itself revealed. The Spirit is destined for ever to be a means to the mutual transparence of others, and hence, like a window, to be imperceptible in his function as intermediary. Yet this self-abnegation is also the Spirit's joy.

In forsaking the possibility of revealing himself like the Father and Son, he becomes the comfort of the Father and Son, becomes the real love between them, and thus is filled with joy.[13]

Thanks to the Holy Spirit, nature in the Godhead – the not-I of the Father as absolute Subject – becomes at last fully hypostatised, fully personal. Yet the divine nature does not lose its own significance in thus being appropriated in the relations of the persons. There are 'depths of life' in God which are not simply subsumed under the relations of the Trinitarian persons. In the Godhead, 'nature' exists not only for the mutual revelation of the persons but for itself as the highest of all powers, that of the *ens realissimum*, the divine Essence. And it is this divine life and power which Bulgakov calls Sophia. It is this which he regards as creation's own foundation, its principle of being.

The Sophiology Crisis

In the midst of writing the 'great trilogy', Bulgakov's daily round of study and teaching was rudely interrupted. In September 1935, Metropolitan Sergei (Stragorodsky) of Moscow announced that he condemned Bulgakov's sophiological teaching as alien to the Orthodox faith.[14] In October of the same year, apparently quite independently, the bishops of the Russian Church in Exile, themselves not in communion with the Moscow patriarchate, wrote to Bulgakov's ecclesiastical superior in Paris, Metropolitan Evlogy (Georgievsky), in yet stronger terms, characterising his theology as heretical.

These attacks were not wholly unheralded. As early as 1924, the former Archbishop of Kiev, Metropolitan Antony Khrapovitsky, presiding bishop of the Church in Exile, had accused both Florensky and Bulgakov of adding a fourth hypostasis (person) to the Holy Trinity. And some phrases in *Svet nevechernii* could indeed give the impression that Bulgakov believed in a quadernity of Father, Son, Spirit and Sophia.[15] To this earlier attack, Bulgakov had written a reply, 'Ipostas i ipostasnost', in which he explained that the Wisdom of God is not a person and yet may be called quasi-personal for two reasons.[16] First, it is the recipient of the love of God. Secondly, being itself the medium whereby the world is made, it is capable of manifesting itself in innumerable persons – namely, in human beings. This answer was, no doubt, as little satisfactory to zealous Orthodox bishops as it was intelligible to ordinary readers.

The charges brought by the Orthodox hierarchy against Bulgakov in 1935 were various and weighty. The Moscow patriarchate in its *ukaz* declared that Bulgakov's teaching was not ecclesial in its intention, since it ignored the Church's own teaching and tradition, preferring at certain points openly to embrace the views of heretics condemned by the councils. Nor was it ecclesial in content, since it introduced so many new elements into the understanding of fundamental dogmas as to be, rather, reminiscent of Gnosticism.[17] Nor, finally, was it ecclesial in its practical consequences, since by presenting salvation as a cosmic process, it undermined the sense of personal sin, personal repentance, and the personal ascetic effort of the individual. Study of the Moscow patriarchate document suggests that its authors enjoyed a rather general notion of Bulgakov's system, though not an altogether inaccurate one.

In the condemnation issued by the Church in Exile, Bulgakov is accused of pride as a converted Russian intellectual who had never ceased to look down on the ordinary clergy and faithful of the Russian Church. He is a rationalist, who ignores the essentially apophatic character of Orthodox theology. And by attempting to describe positively (cataphatically) what was in the divine nature that made possible the Incarnation and Pentecost, he had pried into questions which Scripture and the Fathers would never have dared to ask. At the same time, he is also a subjectivist who allows his own imagination to run riot, and suffers from 'verbal incontinence'. His sophiology is nothing more than a revival of Gnosticism, which consists essentially in speculation about intermediaries between the Creator and the creature. Sophiology has no basis in the Bible, and, so far as tradition is concerned, it is a new doctrine. Unlike the Moscow text, the synodal document is both detailed and circumstantial in its accusations.

A critical memorandum, on behalf of the neo-patristically inclined members of the 'Confrèrie de saint Photius', by that other giant of Russian diaspora theology, Vladimir Lossky, played its part in the formulation of these episcopal asperities. Though not himself a lecturer at the Institut Saint-Serge, Lossky's intervention would lead in time to a rupture in that body, whereby those scholars unsympathetic to Bulgakov's speculative flights, and notably George Florovsky, would depart for North America.

Bulgakov's Defence

How did Bulgakov respond to these charges? An answer to this question involves a positive consideration of Bulgakov's theology of wisdom. This in turn will lead to a critical evaluation of my own.

In part, Bulgakov's response was a formal one, which did not consider the material doctrinal or theological issues involved, but confined itself to the issues of authority raised by the condemnations. I can deal simply with this formal aspect of his reply. Bulgakov defended himself by saying that, Sophiology does not concern the content of the revealed dogmas, but only their theological interpretation. In other words, he had denied no dogma, but was, rather, setting the dogmas in a special framework of philosophical theology. He also pointed out that hitherto Sophiology had been a theological interpretation of dogma permitted in the Orthodox Church, as the careers of Solov'ev and Florensky demonstrated. Furthermore, he considered that the condemnations, made as they were by a single hierarch or else a small group of hierarchs, contravened the Orthodox ethos of decision-making, which is essentially conciliar, and, no less importantly, followed up by regard for reception or rejection on the part of the faithful. Bulgakov held that the condemnations showed a characteristically Catholic tendency to ascribe to the hierarchy an intrinsic, *ex sese*, infallibility in all questions of truth. According to Bulgakov, this violated the freedom of theological opinion and so threatened the life of the Orthodox Church by attacking the vital interests of all theologians, no matter what their tendency.

Turning to the actual issues, Bulgakov took the opportunity to offer a succinct exposé of his doctrine, both in Russian (*O Sofii, Premudrosti Bozhiei*) and in English (*The Wisdom of God*).[18] He maintained that, whereas many of the Fathers identify the divine Wisdom with God and Son, others ascribe it, like Bulgakov himself, to the whole Godhead. Bulgakov justified his further development of the theme of Sophia by reference to Russian Church dedications, to liturgical texts and to iconography, where the Old Testament wisdom texts are linked not only to the Trinity but also to Christ, Our Lady, John the Baptist, the apostles and the Angels. Such liturgies and images, he pointed out, are recognised *loci theologici* in dogmatic writing. Bulgakov interprets them to mean that there is in God from all eternity a spiritual humanity, the wisdom of God, which is itself the object of the common love of the Trinitarian persons. This pre-existent Wisdom reveals itself in the creation. Above all, it reveals itself in man, and more particularly still in Mary of Nazareth and John the Baptist, in whom the Old Testament economy comes to its climax. Then, definitively, it reveals itself in Jesus Christ. Lastly, in dependence on Christ, it finds its revelation in the apostolic Church. The same pre-existent Wisdom is also reflected in the heavenly 'humanity' of the Angels. Thus the ensemble of church dedications, liturgical texts and icons, to which Bulgakov appealed, may be said to represent the divine Wisdom in its two modes. For it represents the Uncreated and the created, the eternal 'humanity' of God and created humanity. (By 'humanity' here is meant, evidently, whatever it is in angelic and divine nature that inclines to inter-action with humankind. Moreover, it represents these two in their interconnecting unity.

All this wealth of symbolism has been preserved in the archives of ecclesiastical antiquities, but, covered by the dust of ages, it has been of no use to anyone. The time has come, however, for us to sweep away the dust of ages and to decipher the sacred script, to reinstate the tradition of the Church, in this instance all but broken, as a living tradition. It is Holy Tradition which lays such tasks upon us.[19]

For good measure, Bulgakov went on to attack the bishops for their deprecation of his own reliance on the imaginative interpretation of Christian symbols. Their criticism of him on this point showed, he said, that they themselves were little better than nominalist rationalists. Unlike his critics, he has drawn on the living tradition of the Fathers and the liturgy, and interpreted them with the controlled intuition of an Orthodox mind and heart – a procedure more genuinely Eastern than dependence on a debased, propositionalist and scholastic theology.

Furthermore, Bulgakov argues that the cataphatic uses to which he has put these traditional materials are fully justified. Basically, he had had two main purposes. First, to show what, positively speaking, relates God with the world; and secondly, on the basis of this first enquiry, to show (positively, once again) what made possible the union of the divine and human natures in the person of Christ. To work out some understanding of these matters is for the theologian a religious duty, whereas the bishops and their advisers are like the lazy servant in the Gospels who buried his talent in the ground. The idea of Sophia is invaluable, since it enables us to say that, in creating the world, God does not produce a reality which stands over against him. If he did so, he would cease to be the Absolute. For the Absolute, of its very nature, must constitute the reality of everything else that is.

In acting as creator, God allows his own wisdom to enter into nothingness. His wisdom begins to exist in the mode of limitation, as process or becoming. It begins to develop, taking the differentiated form of the varieties of creatures found in, and as, the world. It provides those creatures with their fundamental energy. It acts as what Aristotle had called their *entelecheia*, and so provides them with their own immanent finality or goal. It is this natural, ontological union of the world with God which is taken up in the revealed economies of the Son and Spirit. This it is which makes it possible to conceptualise the Incarnation. It is this which makes possible the transfiguration of creatures by the Holy Spirit.

Sophiology Evaluated

How is Bulgakov's sophiology to be evaluated? Almost all critics, whether Orthodox, Catholic or Protestant, seem agreed that Bulgakov undoubtedly ran the risk of pantheism. Though his intention was simply to avoid a radical dualism between God and the world, his position appears to lead towards an identification of the world with God. In his kenotic love for his own creation, God allows his own essence to exist apart from his Trinitarian hypostases, and to become instead enhypostatised in man. In other words, the divine Sophia and the creaturely sophia are apparently the same reality under two different modes of existing. For Bulgakov, the world is the energy of the divine *ousia*, an energy which God has placed outside himself, in nothingness, and which, by fusion with that nothingness, takes the form of process or becoming.

It is interesting to note that Bulgakov called the teaching of Gregory Palamas an incomplete sophiology. Yet Bulgakov's own theology of divine process, like that of his Anglo-American Episcopalian contemporay, Alfred North Whitehead, could be called an incomplete pantheism. To some degree, Bulgakov seems to have allowed a certain rationalism to penetrate his theological thought, in that he refuses to allow creation *ex nihilo* its proper status as mystery. Creation from out of nothingness is a mystery in that by means of it God lets a creature be. He lets it share in his own act of existence without, for all that, transferring to nothingness the quality of being an emanation of his own divine reality.

As a theologian, Bulgakov's most distinctive concern, deriving perhaps from his Marxist period, was the due recognition of the intrinsic value of the visible world, and of the earthly life of man.

He wanted to show how the revelation of the Father in the missions of the Son and the Spirit in Christ and in the Church presupposed the intrinsic value of the cosmos in general and of man in particular; and how, furthermore, they proceeded to fulfil those values by taking them to their furthest term of development. Possibly, as has been suggested by Barbara Newman, Bulgakov's closest kindred spirit in the Western Church was Pierre Teilhard de Chardin.[20]

The enduring significance of Bulgakov's thought lies, then, in the stress he laid on the divine immanence. As he wrote in *The Wisdom of God:*

> Heaven stoops towards earth; the world is not only a word in itself, it is also the world in God, and God abides not only in heaven but also on earth with man.[21]

But the question here is whether it is not precisely by virtue of his transcendence, by his absolute difference from the world, that God can be immanent within all things and intimately present to them.

This is why the most intelligent line of defence of Bulgakov is that pioneered by Constantin Andronikof. In his contribution to the colloquium on Bulgakov's thought held in Paris in 1985, Andronikof emphasised that while, for Bulgakov, the Absolute and the relative have, certainly, something in common, this factor

> does not render them identical but maintains them in ontological distinction ... Their conjunction (*jonction*) does not affect their otherness (*altérité*).[22]

The two worlds of heaven and earth are at once 'absolutely distinct and incommensurable', yet linked by a 'configuration' of 'conformity' which allows God to come down to the level of the creature without pulverising it, and man to mount up without being burnt up.

According to Andronikof, Bulgakov's great question was, how

is it possible for God to manifest himself to us, and for humanity to have, in the Church, a life filled with grace? The answer is given by the very nature of our Creator, who is love and therefore relationship: the creature reflects the Wisdom of God, but not without the 'occultations' of evil.[23] The supreme realisation of this relation is the work of the Word taking flesh by the Holy Spirit, uniting in himself the divine world and the world of man. In his attempt to vindicate the fundamental orthodoxy of this 'realist ontology', expressed as it is in a sophiology and closely linked to the theology of the Incarnation. Andronikof leans for support on the massive study of Bulgakov on yet another theologian of the Russian diaspora, Leo Zander.[24] In his *Bog i Mir* ('God and the World'), Zander held that Bulgakov's early work, and notably *Svet nevechernii* can indeed be convicted of the errors with which the sophiological 'system' has been charged. The book offers a 'monistic' sophiology, with only one Wisdom: Janus-like, it has two faces, created and Uncreate in turn. Moreover, this same Sophia is presented as a true subject, an hypostasis. But with the writing of the 'Chapters on trinitarity', Bulgakov introduces a 'dualist' sophiology, in which the divine *ousia* and the being of creatures are clearly differentiated, and the wisdom theme is integrated with the doctrine of the Holy Trinity. Moreover, starting with the 1925 essay on hypostasis and hypostaseity, Bulgakov insists that Sophia is not a personal principle but rather an 'ontological principle of life'. For Andronikof, Bulgakov's finest statement of an orthodox sophiology is found in his study *Ikona i ikonopochitanie*, where he wrote:

> Sophia is the very nature of God, not only as act but as divine eternal fact; not only as power but also as effect ... In Sophia, God knows and sees himself, he loves himself, not with the mutual personal love of the three super-eternal hypostases, but as loving what is his own, his divinity, his divine life ... So Sophia is the divinity of God or the divinity in God. In this sense, Sophia is the divine world before the creation.[25]

And the passage continues:

For the created realm, God is Sophia, since, in Sophia and by Sophia he discloses himself as the personal tri-hypostatic God and as the creator. The world is created by and in Sophia, since there neither is nor can be any other principle of being. Consequently, the world is also Sophia, but in becoming, as a creature existing in time. Created on the foundation of Sophia, the world is destined for a condition where 'God is all in all' – to become integrally sophianic.[26]

Thus Andronikof calls Bulgakov's work an attempt to point out the positive presuppositions interleaved with the negative disjunctions of the Chalcedonian definition,[27] that famous quartet of adverbs, whereby, in the God-man, the Uncreated and the created are said to be conjoined 'without confusion, without change, without division, and without separation'.

It would be a worthwhile task for Orthodox theologians to investigate more fully the implications – whether positive or negative for Christian doctrine – of the Schellengian philosophy which underlies Bulgakov's conceptual scheme at many points.

In conclusion, I note the balance-sheet of praise and blame drawn up by Barbara Newman, herself a student of the mediaeval Western sophiologist, Hildegard of Bingen. Though Bulgakov's fundamental ontology is flawed, 'heresy' is too harsh a term for the weaknesses of his speculative system. Moreover, he discovered forgotten insights of the Fathers and uncovered elements of Orthodoxy expressed, if obscurely, in such unusual *loci theologici* as the dedications of churches and the forms of popular devotion. Hence, while lamenting Bulgakov's neglect in the English-speaking world, she concludes, in future years:

We may hope that the revelation epitomized by the dome of Hagia Sophia will again receive the attention it deserves.[28]

V
John Romanides and neo-Photianism

The Catholic doctrine of the procession of the Holy Spirit from both the Father and the Son is, with the Roman primacy, the most obvious of the obstacles to reunion between the Latin Church and the Orthodox, so it should be of some ecumenical importance to see how one leading Greek theologian, John Romanides, treats the matter.

Historical Background

The origins of the *Filioque* dispute in Chalcedonian Christendom go back to the patristic age. Although the differences between the Latin and Greek theological schemata of the patristic period have been in much modern historical theology simplified and even distorted, both by overlooking the varieties of currents within Western and Eastern thought, and by ecclesiastical polemic, the existence of some important contrasts, as between Latin West and Greek East, can hardly be denied. First of all, by and large the Greek considered the Father as the supreme principle, *archê*, both of the other two persons and of the creation, whereas the Latins generally regarded the common nature of the triune persons as the 'principle' of creation, and the Father and Son together as the principle of the Spirit. However, it has to be noted, as Bertrand de Margerie points out in his *The Christian Trinity in History*, that *principium* is a more general term than *archê* and lacks the latter's connotation of a *supreme* or ultimate *principle*.

In the post-patristic era the Council of Florence would take this linguistic difference fully into account when it spoke of the Father as *principium sine principio*, the Son as *principium de principio*.[1] Similarly, the Latin term *procedere* has a more general significance than the Greek New Testament's *ekporeusthai*, of which it is a translation. The Latin term refers to origin, like the Greek, but unlike the Greek it does not specify whether this origin is really ultimate or only immediate. The problem of the verb involved only compounds that of the proposition, the Greek *ek* signifies ultimate derivation, the Latin *ab* is much more general. However it should be noted that while for the most part the Greek Fathers would no doubt have objected to the statement that the Spirit proceeds *ek tou Huiou* on the grounds that this suggests that the Son, not the Father, is the ultimate unoriginated source of the Spirit, both Epiphanius of Salamis and Cyril of Alexandria did not let grammatical scruples get in the way of saying precisely that.[2]

As is well known, the Creed of Nicaea-Constantinople, in its original form, affirms only that the Spirit proceeds from the Father. Gradually, however, beginning in Spain, the *Filioque* clause was introduced into the Latin Creed in order to protect the Orthodox confession against various late survivals of Arianism in the Western Church. For several centuries the Roman popes, while approving the doctrine of the *Filioque* (which was common teaching for most of the Latin Fathers – not only Augustine but even figures, such as Cassiodorus, who were in other respects quite non-Augustinian), did not permit its inclusion in the papal liturgy. This was a major cause of tension between the Holy See and the Frankish Church – the Church in the Carolingian Empire – during the eighth and ninth centuries. In the Frankish domains, which extended across present-day France and Germany, as well as the Low Countries and Northern Italy, episcopal leaders became increasingly insistent that the *Filioque* doctrine could not be communicated adequately unless it were actually said or sung by the people in the Creed of the Mass. There are some indications that their doctrinal opponents at this stage were not so much neo-Arians as early protagonists of the Monopatrist position soon to be identified with the Patriarch Photius of Constantinople. Thus for instance at the local council of Friuli in 796, Paulinus of Aquileia (near Venice) declared the addition of the *Filioque* a necessity because of 'heretics who murmur that the Holy Spirit proceeds from the Father alone'.[3]

In time, thanks not least to the attitude of the German rulers of the House of Hohenstaufen who succeeded, eventually, to Charlemagne and his successors as emperors of the West, the resistance of the Papacy to incorporation of the *Filioque* in the Creed gradually crumbled away. In 1014, at the coronation of Emperor Henry II at Rome by Pope Benedict VIII, the *Filioque* for the first time (so far as is known) at any papal liturgy was actually sung at Mass. Not that this guaranteed its automatic inclusion in the Creed throughout the Latin West. For example, at Paris it appears not to have been included as late as 1240.[4] Nonetheless, the *Filioque* doctrine had been itself by this time solemnly promulgated at a general council of the Latin Church, namely Lateran IV, in 1215 and, in the course of a first attempt at reconciliation with the Byzantine East, the Council of Lyons of 1274 specified that the Holy Spirit

> proceeds eternally from the Father and from the Son, not as from two principles but from a single principle, not by two spirations but by a single spiration.[5]

On this formulation the second major reunion Council of the Middle Ages, that of Florence, made a considerable advance. It based the Spirit's proceeding from the Son on the consideration that:

> Everything that belongs to the Father, the Father has given to the Son by begetting him, except for the fact of being Father.[6]

And it proposed that the Greek formula *dia ton Huion*, the *per Filium*, both suggested and prepared the way for the *Filioque*: in maintaining their *per Filium* – in giving the Son a rôle, in dependence on the Father, in the spiration of the Spirit – the Greeks held the essence of the *Filioque* doctrine.

Romanides's Version

Romanides is by background an Athenian theologian whose first work, a study of the doctrine of original sin, was published in 1957 under the title *To protopaterikon hamartêma*. A second edition came out in 1989.[7] The relevance of this book to Romanides's approach to the *Filioque* was that it made clear his profound antipathy to St Augustine. According to Romanides, the Augustinian understanding of the Fall of man as involving morally all later human beings is not accepted, and cannot be accepted, by the Orthodox tradition. Claiming to base himself on the consensus of the remaining Fathers, he offered his own version of what the Fall is by way of an attempted synthesis of patristic anthropology and modern physiology. Whereas, for Romanides, the human brain is the centre of man's adaptation to the environment, *nous*, which he understood, with the Byzantine ascetic tradition, as the noetic faculty, or power of understanding, in the heart, is the primary organ for communion with God. The Fall of man, or the state of inherited sin, is, he went on, first, the failure of the noetic faculty to function properly, or at all; secondly, its confusion with the functions of the brain and the body in general; and thirdly, its resulting enslavement to the environment. Opposing himself to the Augustinian doctrines of election and reprobation, Romanides insisted that all human beings have this noetic faculty in the heart, and so all are placed in direct relation to God in various ways, or at different levels – in dependence on the degree whereby the individual personality resists such enslavement to his or her physical and social surroundings and allows themself to be directed by God. For Romanides, every individual is sustained by the uncreated glory of God, and is the dwelling place of that uncreated creative and sustaining Light, which is called the rule (or kingdom), power, and grace of God. Human reaction to this direct relation or communion with God ranges from hardening of the heart, by which the spark of grace is extinguished, to the experience of glorification attained by prophets, apostles and saints. Upon such purification and illumination of the noetic faculty, selfless love is transformed in them into selfless love, egoism into charity – as the New Testament predicts.

In 1975 Romanides published a study of the relations between early Germanic Christianity and the Byzantines, which was at the same time an historical and dogmatic attack on the *Filioque* doctrine. It bore the fine alliterative title, *Rômaiosunê, Romania, Roumeli,* which we can translate very inadequately as 'Romanità, Byzantium and the Frankish Empire'.[8] Six years later, invited to give the Patriarch Athenagoras Memorial Lectures at the Greek Orthodox theological school at Brookline, Massachusetts, he brought out an English resumé of this curious work, with the title, *Franks, Romans, Feudalism and Doctrine. An Interplay between Theology and Society.*[9] That he approached the *Filioque* in both historical and systematic ways was in itself perfectly intelligible, since all studies of the *Filioque* issue are bound to address *both* the canonical question of the origins of the *Filioque* clause, *and* the dogmatic question of the validity of the *Filioque* doctrine. What was less expected was the virulence of his polemics.

Historically, Romanides presents the *Filioque* as an imposition of Frankish barbarians on what he calls *Rômaioi* – 'Romans', meaning by that both the West Romans of Rome itself and the East Romans of Constantinople. As he wrote:

> The cause of the Filioque controversy is to be found in the Frankish decision to provoke the condemnation of the East Romans as heretics so that the latter might become exclusively 'Greeks' and therefore a different nation from the West Romans under Frankish rule. The pretext of the Filioque controversy was the Frankish acceptance of Augustine as the key to understanding the theology of the First and Second Ecumenical Synods [namely, Nicaea and Constantinople I], that is, the Creed.[10]

In pursuit of their aim of dividing from the East the non-Frankish West, the West of the ancient Latin portion of the Byzantine *oikoumenê*, the Franks used Augustine as a tool. They took advantage of his idiosyncrasies *vis-à-vis* the patristic tradition at large to distort the Christianity of the West, sundering it from its Eastern counterpart, by forcing patristic tradition into an Augustinian mould. And if this seems, in relation to what other Church historians and historians of doctrine have to say, a rather exaggerated account, Romanides has an explanation:

> European historians have been sucked into the Frankish perspective, and thereby deal with Church history as though there were a Greek Christendom as distinguished from a Latin Christendom. Greek Christendom consists of, supposedly, the East Romans, and Latin Christendom of the Franks and other Germanic peoples using Latin, plus, supposedly, the West Romans, especially Papal Romania, that is the Papal States. Thus the historical myth has been created that the West Roman Fathers of the Church, the Franks, Lombards, Burgundians, Normans and so forth are the continuous and historically unbroken Latin Christian tradition, clearly distinguished and different from a mythical Greek Christendom.[11]

What, then, should historians have said? Romanides is not slow with his answer. He remarks:

> A much more accurate understanding of history, presenting the Filioque controversy in its true historical perspective, is based on the Roman viewpoint of Church history, to be found in (both Latin and Greek) Roman sources, as well as in Syriac, Ethiopic, Arabic and Turkish sources. All these point to a distinction between Frankish and Roman Christendom, and not between a mythical Latin and Greek Christendom. Among the Romans, Latin and Greek are national languages, not nations. The Fathers are neither Latins, nor Greeks, but Romans.[12]

The main problem with this historical thesis is that Western barbarians, so far from wanting to remake the Western Roman Empire in their own image, and so rupturing its links with the East, were only too glad to accept whatever of its patrimony, whether cultural, linguistic or religious, the Greco-Roman world at large could offer them.

But so far Romanides has not explained in what way Augustine could offer the Franks an instrument to differentiate and ultimately divide the Western portion of 'Romania', under their control, from its Eastern brothers. This he now goes on to do. In the *De Fide et Symbolo*, chapter 19, Augustine remarks of the Holy Spirit that those who study and enquire into Scripture have not yet discovered, really, what constitutes the Spirit's *proprium*, that is, his hypostatic particularity – what, essentially, makes him the unique person that he is. According to Romanides, this was, on Augustine's part, a foolish remark, for Constantinople I had already answered this question in speaking of the Spirit's origin as his procession rather than filiation. The Augustinian *Filioque*, then, was an answer to a non-existent problem. But, once this answer was given, it served the Franks' purpose well.

> It is no wonder that the Franks, believing that Augustine had solved a theological problem which the other Roman Fathers had supposedly failed to grapple with and solve, came to the conclusion that they uncovered a theologian far superior to all other Fathers.[13]

But just as the answer was superfluous and in fact erroneous, so was the method of arriving at it misplaced. And this is the other principal objection Romanides has to Augustine, aside from his difficulties with Augustine's account of original sin and the Spirit's procession. Augustine's method in theology was, admittedly, based on faith, in the sense that its starting point was revelation as accepted by faith. But after that it was, according to Romanides, one of sheer speculative virtuosity, an intellectual matter in the sense of concepts arranged by the reasoning faculty – what Romanides calls 'brain' – rather than by the noetic faculty in the heart, the organ of supernatural communion. He writes:

> For Augustine, there is no distinction between revelation and the conceptual intuition of revelation. Whether revelation is given directly to human reason, or to human reason by means of creatures

or created symbols, it is always the human intellect itself which is being illuminated or given vision to. The vision of God itself is an intellectual experience, even though above the powers of reason without appropriate grace.[14]

What the Frankish theologians did was to transfer to the level of the corporate Church what Augustine has to say about the possibility of a development of individual Christian understanding of revelation through theological enquiry, and so come up with the notion that the *Filioque* is a development of doctrine – something which, then, the whole Church must accept – hence their intransigence in demanding its addition to the Creed in the face of the reluctance of the Papacy in the ninth century. In eventually succumbing to the demands of their German successors in the eleventh century, the patriarchate of Old Rome ceased to be a Roman, that is, patristic, and became a mere Frankish, institution.

But what, according to Romanides, is proper theological method, the kind which will save us from belief in the *Filioque*? If we turn to his general dogmatics, the *Dogmatikê kai symbolikê theologia tês Orthodoxou katholikês Ekklêsias*, we find an answer. Having told his readers that Holy Tradition cannot be found outside the communion of Christ's visible – that is – Orthodox Church, Romanides goes on to explain that the apostolic tradition, as taught according to the mind of the Fathers, is not received in later generations simply by virtue of possession of a valid ministry, a tactile succession, *cheirotonia*, but also requires 'right teaching', *hê orthos peri Christou didaskalia*, as well as (and this is the point to note here) 'right spirituality', *hê orthos kata Christon kai en Christô pneumatikotês*, 'right spirituality according to and in Christ'.[15] Applying this to the *Filioque* dispute, and, in particular, the claim of Augustine and his disciples to furnish in the *Filioque* a more coherent understanding of Scripture, Romanides writes:

For the Fathers, authority is not only the Bible but the Bible and those glorified or divinised as the prophets and apostles. The Bible is not in itself inspired and infallible. It becomes inspired within the communion of saints because they have the experience of the glory described in the Bible. The presuppositions of the Frankish Filioque are not founded on this experience of glory. Anyone can claim to speak with authority and understanding. However, we follow the Fathers and accept only those as authority who like the apostles have reached a degree of Pentecostal glorification.[16]

But how can Romanides be so sure that Augustine, and later Latin divines who accepted a broadly Augustinian understanding of the inter-relation of Father, Son and Spirit, lacked this 'experience of glory'? The answer seems to lie in his angry rejection of Augustine's proposal that the theophanies of the Old Testament were not genuinely experiences of the Word, the Logos, but were, rather, perceptions of purely symbolic realities put forth by the Trinity as media of their provisional self-disclosure, and that, similarly, the tongues of fire which alighted on the heads of the apostles at Pentecost were not so much the uncreated energies of the Holy Spirit as creatures, once again, brought into existence by God to serve the purposes of revelation. To Romanides, such down-playing of Old Testament theophanies smacks of rationalism, a refusal to believe that God and man can really enter into reciprocal communion. As he puts it:

> In the patristic tradition all dogma or truth is experienced in glorification. The final form of glorification is that of Pentecost, in which the apostles were led by the Spirit into all the truth, as promised by Christ at the Last Supper. Since Pentecost, every incident of the glorification of a saint is an extension of Pentecost at various levels of intensity. This experience includes all of man, but at the same time transcends all of man, including man's intellect. Thus the experience remains a mystery to the intellect, and cannot be conveyed intellectually to another.[17]

The effect, and the purpose of this statement is to disqualify any argumentation offered for the *Filioquist* position.

Romanides concludes that, in terms of its threat to the

monarchy of the Father, so well identified by *ho megas Photios*, the 'great Photius', the *Filioque* is an error as serious in its own way as was Arianism to the Sonship of the Word. The only proper response is to identify its main author, Augustine, and remove him from the list of Orthodox Fathers. According to Romanides, Augustine was not genuinely part of the patristic tradition but rather interpreted Scripture

> within the framework of Plotinus and under the pressure of his Manichaean past.[18]

As even today little of Augustine's writings are available in Greek, it is a pity that Romanides has used the Greek language to spread this jaundiced view of the great North African doctor whom in effect he states to be no less a heresiarch than Arius.[19]

The Ecumenical Dimension of the Filioque *Issue*

It is true that the removal of the *Filioque* from the Western Creed is a major objective of the Orthodox within the ecumenical movement. As we shall now see, some progress has been made in that direction, though uncountenanced by Rome. But the responses of other Western confessions, and even indeed the official positions of the Orthodox themselves, are a good deal more nuanced than the neo-Photianism of Romanides.

Not all Christian churches have a creed at all. And so for many of them there is no clear context for discussion of the *Filioque* problem. However, in the last two decades or so it has become an important aim of the more theologically minded organs of the World Council of Churches to secure the adhesion of its member denominations to at least the general idea of having a creed. This is well illustrated in the document entitled 'Towards a Confession of the Common Faith: a Plan of Work of the Joint Working Group of the Roman Catholic Church and the World Council of Churches, 1980', which has as its Catholic signatory Père (now Bishop) Pierre Duprey of the Vatican Secretariat, now Council, for Promoting Christian Unity.[20] That text remarks of the great creeds:

> Inserted into the baptismal and eucharistic liturgies, these creeds will be important for the course of tradition. They will, in fact, be the sign and test of fidelity to the apostolic faith.[21]

Noting that, in the interim, major disagreements in the interpretation of the Creed have arisen, the signatories summon the contemporary divided confessions to make a choice.

> The churches have ... to state what in their corpus of doctrine they judge to be either a point on which they must require an explicit affirmation from other churches so that the unity God himself wishes to give to his Church may become reality at the level of faith, or, on the contrary, to be an aspect which can remain implicit without radically compromising the unity of faith.[22]

This 1980 document speaks only, in quite general terms, of creeds at large, but in 1981 the Faith and Order Commission of the World Council of Churches took a further step of relevance to the *Filioque* issue by publishing the conclusions of a meeting held under the auspices of the Moscow Patriarchate at Odessa: 'The Ecumenical Importance of the Nicene-Constantinopolitan Creed'.[23] The Odessa Report was in part a commemoration of the sixteenth centenary of the First Council of Constantinople, whose Creed this is. But more importantly, it constituted a response to criticisms of the World Council of Churches made at least since its New Delhi Conference of 1961 to the effect that the doctrine of the Holy Trinity played an insufficient part in the Council of Churches' deliberations and concerns. Pointing out that this Creed has been used as both a baptismal confession and a central doctrinal statement, in liturgical rites and notably at ministerial ordinations, and that it has inspired theologians, hymnwriters, preachers and artists down the centuries, the Odessa Report claims for it that, as the product of a universally accepted Council, it has served as a lighthouse in times of confusion and strife. The Report invites churches which do not use the Creed to examine it, with a view to adopting it, and those that do to look in its light at their other credal and confessional statements. We then find a statement of close relevance to the *Filioque* issue when the signatories continue:

> If the Creed is regarded as a sufficient formulation of faith, this sufficiency does not mean that the Creed cannot be interpreted, applied, explicated, and even expanded on – as long as proposed consequences and additions cannot be understood as contradictory to the Creed. How far is it possible to regard the dogmatic decisions of later Ecumenical Councils as following the inner logic of the Creed? How far may modern 're-interpretations' be stretched without going counter to the original meaning?[24]

So far as the *Filioque* itself is concerned, the World Council hosted in 1978 and 1979 an unofficial consultation of theologians from all the main Eastern and Western confessions, at Schloss Klingenthal in Alsace, discussions which produced the so-called 'Klingenthal Memorandum', whose full title was *The* Filioque *Clause in Ecumenical Perspective*, in 1979. Later that year, at Taizé, the Memorandum was recommended by the World Council to the churches. Both in status and content it is sufficiently weighty a document to merit attention here.

The Memorandum opens by asserting that, where the *Filioque* clause is concerned, three main questions need to be addressed. They are: first, divergences in approach to the Trinity; secondly, the particular problem of the wording of the Creed; and thirdly, the potential ecumenical significance of the Nicene Creed itself – an anticipatory reference to the two wider documents we have considered so far.

Next: the Memorandum undertakes to review, in brief compass, the history of the *Filioque* debate. It refers to 'some Latin writers' speaking of the Holy Spirit as 'proceeding from the Father and the Son', and of Augustine as so developing this conviction that between his day and the eighth century *'Filioque* theology' became deeply embedded in the minds and hearts of

Western Christians. Recalling such milestones in the story as the appearance of the *Filioque* addendum to the Creed in Spain, its support by the Frankish Church and its adoption by the eleventh century Papacy, the Memorandum then tackles the reunion councils of Lyons II and Florence which it has no hesitation in calling unsuccessful – on the grounds that, in the long run, their effect was to intensify the bitterness felt in the Eastern Church at the unilateral action of the West, not least because of the anathema which Lyons laid down against all those who knowingly rejected the clause. Although the Reformers did not question the *Filioque* either as a doctrine or as a clause, in the modern period fresh contacts between non-Catholic West and the separated East have influenced a number of Western confessions to reconsider the matter. The Old Catholics have in fact abandoned the *Filioque* clause, and the 1978 Lambeth Conference called on the provinces of the Anglican Communion to do likewise. The Memorandum states that even those churches which use the Creed very little or not at all are interested in this matter, since they too are heirs of the Western theological tradition.

The authors of the Klingenthal Memorandum now turn to a substantive, rather than historical consideration of the issue involved. They open by declaring that:

> From its beginnings in the second and third centuries, the doctrine of the Trinity was intended to be a help for Christian believers, not an obstacle or an abstract intellectual super-imposition upon the 'simple faith'. For it was in simple faith that the early Christians experienced the presence of the triune God; and it was in that presence that they were gathered and held together in remembrance of the God of Israel, the presence within the congregation of the crucified and risen Christ and, from Pentecost, the power to hope in God's coming Kingdom which is the future of mankind.[25]

The Memorandum suggests that theologians today, in reconsidering the development of Trinitarian concepts, should retrace the cognitive processes of the early Church. The Fathers did not

deduce their theological conclusions from a pre-conceived Trinitarian concept. Any reference to the Trinity was originally
doxological in character. Trinitarian thought emerged in the
context of giving glory to God. The conceptual distinction
between the 'economic' and 'immanent' Trinity should not be
taken in the same sense of two different realities which must then
be somehow re-connected. Both serve to show the triune God as
the living God. As the Memorandum puts it:

> In calling upon God, we turn and open ourselves to the God who is
> none other than he has revealed himself to be in his Word. This
> calling upon his Name is the essential expression of doxology, that
> is, of trust, praise, and thanks, that the living God, from eternity to
> eternity, was, is and will be none other ('immanent Trinity') than he
> has shown himself to be in history ('economic Trinity').[26]

Moreover, such Church Fathers as Basil and Athanasius make it
clear that all such doxological references to the inner life of God
must be controlled by the biblical message concerning God's
activity and presence with his people. Looking, then, at the New
Testament, the authors of the Memorandum assert that the
Scriptures do not present the relationship between Jesus and the
Holy Spirit in a linear or one-directional fashion. The Spirit
precedes the coming of Jesus, the Old Testament witnessing to
his presence and activity as the Spirit of Israel. The Spirit is,
furthermore, active throughout the life, death and Resurrection
of Jesus, though the Spirit is also sent by Jesus – as the *Filioque*
classically insists.

At this point, the Memorandum raises some serious questions
about the validity, or at any rate sufficiency, of Filioquist belief.
It does so, we shall see, with considerably more circumspection
than Romanides. The authors ask:

> Does it [the *Filioque*] involve an unbiblical subordination of the Spirit
> to the Son? Does it do justice to the necessary reciprocity between
> the Son and the Spirit? If its intention is to safeguard the insight that
> the Holy Spirit is truly the Spirit of the Father in *Jesus Christ*, could

other insights and formulations defend that insight as well or even better? Is it possible that the Filioque, or certain understandings of it, may have been understandable and indeed helpful in their essential intention in the context of particular theological debates, but yet inadequate as articulations of a full or balanced doctrine of the Trinity?[27]

In its own effort to be balanced, the Memorandum displays sensitivity towards both the Eastern and Western positions. It notes the fear of many Easterners that the *Filioque* obscures the Father's Trinitarian *proprium* of being cause of Son and Spirit, and the anxiety of numerous Westerners that Monopatrism makes the Spirit a stranger to the Son. Actually, the Memorandum commits itself to a modified Monopatrism by declaring that the Spirit proceeds from the Father alone while at once adding that this procession is yet from this Father as, precisely, Father of the Son. Such a *prise de position* can be expressed, so its authors think, in a whole cluster of formulae, such as: 'The Spirit proceeds from the Father of the Son'; 'The Spirit proceeds from the Father through the Son'; 'The Spirit proceeds from the Father and receives from the Son'; 'The Spirit proceeds from the Father and rests on the Son'; 'The Spirit proceeds from the Father and shines out through the Son'. Here we can detect the influence of some later Byzantine theologians who felt the force of the Latin critique of Photian Monopatrism in its pure form.

The desire to have one's cake and eat it is not unknown among ecumenists. And so we find that, while the Klingenthal Memorandum on the one hand, in the spirit of Barth, praises the *Filioque* for underlining the fact that the Holy Spirit is none other than the Spirit of Jesus Christ, it also, on the other hand, in obeisance to the shade of Lossky, wonders whether the *Filioque* has not subordinated the Spirit to Christ, depersonalising him and turning him into a mere instrument of power, rendering him tributary to the Church which ossifies, consequently, into an authoritarian institution.[28] Such havering is, at any rate, absent from the recommendation with which the Memorandum ends, namely the excision of the *Filioque* clause from the third article of the Creed.

The World Council of Churches memorandum is in full accord with the conclusions of a bilateral dialogue involving the Orthodox, not with Catholics (evidently), but with Anglicans. In 1976 the International Anglican-Orthodox Commission, meeting in Moscow, resolved that

> because the original form of the Creed referred to the origin of the Holy Spirit from the Father; because the *Filioque* was introduced into the Creed without the authority of an ecumenical council and without due regard for Catholic assent; and because this Creed constitutes the public confession of faith by the people of God in the Eucharist, the *Filioque* clause should not be included in the Creed.[29]

In 1984 the Dublin Agreed Statement of the Anglican-Orthodox Commission confirmed its 1976 Moscow predecessor, while at the same time distancing itself from the shriller voices of anti-Latinism among the Orthodox and philOrthodox Anglicans.[30] The Orthodox members put it on record that at least St Augustine's way of expressing the *Filioque* is capable of an Orthodox interpretation (as already implied in the work of Maximus the Confessor), and noted that some of their recent theological predecessors regarded it as a legitimate theologoumenon – opinion, not doctrine – for the West. Their Anglican counterparts, meanwhile, though repudiating the claim that the Son 'causes' the Spirit to be, defended the *Filioque* against the charge that it had destroyed authentic Trinitarian theology in the Latin Church, abrogating belief in the Father as sole fount of deity, and ascribing the origin of the Spirit to an undifferentiated divine essence rather than to the persons of Father and Son.

The Catholic Church, via the Roman Secretariat for Christian Unity, was invited by the Anglican-Orthodox Commission to comment on its own deliberations so far. The Secretariat clutched the nettle, and addressed itself to the issue of the *Filioque* clause – by far the more intractable, ecumenically, of the two issues, clause and doctrine. It responded by noting what it called

the importance of an underlying question about authority in the
Church here. The addition was not 'imposed' by the Papacy (indeed
it met with initial papal opposition), but arose from the needs and
experience of very widely scattered parts of the West. This consensus on a matter of truth is a theological fact, and its acceptance
expresses an understanding of tradition, development, etc., that was
later 'canonized' in the West. If the addition is a *licit* addition that the
West does not seek to *impose* on our Orthodox brethren, then this
seems to be a further reason for a pluralism of expression – even in
the Creed.[31]

Nor was there much indication that Catholic theologians close to
the Holy See would yield much ground on the less intractable
issue, the *Filioque* doctrine. Writing in the semi-official *Civiltà
Cattolica* in 1982, between the Moscow and the Dublin statements
of the Anglican-Orthodox Commission, Giovanni Marchesi of
the *Gregoriana* presented the *Filioque* teaching as the filling of a
major *lacuna* in doctrinal tradition. It was necessary to explicitate
what the Nicene-Constantinopolitan 'proceeding from the
Father' had by way of implicit content on the rôle of the Son in
the Spirit's origination.[32] Similarly, de Margerie, a member of the
Pontifical International Theological Commission, has had much
to say about the biblical wellfoundedness of the *Filioque* doctrine.[33]

The solution of the Roman see is clear: to insist on the *Filioque*
in the Latin Church and to both as doctrine and as clause, and to
require it as *doctrine* for the Eastern Churches but *not* as clause.[34]
It is simply unthinkable that the Catholic Church should abandon
the *Filioque* as doctrine, because to do this would be to abandon
by the same token its own claim to teach with the authority of
Christ and his apostles, to have guarded faithfully the apostolic
deposit, to have developed its original understanding only in a
homogenous not a heterogeneous way. What *is* possible is that
the see of Rome could legislate that on occasions when different
rites are represented, the Creed will always be said or sung
without the *Filioque* clause. But whether such a modest measure
will satisfy Orthodox intransigence, not least of the kind represented by Romanides, is open to every possible question.

VI
Panagiotis Trembelas and Orthodox Christology

It can be said at once, and with conviction, that Orthodox Christology today is overwhelmingly classical in character. The great bulk of Orthodox writing on this subject consists in a restatement, or even a repetition, of the Christological teaching of the first seven Ecumenical Councils. For many Orthodox, after all, the entire dogma of the Church comes from these seven Councils, from Nicaea I in 325 to Nicaea II in 787. When Bishop Kallistos Ware's *The Orthodox Church* was translated into French, he accepted as its new title *L'Eglise des Sept Conciles* – the 'Church of the Seven Councils'. The Orthodox regard these seven Councils as internally related, a kind of symphony rendered one by a single major theme. That theme is the affirmation that in Jesus Christ there is one person, who is divine, and in two natures, divine and human. Even the seventh Council, which dealt with the Iconoclast controversy, belongs to this symphony. According to the Orthodox, that seventh Council teaches, in effect, that the divinity of Christ can be portrayed through his humanity because of the single personhood which unites them both. In other words, the self-same Christological faith of the Church was at stake in this Council as in the other six. Naturally, were this wholly true, then an essay on Orthodox Christology today would be an essay on the conciliar Christology.

In point of fact, however, there are two dimensions to Orthodox Christology which go beyond what we in the West normally think of as the classical conciliar Christology. These are, first, the specific perspective of the Greek tradition after Chalcedon, as distinct from the Latin; and, second, the speculative Christology developed in Russia, or in the Russian diaspora, in the nineteenth and twentieth centuries.

First, then, the specific development of the Greek patristic tradition after Chalcedon compared with the customary Western perspective. In the West, Chalcedon is generally regarded as the definitive statement of the conciliar Christology.[1] The meaning of the Chalcedonian definition is taken to be fairly self-evident, and if elucidation is looked for anywhere, it is sought in the Tome of Leo – the Christological letter of Pope Leo the Great read out with approval at the Council. Thus Western theologians often regard the next three Ecumenical Councils – Constantinople II in 553, Constantinople III in 680 and Nicaea II – as simply mopping-up operations, clarifying or applying Chalcedon in various ways. But the Orthodox do not normally share the Western tendency to make 451 the climax of the story. The reason for this lies in the greater influence on the Eastern Church of the so-called neo-Chalcedonian school.

The contours of this school are only now becoming clear, but it can be said to have four main members – Leontius of Jerusalem, John the Grammarian, John Maxentius and Cyril of Scythopolis, together with one important hanger-on, Leontius of Byzantium. The latter's thought was a kind of blend of Chalcedonianism with Origenism, but Leontius came up with some categories which the neo-Chalcedonians found helpful. The essential aim of the neo-Chalcedonian school was to justify the episcopal cry which greeted the reading of Leo's Tome: 'Leo and Cyril teach the same thing.' In other words, it was to reconcile the Tome of Leo, or, more broadly, the Chalcedonian definition itself, with the teaching of Cyril of Alexandria – the latter being thought of as summed up in two formulae: 'One nature of the Word incarnate', and 'One of the Holy Trinity has suffered for us'. The neo-Chalcedonians tried to show that a Chalcedonian sense can be given to these phrases, the first of which Cyril borrowed unconsciously from the heretical writer Apollinaris of

Laodicea, condemned at the First Council of Constantinople in 381, and the second of which was not Cyrilline at all, but was used by Syrian Monophysites devoted to Cyril's memory.

The way that neo-Chalcedonians defended these formulae was by interpreting Chalcedon in the light of Cyril's idea of the hypostatic union. Chalcedon itself does not use that phrase, nor does it say explicitly that the hypostasis of the union is the pre-existent hypostasis of the eternal Word. We may believe that this point was not pressed at the Council so as to avoid alienating the moderate Antiochenes present there, whilst its absence *expressis verbis* was compensated for by the eightfold assertion that there is only one subject of the divinity and humanity in Christ. Like Monophysitism, neo-Chalcedonianism takes as its starting-point the personal identity of the Incarnate Word with the pre-existent Word. But, unlike Monophysitism, it does not regard Christ's humanity as simply a 'state' of the Logos, something expressing itself in human actions but without an ontologically consistent human existence to provide those actions with their stable foundation.

Although in the generation following Chalcedon, the Byzantine patriarchs were not themselves neo-Chalcedonians but rather strict Dyophysites, favourable not only to Roman Christology but even to moderate Antiochenism, the Byzantine Church at large swung round to the new Christology. Constantinople was, after all, the imperial city, and it was in the imperial interest that Chalcedonians should move closer to moderate Monophysites of the ilk of the great Syrian theologian Severus of Antioch, in the hope of winning back both Syria and Egypt to unity of faith, and so of cohabitation within a single Christian empire.

But while in Byzantium, Chalcedon was increasingly interpreted as a Cyrilline council, a victory over the vestiges of Nestorianism, in the West it was seen as essentially an anti-Monophysite council. For strict Dyophysites, Chalcedon represented the position of moderate Antiochenes like Theodore of Mopsuestia and Theodoret of Cyr. It was a great shock to the Western Church when Emperor Justinian secured the posthumous condemnation of Theodore at the Fifth Ecumenical Council in 553. Large areas of the Western Church, such as the Ambrosian or Milanese Church, broke off communion at this point with the East, and it remains unclear whether Pope Vigilius finally confirmed the condemnation of Theodore though under heavy imperial pressure so to do.[2]

As a result of this difference, two differing images of Chalcedon have been constructed in East and West. In the West, one *can* find much neo-Chalcedonianism: a great deal of the high mediaeval Scholastic theology found its own way to the neo-Chalcedonian position. But Chalcedon is not seen as in itself a neo-Chalcedonian affair, and so room is left for other options, as is witnessed by the survival in the West of the *homo assumptus* Christology espoused or at any rate tolerated by Augustine, and today best represented, perhaps, by the Christology of the German Walter Kasper.

In later Greek Christology, Byzantine and modern, we have what can be called a 'high church' or Cyrilline view of the conciliar Christology. Very schematically, we may say that Greek Christology is clearer about Christ's unity and his divinity than it is about his humanity. In the West, by contrast, we have a 'low church' or Leonine view of the conciliar Christology which, being less clear about the unity of Christ, is less sure about how to interrelate the factors of divinity and humanity. It is surely not by accident that Christology from below, for example, has emerged in Western, not Eastern, theology. Of course one can argue that the origins of this type of Christology lie in Protestantism, but even so it has marked affinities with the neo-Scholastic tractate *De Christo legato divino*, regarded by its authors as a piece of fundamental theology and with roots going back to, at least, the Renaissance.[3]

Greek neo-Chalcedonianism was sanctioned by the Fifth Ecumenical Council which explicitly taught that the union of natures in Christ takes place within the hypostasis of the pre-existent Word. The humanity has no hypostasis of its own but is 'enhypostatised' or received into, the divine hypostasis itself.

Since the Council of 553 also insisted on the presence in Christ of a rational soul, in other words a fully human mind, it made it clear that the hypostasis is not the same as mind or self-consciousness. The hypostasis is the 'I' which was the subject of the birth, temptations, passion and death of Christ – all these aspects of human existence being freely assumed by the Word itself. As John Meyendorff puts it, the hypostasis here is an ontological foundation, not an ontological content. And so the enhypostatisation of Christ's human nature in the Word does not prevent his energies, his activities, from being themselves fully human.

In this way, the Byzantine Church was able to recover much of the Antiochene (and Leonine) stress on the full humanity of Jesus. This became clear at the Sixth Ecumenical Council of 680–81 where the Greek East, after an enormous struggle, finally came down on the side of Western Dyothelitism, the doctrine of the two wills of the Redeemer. The incorporation of Antiochene elements within a neo-Chalcedonian framework which made this possible was the work of the last creative Greek patristic Christologist, Maximus the Confessor. It can be said that the Greek theological tradition, even today, regards Maximus as the supreme Byzantine theologian, the synthesiser who fitted together the best aspects of the preceding tradition into a unity. This was not simply because he managed to regain the Christological balance of Leo in a more sophisticated form and with a better articulation of the Lord's unity. It was also because he contextualised his Christology within an entire Christian metaphysic, in a way comparable to the achievement of Thomas Aquinas in the Latin West. For Maximus, the Logos by whom and in whom, at the beginning, all things were made, re-orientates and re-integrates the entire creation by assuming it in incarnation. The creation had abandoned the 'movement' which God had established for it, and in it, but now, through Christ, this movement is taken to its goal or permanent fulfilment. There are, then two movements involved: one from God towards man, and this consists in God making himself accessible to his creation. The other is from man towards God, a movement willed from the beginning by God and restored in Christ. In the Incarnate Word these two movements are hypostaically united. The two energies or wills – divine and human – become one.[4]

But while in this case giving Christology a speculative context enriches it, rather than diminishes it, it has not been ever thus in the Orthodox tradition. This becomes clear when we turn to look at the Church of Russia. The Russian Church of the Middle Ages produced no Christology to speak of. From the sixteenth to the mid-nineteenth centuries its Christological teaching, like its theology at large, was based on Western models – whether Catholic, as in the school of Kiev, associated with the name of Peter Mogila, or Lutheran as in the school of Moscow whose leading light was Feofan Propokovič.

But as soon as an independent tradition of speculative Christ-ology got underway, it ran into major problems. From Vladimir Solov'ev to Sergei Bulgakov, the Russian Church has known a series of attempts to write a speculative Christology, most of which seem ill-judged – theosophical, rather than theological, a mixture of questionable mysticism with somewhat strange philo-sophy. In each of the two cases just mentioned, Solov'ev and Bulgakov, many students report that Christology is handled much less successfully than pneumatology, the doctrine of the Spirit. For Russian speculative Christology belongs with a wider attempt, which we have already glimpsed in the sophiology of Bulgakov, to identify categories that can embrace both the divine and the human – most commonly, *sophia* or Godmanhood. These two key ideas, in fact, are used to construct an account of how, in general, God is immanent in man, and man in God, of how the Incarnation can be not only possible but in a sense natural. Not only Solov'ev and Bulgakov but also others deeply influenced by them, such as Florensky and Berdyaev, ascribe to the God-world relationship something which is, rather, the work of the Holy Spirit in the saving economy, where he carries out his task on the basis of the activity of the Incarnate Son in his life, death and resurrection. Thus for Bulgakov, as we have already seen, the Chalcedonian definition is only possible if the *Sophia* or foundational content of humanity and the *Sophia* or foundational content of divinity already in some sense coincide, the single *Sophia* existing in two modes, one created, the other uncreated. Thus the effective capacity of human nature to be, in Jesus' case, assumed in the Incarnation, and, in our case, to be deified by grace, is ascribed to the Spirit of God as the Creator Spirit, rather than to the special dispensation of the Holy Spirit through the mission of the Son.

The danger with all these thinkers is that the significance, or implications, of the Incarnation will be severed from the actual history of the One who was incarnate. If what the Incarnation signifies is erected into a general system of thought about the God-world relationship, it may be that, being thus in possession of the idea of the total compenetration of God and man, we no longer need Jesus Christ who gave it to us. This danger is highly reminiscent of that found in the idealism of Hegel whose philosophy deeply influenced the Russian religious thinkers of the nineteenth century. In Hegel, for God to be God he must incarnate himself into man, in whom he knows himself as God for the first time. Similarly, for man to be man he must know himself to be one reality with the divine. This is the doctrine of *Geist*, or of divine-human unity, in Hegel and it provides the general ambience in which Russian speculative theology moved until the partial victory of the neo-patristic school after the Second World War. With Bulgakov's death in 1944, the stream represented by Lossky and Florovsky over-mastered the other currents of Russian theology in the diaspora, and so it remains. In effect, this was a return of Russian Christology to its own origins in the Greek patristic tradition, and as Lossky and Florovsky would maintain, a return of the prodigal son to his father.[5] And certainly, whereas in the development of Russian theology we can see a speculative mysticism of the Spirit threatening to engulf the Christ of the Church, study of Greek Christology makes it hard to see that there is much truth in the prediction of St Thomas Aquinas that denial of the *Filioque* will lead ultimately to depreciation of Christ.

So much for the background to the Christology of Panagiotis Trembelas. Trembelas was born in 1886. He is a classical Athenian theologian of the conservative school. Professor of dogmatics at Athens from 1939 to 1957, he remained extremely active as an *emeritus* until the 1970s. He was a highly prolific writer: the chief Greek theological encyclopaedia – *Thrêskeutikê kai ethikê enkyklopaideia* (Athens 1962–1968) – lists eighty-seven books by him to which a host of periodical articles should be added. On his death in 1977 Trembelas left commentaries on all the New Testament books; he edited the texts of the Byzantine rite for the Eucharist, the other sacraments and the Offices of Matins and Vespers. His *Dogmatikê*, 'Dogmatics of the Orthodox Catholic Church', in three volumes is, however, his *magnum opus*. His Christological work does not consist in a so-called 'separate Christology' but is found enclosed within his dogmatics, itself published in Athens in the years 1959 to 1961 by the Zoe Brotherhood. The Zoe Brotherhood is an evangelical movement within the Church of Greece, consisting mainly of laymen, a number of them being theologians. Though the aim of the Zoe Brotherhood, to which Trembelas belonged, is the renewal and re-invigoration of the Greek Church, this should not be taken to imply that their theology is especially liberal or progressive. The work of Trembelas is, in fact, a very solid piece of traditional theology, founded on conservative biblical exegesis and the Fathers, with – in Christology in particular – a strong bias towards Cyril and the neo-Chalcedonians. In 1966 Trembelas's dogmatics were translated into French by a monk of Cheve-togne, Pierre Dumont, as a contribution to Ecumenical *rapprochement*.[6] Cardinal Augustin Bea, at the time President of the Secretariat for Christian Unity, wrote Dumont a public letter to mark the event in which he stresses the representative character of Trembelas's work. It is the expression of the classical contemporary teaching of the Greek Church. Dumont's preface confirms this, pointing out that the holy synod of the church of Greece had made Trembelas its representative in Ecumenical negotiations with the Old Catholics and the neo-Chalcedonian

Orthodox, thus demonstrating their confidence in his ability to put their point of view.

To acquire an idea of how Trembelas approached the creation of an Orthodox dogmatics, and so of an Orthodox Christology, it may be useful to look first at his opening sections in volume I before plunging into his Christology in volume II. Dogmatics, Trembelas declares, is that

> theological discipline which concerns itself with the truths of faith contained in divine revelation and which seeks to give them an organic unity through a scientific exposition.[7]

In what sense does he see dogmatic theology as 'scientific'? In two senses. First, as a derivation from dogma, dogmatic theology shares in the authoritative character of revelation itself. Though it deals with a super-sensuous realm where other sciences fall silent, dogmatic theology provides objectively true knowledge which engenders in the Church's members genuine information and legitimate certitude. Secondly, dogmatic theology is scientific because, as already mentioned, it seeks to unify the teachings of revelation as a coherent whole. As to dogma itself, Trembelas ascribes to it a twofold character. The internal or objective character of dogma comes from the fact that it is based on the sources of revelation: Scripture and the apostolic tradition. As he explains:

> ... dogmas are not images, representations or symbols, which interpret the personal feelings or religious impressions of the persons who constitute the Church.[8]

But, independently of this internal, objective character which dogma derives from its divinely revealed origin, it also possesses what Trembelas calls an 'external and ecclesiastical' character. This stems from the fact that the depositary or guardian and the authoritative interpreter of divine revelation is the Church. She it is who develops and infallibly interprets the teaching of faith, offering new explanations of the revealed teaching or throwing fresh light upon it, so as to render it more accessible to believers while at the same time protecting it from false interpretation. This, for Trembelas, is what was happening when the Fathers of the fourth and fifth centuries, and the Ecumenical Councils which drew upon their work, applied such terms as *ousia*, *hypostasis* and *prosôpon* to Trinitarian theology and Christology. Reason, aided, Trembelas adds, by the Christian experience of the believer, can to some degree penetrate the content of faith. Gradually, reason and experience, working together, are illuminated by supernatural truth, and thus led from knowledge to knowledge. But if Trembelas gives an auxiliary rôle here to philosophy and Christian experience *vis-à-vis* dogmatic theology, he makes it clear that the main foundations of the dogmatician's work lie elsewhere – in the assured results of the exegete and the historian of doctrine. Dogmatic theology, he writes,

> examines, in relation to the past, what it was that, from the beginning, the Church confessed and believed, but it expounds this systematically, so as to explain and present in a methodical manner what the Church must strongly maintain, even at the present time.[9]

Theology's sources, then, are the Bible and Tradition, which latter Trembelas defines in a somewhat restrictive sense. Tradition is

> a teaching transmitted vocally and verbally by the Lord and the apostles, and, through the action of the grace of the Holy Spirit, engraved in the hearts of those who constituted the first Church. Fashioned under the direction, and by the attentive solicitude, of those pastors who succeeded the apostles, it was interpreted in a Catholic ecclesiastical thought or an apostolic thought, and conserved in the ancient symbols, the definitions of the Councils, the consensus of the Fathers and in all the action and teaching of the Church of the seven Ecumenical Councils.[10]

This statement is necessarily momentous for the theological method of Trembelas. Tradition is no longer, for him, directly available to us after the close of the patristic age. It is only accessible via its monuments – the Creeds, the definitions of the Councils and the *consensus patrum*. These things, therefore, must be our main guides in the interpretation of Scripture. It follows that his theology will be, in its own way, a neo-patristic theology: no fundamentally new insights are on offer after the epoch of the Fathers, though the insights inherited from them may themselves be further penetrated by philosophy assisted by Christian experience. Trembelas shows himself especially concerned to exclude Schleiermacher's view that the main source of dogmatics lies in Christian awareness or consciousness. Schleiermacher has put the cart before the horse. Consciousness can only be a certain source of saving truth if the mind and heart have already accepted the gospel as the truth and been enlightened by it. Consciousness can witness to the fact that the gospel has been revealed, but it cannot re-constitute its content from within itself, from out of the materials of subjectivity.

What kind of systematic organisation will Trembelas give to his dogmatics, thus understood? A number of different schemes are, he says, possible, but the best of them is salvation-historical and Christocentric. However, he warns against simply regarding theological method as synthetic: that is, as synthesising the truths of faith in relation to God's plan of salvation and its centre, Jesus Christ. Method in dogmatics must also be analytic, so as to deepen our grasp of particular dogmas. It must be, moreover, historical, in the positive or technical sense of that word, showing how particular dogmas were hammered out in the controversies of the patristic Church.

The particular salvation-historical scheme of Trembelas is (despite what Dumont and Bea have to say about how Greek Orthodox he is), borrowed from Western models, and notably from the Dutch Reformed dogmatician van Oosterzee whose 'Christian Dogmatics' was put into English in 1891.[11] The idea of Van Oosterzee was to lay out all the dogmatic themes in terms of the master-theme of the Kingdom of God – its eternal foundation in the Holy Trinity; its temporal beginning in creation and providence; its subject: man, fallen into sin; its founder, Christ, and his redemptive work; the earthly form of the Kingdom, the Church, and its final consummation in the Last Things. What Trembelas does, as an Orthodox, is to give all of this a more resolutely Christocentric character. As he puts it:

> As he (Jesus Christ) is the king of truth and the head of the Church, he must be the heart and soul of an Orthodox Christian dogmatics.[12]

Whereas, he points out, with a retrospective glance at ancient Hellas, the Sophist Protagoras had called man 'the measure of all things' and Plato in the *Laws* had corrected him, saying that God is that measure, the Orthodox dogmatician will take one step further still and say, 'God, the measure of all things, in our Lord Jesus Christ': a suitable note on which to pass into a consideration of his Christology in its own right.

It falls into three clear parts. First, by way of context, Trembelas offers his readers an account of God's redemptive plan in its overall structure, with a view to showing how the person, life and work of Christ forms the climax of that plan. Secondly, he gives us an ontological essay on the being of Christ as the Word Incarnate. Thirdly, he presents an account of Christ's offices or functions as prophet, priest and king.

I shall now outline each of these three sections before making some comments on Trembelas's approach and its wider ecumenical implications.

First, then, the general redemptive context of the coming of Christ. Trembelas's account of man in need of redemption is based above all on John Damascene and Augustine. Damascene, in his *Against the Manichaeans*, had noted that, while the Devil had instigated or invented evil, man had merely committed it at Satan's prompting. In Damascene's view, this difference means that man's crime is less serious than Satan's. Accordingly, the results of his crime or sin are less radical also. With the abuse of freedom, the very nature of Lucifer, the glorious archangel, was transformed, so that it became impossible for the Devil to repent. To conceive of Satan's future salvation is impossible. With man, however, this is not so. Human beings, as a matter of empirical fact, frequently express sentiments of guilt and shame at their own sinful actions, thus showing that they are prisoners, merely, of sin. They have not been re-made by sin into a different kind of being. Following Augustine, Trembelas sees in man's sorrow for sin evidence that in the depths of his nature there is a remnant of goodness. This remnant of goodness moves him as if by an instinct to seek reconciliation with God and purification from evil. Redemption, should it occur, will be above all a transformation of the inner man. It is our name for liberation from slavery to sin and the consequent beginning of a new life in which we become what we were always meant to be: sharers in the divine nature.

Trembelas goes on to say, however, that such a radical change in the sinner, though perfectly conceivable from our side, is only practically possible from the side of God, through a divine act. This act was prepared by divine Providence in both Israel and the pagan world. Under the heading of the providential preparation of the redemptive act in *Israel*, Trembelas considers – as we should expect – the principal stages of the biblical history from the covenant with Noah, through the covenant with Abraham (seen by Trembelas as the fundamental covenant of the Old Testament period), to the covenants with Moses and with David. The preparatory history continues with the divinely inspired rise of the prophetic movement, especially in the Messianic expectations which that movement fostered. The prophetic movement and its messianic hopes reached their most intense point in the preaching of John the Baptist, a preaching all the more readily heard since it came after an accumulation of Jewish national misfortunes. Trembelas holds that, in an analogous though lower manner, God also providentially prepared the *pagan world* for the coming of the Redeemer. This he did in basically three ways. First, following the Paul of Romans and the unknown author of the Letter to Diognetus, Trembelas presents divine Providence as permitting ancient society to fall into a moral chaos so complete that it became consciously aware of its own need for redemption. Secondly, following this time Clement of Alexandria, Trembelas sees ancient philosophy as preparing the Gentiles for the reception of Christ's revelation by breaking down superstition and idolatry. In particular, the general religious syncretism of the Greco-Roman world in the Hellenistic period disposed people towards religious independence and tolerance, and this facilitated the activities of the first Christian preachers to the Gentiles. Thirdly, the Jewish diaspora created a network of synagogues from Rome to Babylonia which communicated the truths of the Old Testament to many non-Jewish proselytes, thus putting them in contact with the direct providential preparation for the Redeemer found in the history of Israel. As Trembelas puts it:

> It is not only Greek philosophy but also Israel herself who served for hundreds of years among the pagans as 'pegadogues in Christ'.[13]

Thus we come to the second Christological section of Trembelas. After the contextualisation of the coming of the Redeemer in salvation history, we have his ontological analysis of the event of the Incarnation. Whatever term we may use for this event – Incarnation, epiphany, theophany, *kenôsis* – the reality we are talking about is the assumption of human nature by the only Son of God and his perpetual union with that human nature. Trembelas prefaces his account of the Incarnation by a modest declaration of the need for *apophasis*. We cannot expect theology to deal exhaustively with what is, after all, a unique mystery. He considers the objection to the Christian claim to incarnational uniqueness that world religions, myths, legends, are in fact full of accounts of unions between a divinity and a human being. All such apparent pagan analogues to the Incarnation are based, however, on an ontological confusion of the world with God, something well-nigh universal outside of Israel. What is distinctive about Christian belief in the Incarnation is that it arose in a context where the distinction between the Uncreated and the created was already absolutely clear, and hence there was no human temptation to project fantasies of incarnation onto God.

Having said so much by way of preface, Trembelas basically considers two questions. First, was it 'convenient', fitting, appropriate, that God, and specifically the Son or Word of God, should become incarnate? Secondly, granted that it was thus *conveniens*, what is the ontological make-up of the person of the Word Incarnate, Jesus Christ? Trembelas asks, in an inversion of what may seem the logical order, first, whether it was convenient for the *divine Son* to become incarnate and only after that whether it was convenient for *God* to become incarnate. Fundamentally, Trembelas offers three considerations which show why it was the Son, and not any other divine person, that properly became man. In the first place, since the Son already has the property of filiation within the Godhead, it was right that he should be on earth the Son of man. The distinctive hypostatic property of the Son was preserved unchanged when he began to exist as man at the Incarnation. In the second place, since it was the divine Logos who first fashioned man from the clay as the living image of the Father, it was only right that the same divine Logos should re-fashion him to the same image after the partial dissolution of that image by sin. In both these arguments, Trembelas is much indebted to St Athanasius. In the third place, Trembelas draws attention to a difficult notion of St Irenaeus, the 'recapitulation' of man in the Word. This Trembelas understands along the lines suggested by the nineteenth-century Danish Lutheran dogmatician Hans Lassen Martensen, better known for his quarrel with Sören Kierkegaard, who attacked his tendency to harmonise faith and reason.[14] Martensen, just one of a number of Protestant writers used by Trembelas, argued that as the ultimate presupposition of the creation is the divine Logos, the final goal or purpose of the creation could only be revealed by the disclosure of the Logos through the Incarnation. Along with the generality of Christian theologians, Trembelas admits that, though only the Son became incarnate, all three persons co-operated in the act of the incarnation in ways appropriate to them. Granted, then, that if God were to become incarnate, it would rightly be the divine Son who took flesh, was it proper for God to become incarnate at all? Trembelas argues that the Incarnation was (as he puts it) excellently fitting to God since it was a wonderful manifestation of the divine perfections. It manifested God's goodness, wisdom and power, in a way which fully corresponded to the needs and desire of human nature. But this does not mean that God was obligated by his own nature to become incarnate. It was in his absolute freedom and sovereignty that he was pleased to do so. But having determined himself to become incarnate, the act of Incarnation is a supreme glorification of the divine properties, as Trembelas seeks to show by a whole host of citations from the Greek Fathers. Yet Trembelas goes on to say, that if from the viewpoint of the divine action the Incarnation was absolutely gratuitous, from the viewpoint of man it was absolutely necessary. He concedes that the Fathers often speak as though in principle God could have redeemed man by some other way, even, for instance, by a simple word of forgiveness, but he rejects this view, holding that the Fathers only formulated it as a theological opinion and one moreover which they surrounded by reservations and limitations. Had God redeemed man by any other way than the Incarnation, man would have been saved only in an external sense, from without. Whereas through the Incarnation, as Cyril of Alexandria had earlier realised, we were able to have a rôle ourselves in the restoration of our communion with God. And so we are saved from within, from within our own freedom.

Granted then that it was convenient for God to become incarnate, and in particular, as already set forth, for the divine Son to become incarnate, what is the being of the Incarnate Son whom the Church calls on as Jesus Christ? Trembelas deals with this in four parts, which take us to the end of his central section on Christology. The four parts are: the divinity of Christ; the human nature of Christ; the hypostatic union of the two natures in the theandric person of Christ; and the consequences of the hypostatic union. I shall not say very much about Trembelas's comments on the divinity and human nature of Christ which simply consist in putting forward the evidence from the New Testament and early Christian writers that the Church did always consider Jesus as both divine and human. His amassment of evidence on belief in Christ's divinity runs from the New Testament to Origen; the corresponding section on belief in Christ's humanity takes the story somewhat further, indeed up to the end of the patristic period. At the Incarnation, so Trembelas concludes from this survey, the divine Saviour assumed a complete human nature with all of those natural passions that can be called 'irreprehensible', that is, those which cast no moral blame on their subject, their possessor. Gregory Nazianzen had explained the soteriological necessity of a *full* assumption of humanity in the words, 'What was not assumed was not healed; only what was united to God has been saved'. However, following Damascene (who was himself dependent in this regard on Maximus the Confessor), Trembelas goes beyond the explicit teaching of the Cappadocian Fathers in distinguishing between two sorts of assumption of the human condition by the Saviour. Through a natural liaison, Christ assumed our irreprehensible passions, while through a personal liaison he also took our dereliction, our abandonment and sense of estrangement by God.

Thus we come to the heart of Trembelas's Christology, the account of the hypostatic union. As already noted, the term hypostatic union does not occur in the course of the Chalcedonian definition itself, being rather the personal theology of Cyril of Alexandria. Though frequently invoked in order to refer to, or sum up, the teaching of the council of Chalcedon on the two natures and single person of the Word Incarnate, it is not in itself part of the Chalcedonian definition. Trembelas, who is perfectly aware of this fact, thus commits himself in the very title he gives his discussion to a *Cyrilline* Christology. Implicitly, he holds, therefore, that the Christological confession of those who accept the Council of Chalcedon cannot be divorced from this special insight of Cyril of Alexandria that the union of the divine and human natures in the single person of Christ is itself a union *kat'hypostasin*, a 'hypostatic union'. We shall see later that this claim, which is also made by the Christology of St Thomas, is not accepted by some modern Catholic writers, and that a decision on the matter has considerable ecumenical implications.

Trembelas considers that the New Testament testifies to the hypostatic union both indirectly and directly. It testifies indirectly to that union on all the occasions when it ascribes divine properties to the Son of man, and human properties to the Son of God. It testifies directly to the union in two vital texts, the Prologue of the Fourth Gospel and the Christological hymn embedded in Paul's Letter to the Philippians: 'Though he was in the form of God, he did not consider equality with God a thing to be grasped but emptied himself, taking the form of a servant'. Trembelas admits that early writers, indeed all the Fathers until the years immediately preceding the Council of Ephesus, use terms for the Incarnation which could be interpreted in a sense other than that of hypostatic union. They speak, for instance, of the mingling or mixture of the divinity and humanity; or of the human nature becoming the house, temple, clothing or ornament of the divine Word. They use terms like the conjunction, composition, cohesion, of the divine and human elements in Christ. However, Trembelas believes that, through all these inadequate linguistic instruments, the Fathers were giving expression to the belief later brought to lucid articulation by Cyril. As he puts it:

> By all these expressions, understood correctly, one would show the union of the two natures in one person and hypostasis, and not an extrinsic or moral union, or a parallel existence, but a natural and substantial union without any confusion or mixing up of the two natures, but rather with each conserving its particular properties.[15]

Nestorius provided the opportunity for the clarification of the Church's faith. Under the influence of Aristotelean theses, or so Trembelas maintains, Nestorius maintained that where there exists a true nature there must also exist a true person, so that if Christ is truly man he must truly have a human personhood.

Consequently, for Nestorius the union of the two natures in Christ must take place as the union of two persons. This union is carried out by their reciprocal moral interpenetration, in such a manner that they form morally one single person. In this moral union, the two persons remain two distinct 'I's. In the providence of God, Cyril of Alexandria was able to discern the insufficiency of the position of Nestorius as a statement of the faith of the Church. Through the work not only of Ephesus and Chalcedon but also of Constantinople II and the neo-Chalcedonian movement associated with, among others, Leontius of Byzantium, the Cyrilline Christology triumphed and became the received understanding of Orthodoxy. The hypostatic union of the two natures in Christ constitutes, Trembelas declares, 'the inaccessible and incomprehensible mystery, really new, unknown even to angels', a mystery which, however, though going beyond reason does not contradict it. The human nature of Jesus Christ does not exist in an hypostasis of its own but in the divine Word to whom it belongs and who, in assuming it, gave it existence. This in no way mutilates the integrity or fullness of Christ's humanity. On the contrary, by its union with the personhood of the Word, that humanity acquires a more complete personal perfection. It possesses all the perfection and elevation which human nature can receive. Closing his central section on the ontology of the Word Incarnate, Trembelas draws attention to the transformation of human powers which the assumption of humanity by the Logos brought about. In his intellect and will, Christ shares in the divine self-knowledge and holiness insofar as that is possible within the limits of human nature. Christ knew the Father humanly by an immediate contemplation, and he sanctified human beings by his own human action, since that action was also that of God the Word. The account given by Trembelas of the consequences of the hypostatic union is, quite frankly, in George Florovsky's term, 'asymmetrical'. As Trembelas puts it:

Here we are dealing with two essences or natures of which only the divine one is infinite while the human one is limited. It is fully penetrated by the divine, but by reason of its finitude does not insert itself into the divine nature in the same fashion.[16]

Before moving on, in conclusion, to Trembelas's account of the offices of Christ, the *triplex munus* of prophet, priest and king, I want to pause here to consider the implications of this neo-Cyrilline Christology which is, in every respect, identical with that of St Thomas.

Until the early 1930s, it was generally believed by both Orthodox and Catholic theologians, that the so-called Twelve Anathemas of Cyril, which are the main source for Cyril's developed teaching on the hypostatic union, had been officially received by the Councils of Ephesus and Chalcedon. This being so, the High Cyrillian or neo-Chalcedonian Christology was quite simply *the* Christology of the Church, an irreformable teaching. But in 1933 a French patristic scholar, Paul Galtier, showed that at Ephesus the Anathemas had been read but not voted on, while at Chalcedon they had not even been read.[17] Moreover, in a follow-up some four years later, his co-national, Auguste Gaudel, argued that Pope Vigilius had given his approval to the Second Ecumenical Council of Constantinople – the Council generally believed to have secured the final victory of Cyril's Christology – only to the extent that its teachings agreed with Chalcedon. Gaudel went on to examine the reasons of St Thomas for rejecting the phrase *assumptus homo* the 'man assumed' in Christology, and showed that Thomas had been misled by his sources into thinking that the concept of the 'man assumed' had been formally condemned by the Church.[18] These somewhat startling discoveries, or alleged discoveries, coincided with a controversy in dogmatic as distinct from historical theology. This centred on the work of the French Franciscan Déodat de Basly who in 1918 had gained Pope Benedict XV's permission to explore the possibility of writing a neo-Scotist Christology more conformable to Franciscan sources. De Basly's method was to show that the *assumptus homo* tradition was at least as respectable as Cyril's, indeed that it was essentially *the* traditional Christology of the Western Church in the patristic age, being held by Pope Damasus, Augustine, Cassian and Leo. The Cyrilline-Thomist denial of human autonomy to Christ (as the modern writer saw it) had come in from the East in the sixth century.[19] De Basly's work was hotly disputed by Thomist writers, and above all by H. Diepen, who pointed out that, whatever the theological opinions of certain of the Latin Fathers, the Christological councils of the fifth to seventh centuries had affirmed the single divine person of the Word Incarnate and *not* the man assumed.[20] In 1951 Pope Pius XII was held by many to have in effect condemned 'Baslyisme' in his encyclical *Sempiternus Deus*. There the pope rejected outright any theology which posited a *homo assumptus*, psychologically *sui juris*, and he re-affirmed that in Christ there was but one person, that of the Logos. Other historical theologians had already provided some backing for this action by suggesting that, though the Anathemas were not in themselves dogmatic definitions, the use traditionally made of them since Cyril's lifetime conferred on them the equivalent value of a solemn definition.[21] However, if we turn to Walter Kasper's *Jesus the Christ*, there we find an attempt at a vindication of Déodat de Basly, though the philosophical categories which Kasper uses for positing a two-fold personality in the Word Incarnate are drawn not from Scotus but from Schelling.[22]

All of this carries considerable ecumenical implications – surprising as the thought may seem at first sight. At stake are the relations of the Catholic Church with three other communions: the Eastern Orthodox themselves; the Oriental or non-Chalcedonian Orthodox, commonly referred to as Monophysites; and the Assyrian Church of the East, often known as Nestorians. The ecumenical implications *vis-à-vis* these three groups emerge if we ask ourselves three questions. Firstly, if the Catholic Church officially permits a non-Cyrilline, *assumptus homo* interpretation of Chalcedon, will it not create an obstacle to reunion with the Eastern Orthodox, where such a Christological tradition is quite unknown? Secondly, if the Catholic Church officially permits such an interpretation of Chalcedon will it not confirm the

Oriental or non-Chalcedonian Orthodox in their belief that Chalcedon was fundamentally a sell-out to Nestorianism, being so ambiguous that it could be accepted even by the dogmatic opponents of Cyril? Thirdly, if the Catholic Church officially permits, once again, a non-Cyrilline interpretation of Chalcedon will it not be in a better position to invite the Assyrian Church of the East to re-enter Catholic unity, by showing that the Antiochene doctors, the founding fathers of the Assyrian tradition, were in no sense anathematised at Chalcedon? The answer to these questions would appear to be affirmative to each case. Looked at from the point of view of *numbers*: the revival of a Christology of the man assumed will bring the Catholic Church ecumenically nearer to some sixty thousand people, and ecumenically further away from some two hundred and fifty millions! Such considerations can play no part in dogmatic theology, but they must be taken into account by Church leaders concerned with ecclesial and human realities.

However, before taking leave of Trembelas, we must for the sake of completeness have a quick look at the third and closing section of his Christology, the account of Christ's threefold function or work. The work which the Father gave to the Son made man was that of human redemption. Christ fulfilled this work in a threefold way. As prophet or teacher, he enlightened man's intelligence which hitherto had been darkened by the passions. As priest, he obtained man's justification through his sacrificial death on the cross. As king he subjected every sinful power to the will of man as fortified and sanctified by grace. Thus Christ redeemed us by enlightening us, by obtaining our forgiveness and by giving us the ability to persevere in holiness despite the persistence of the wounds of sin in our nature. Trembelas rightly claims that this notion of Christ's prophetic, priestly and royal office in our regard has patristic roots, notably in Eusebius of Caesarea and John Chrysostom. But he also candidly admits that it is most fully worked out in a number of Protestant writers, and above all in Calvin. It was in fact from Calvin that John Henry Newman picked it up and introduced it into modern

Catholic theology, and it is difficult to see why what Newman did in the West Trembelas should be forbidden from doing in the East. Trembelas, one imagines, was gratified to discover, as he probably did, that the Second Vatican Council had incorporated the notion of the *triplex munus* into its own Christology in the course of outlining the dogmatic background to the mystery of the Church in *Lumen Gentium*. Such openness to the usefulness of theological instruments taken, at any rate, in an immediate sense from a tradition not our own is part of the process of ecclesial reception of one Christian community by another. It brings home once again, however, the paradox that the most conservative Greek Orthodox circles would be inarticulate without the help of the Lutheran and Reformed as well as Catholic dogmatics they have discovered in the West.

VII
Nikolai Afanas'ev and Ecclesiology

Contemporary Orthodox ecclesiology is made up of several elements, or traditions, or movements. In other words, it is pluralistic, just as in modern Catholic ecclesiology. To remind ourselves of the situation in the Catholic communion – and so to provide ourselves with a way of getting our directions in observing the communion of other people, we can identify at least four ecclesiological strands of some importance today. First, we have a model of the Church as an hierarchical society. This ecclesiology has roots in the Latin Fathers, especially Cyprian, and achieved great importance during the Catholic Reformation. Secondly, there is the idea of the Church as a supernatural organism, developed by such nineteenth century thinkers as Möhler and Newman. Thirdly, there is the mid-twentieth century revival of the biblical and patristic notion of the Church as the body of Christ, associated with the Jesuit Emil Mersch and given striking impression by Pope Pius XII in his encyclical *Mystici Corporis*. Finally, there is the people of God idea, which stands at the centre of ecclesiology among the liberation theologians. At the Second Vatican Council, an attempt was made, in the dogmatic constitution *Lumen Gentium,* to synthesise these various pictures, but, to the extent that an individual theologian stresses one more than another, certain tensions or strains tend to emerge in Catholic discussion about the nature of the Church.

In Orthodoxy, three elements, traditions or movements can be identified. First, there is the idea of the Church as an hierarchical society, just as there is among Catholics. This type of ecclesiology is especially common among writers who look to Western theological method and concepts for inspiration such as the members of the Athens school. But it is more widespread than this, and reflects an essential aspect, in fact, of the nature of Orthodoxy. In practice, the Orthodox Church is a society of baptised persons, taught, governed and sanctified by a threefold ministry of bishops, priests and deacons. That this is so is manifest from the liturgical life and the canon law of the Orthodox, and it finds its most obvious reflection in the 'hierarchical society' model. I do not propose to say anything more about this kind of ecclesiology, on the grounds that it is too familiar from Latin ecclesiology to count as distinctively Orthodox.

The second of the three elements in Orthodox ecclesiology is Slavophilism, which will be treated here as a vital aspect of the background of third and last component, the so-called 'eucharistic ecclesiology'. Both of these streams are Russian in inspiration, and while that of the eucharistic ecclesiology has met with *some* approval in the more conservative Greek church, the Slavophile tradition is often looked on with a jaundiced eye as excessively 'democratic' and fundamentally non-Orthodox by not only the Greeks and the Romanians but also numerous Slav Orthodox as well.

The word 'Slavophile' means, of course, 'Slav-loving', and this may seem an odd description for an ecclesiology anywhere. In point of fact, the word is simply a handy tool for denoting a kind of ecclesiology which emerged in mid-nineteenth century Russian among a group of thinkers who shared sociological as well as theological interests in Russian Christian reality. By far the most important of these thinkers, all laymen, was A. S. Khomiakov.[1] Their basic ideas can be briefly stated. The Slavophiles believed that Russian culture was a product of two forces: Judaeo-Christianity, and the Byzantine church in its evangelisation of the mediaeval Russian State. In lacking Roman law and Greek philosophy, Russian culture had been in one sense impoverished but in another sense it was advantaged. It was advantaged in that it was the only Christian culture which was purely constituted from Christian sources, with no significant admixture of non-Christian influence. Therefore, to find the true spirit of a Christian society, one must look to what survives of indigenous Russian institutions as distinct from those borrowed later from the West. The one social institution which represents the true Christian spirit then turns out to be the peasant commune or *obschchina* with its corporate assembly, the *mir*. This commune where all are equals and yet none is an isolated individual provides a kind of hermeneutical key for understanding the nature of the Church – that Church from out of which the commune and its assembly originally came. The essence of the commune is mutual concern or mutual love, and so this must be the essence of the Church as well. Whereas the organising principle of Catholicism is authority, and the organising principle of Protestantism is liberty of private judgment, that of Orthodoxy is mutual love, and in this the claims of the Orthodox Church to be the Church of the New Testament itself are vindicated. The true Church is a union of communes or communities. Mutual love, *agapê*, unites the members of each community one to another, and the same *agapê* brings about the union of all in a single Church. The principle mark of this Church is *sobornost'* which can be translated as 'communality' or 'conciliarity'. The term *sobornaya*, the adjectival form of *sobornost'* had replaced the word *kafoličeskaya*, 'catholic' in the Church Slavonic version of the Creed of Nicaea-Constantinople shortly after the Russian rejection of the Council of Florence – in order, it would seem, to underline the difference between Orthodoxy and Roman Catholicism.[2] In the mid-nineteenth century, the Slavophiles argued that this 'note' of the Church, *sobornost'*, constituted in effect the source of the other three, namely: unity, holiness and apostolicity. Only the *sobornaya tserkva* could be one holy and apostolic.

So much for the central intuition of the Slavophile theologians. Naturally, there is a good deal more to their ecclesiology than just this stress on reciprocal *agapê*. In particular, if we may take Khomiakov as the central and representative Slavophile thinker, we can say that the definition of the Church as *agapê* is rooted in a systematically Trinitarian vision of the Church.[3] Khomiakov defines the Church as the revelation of the Holy Spirit in the mutual love of Christians. This love, he remarks, brings them back to the Father, through the Incarnate Son. Thus the Church comes about through the activity of Son and Spirit, an activity whose aim is to lead humanity to the Father.

In his account of the Trinitarian foundation of the Church, Khomiakov presents the Spirit as that divine person who interiorises Christ's external revelation of the Father. The truth which Christ taught externally during his lifetime becomes at Pentecost an interior reality – simultaneously truth and love – within the Church. Through the Spirit, Christ vivifies the Church with his love, and this infusion of love into mankind guarantees the truth of the Church. Christ leads the Church interiorly into all truth, but he does so precisely by means of the mutual love of the Church's members. This may seem an implausible notion until we realise that, for Khomiakov, the truth taught by the Church is simply the intellectual expression of her life, and her life is, in fact, a participation in the divine life, as realised by mutual love. Khomiakov cites tellingly in this connexion the introduction to the Creed in the Byzantine liturgy, 'Let us love each other so that we may confess the Father, the Son and the Holy Spirit'.

On the other hand, in the Western churches, so Khomiakov held, there is no interior presence of Christ. In Catholicism Christ remains what he was in the days of his flesh, namely, an external power, represented in the person of his earthly vicar, the Roman pope. In Protestantism he is likewise external, represented by a book, the Bible.[4]

Father Paul O'Leary, in his thorough study of Khomiakov's ecclesiology, stresses the great importance for the Slavophile writer of the distinction between interior and exterior.[5] That distinction is found in his philosophy, where interior understanding is an integral knowledge arrived at by the simultaneous exercise of all our powers. Exterior understanding, by contrast, is defined by Khomiakov as merely rational, and therefore inevitably partial. The same distinction is found in his Christology, where the interior truth of Christ is, as we have seen, his complete revelation in the Spirit, whereas his exterior truth is simply his partial revelation in historical time. The distinction is also found in Khomiakov's pneumatology, where he talks about a twofold mission of the Spirit to man. The interior mission follows Pentecost, is given only to the Orthodox Church and is manifested in an understanding of the eternal procession of the Spirit from the Father alone; the external mission is a general presence of the Spirit to all human beings, and it includes those who do not understand the Spirit's origin, such as those Westerners who uphold the *Filioque*. The effect of this sharp and surely somewhat unconvincing way of distinguishing between interior and exterior in the economy of salvation is that Khomiakov is strong on the Church as mystery, but weak when he deals with her as a mystery embodied in, precisely, a society.

The most searching criticism of Slavophile ecclesiology offered by fellow-Orthodox is that it reduces the unity of the Church to the unity of grace. This is certainly the direction in which Khomiakov's thought is tending, but in fairness to him we should note that it stops short of a final conclusion. Khomiakov assuredly stresses the interior unity of grace. Nevertheless, he also calls unity the visible sign of the Lord's presence on earth and so ascribes it to an external aspect also: for visibility, by definition, can only attach to what is without. This external aspect is found in the fact that in the Church, people enjoy communion in the same sacraments, and adhere to the same doctrines. Here Khomiakov seems to be at one with Catholic ecclesiology, but to his own mind there was an essential difference. He believed that the Catholic Church was not a genuine Church but rather a State in religious disguise, that it was a fundamentally political entity. The unity of the Catholic Church was imposed from above by the pope and so was not true unity. At one level, the unreality of its apparent unity was shown, Khomiakov thought, by the co-existence of divergent and ultimately incompatible theological ideas within Catholicism (such as, in his day, Gallicanism and Ultramontanism). But more profoundly, its unity is a sham unity because, being papally constitutued, it does not spring from the principle of mutual love and therefore is unfree. Thus Khomiakov's dislike of Catholicism restrained him from arguing that the interior unity of the Church as a mystery should be expressed in the exterior unity of the Church as a society with a single government.

From what did this dislike of Catholicism arise? Ostensibly, from distaste for the idea that one local church may have authority over another local church. For Khomiakov, it follows from the definition of the Church as mutual love that there can be no power-relations between local churches, no hierarchy or *taxis* among them, no ordering into greater or lesser within the Christian commonwealth. The pretension of the Roman Church to rule in jurisdiction and to dictate in teaching, expressed above all in the addition of the *Filioque* to the Creed, removed her from *agapê*, the mutual love of Orthodox Christians, and at the same time, indeed in that very moment, de-natured her as a Church.

Unfortunately, Khomiakov's axiom, to the effect that there is no order among local Churches, is itself quite untraditional in Orthodoxy. If generally admitted, it would do away with the principles of patriarchal and metropolitical authority – the notion that in every constellation of local churches there is always *ho prôtos*, one which takes the rôle of primacy – and on that principle the Orthodox Church is itself in its own governance constructed.[6] However after Khomiakov's time it proved possible to re-state his ideas in this area in a more moderate form. Later theologians influenced by Khomiakov accept the ontological equality of all local churches, whilst affirming a functional inequality between them.

Nor was this, however, the only point on which Khomiakov diverged from the Orthodoxy of his time. The most fateful aspect of his influence was his denial that the episcopate is the bearer of truth in Christian doctrine, and, connected with this, his repudiation of the idea of the intrinsic authority of Councils. Stimulated by the 1848 letter of the Eastern patriarchs to Pope Pius IX which spoke of the bearers of the faith as the Christian people at large, Khomiakov believed that he was representing the authentic Eastern tradition on this point.[7] The notion that episcopal or conciliar teaching is not authoritative until received has, since his time, deeply influenced Orthodox theology, and has made something of an impact on Catholic ecclesiology also. For some, it is an obvious conclusion from Church history; for others, it introduces anarchy into the Church's tradition and dissolves the claim to teaching authority into either a head-counting of a democratic kind or, worse still, an appeal to the eventual victors in Church politics, though who these will be we shall not know until the Parousia. O'Leary, in his study, argues that Khomiakov never faces the question why do bishops in council declare dogma if only the whole Church can decisively determine it. Would not, he asks, a group of theologians do just as well or better in thus giving the rest of the Church something to think about, a thesis on which to make up its mind?

The hostility of many Orthodox to Khomiakov's ecclesiology became clear in his own lifetime.[8] Legally, the Russian Church was an aspect of the Tsarist autocracy, and the Tsar's censors would not at first allow the publication of Khomiakov's writings on the grounds of their incompatability with Church doctrine. When eventually they were published they were accompanied by a monitum to the effect that their author was not a trained theologian and had therefore made a number of mistakes in his writing. The controversy within Orthodoxy over the Slavophile inheritance still continues.

Let us sum up Khomiakov's ecclesiology. The essence of this ecclesiology was the idea of *sobornost*, or communality. The Slavophiles held that the basic nature of the Christian society, the Church, can be determined by looking at the form of traditional Russian society, regarded as a synthesis of biblical and Byzantine Christian influences. Using this approach, they came to the conclusion that the nature of the Church is mutual concern or mutual love, brought about by the action of the Holy Spirit. For

Khomiakov, the historical teaching of Christ was a purely external revelation. As such, it was not appropriated by human beings in a way that changed their lives. Only the economy of the Holy Spirit, beginning with Pentecost, interiorised the Son's revelation of the Father and so made it actual in the fullest sense. There is here a radical subordination of the Son to the Spirit; at the same time, there is a sharp distinction between the inner and outer, with the inner – man's interior life – given a marked primacy over the outer – his public life of inter-relationship with others. The upshot of this twofold subordination is that Khomiakov sees the Church as an essentially invisible reality, a union of persons on the basis of their common faith in and love of the Christian God. Whilst not denying the importance of the sacraments, Khomiakov had difficulty in placing them within a scheme which downplayed the historical institutional arrangements made by Christ. As to the idea of an episcopal magisterium in the Church, continuing the work of the apostles, here Khomiakov abandoned the normal teaching of the Russian theological schools. For him, the whole Church, clergy and laity together, inherit the charism of the apostles, and thus teaching of the episcopate, even in solemn council, cannot be regarded with certainty as Christian truth until it has been accepted by the rest of the Church. Khomiakov's doctrine of reception remains the most influential part of his work and has been accepted by Orthodox and Catholic theologians not otherwise in sympathy with his wider theology. Perhaps the main continuing attraction for the Orthodox here is that it justifies their rejection of the Council of Florence, itself outwardly a fully ecumenical council by the tests of developed Byzantine ecclesiology, since all five patriarchs were present or represented, and agreed to its decisions. The attraction for some Catholics is that such a theory gives the non-episcopal members of the Church an active, not just a passive, rôle, *vis-à-vis* ecumenical councils.

I have spent quite a lot of time on the Slavophile ecclesiology since the strengths and weaknesses of that ecclesiology need to be understood before the advent of the eucharistic ecclesiology, and its wide success, can be appreciated. The eucharistic ecclesiology is, from one viewpoint, an attempt to resolve the inherent problems of an ecclesiology of the Khomiakovian type. But before dealing with eucharistic ecclesiology as such, I want to look briefly at the linking period between Khomiakov and Afanas'ev.

In the early years of the twentieth century, a reaction set in against Khomiakov's thought even in those circles where it had at first been well received. The best example of this is the early ecclesiological writings of Bulgakov, produced in the years around the First World War: in other words, in the years around the Revolution of 1917.[9] Bulgakov argued that the reason for Khomiakov's relative indifference to the visible, external aspects of the Church – and notably the Church as an hierarchical society – lay in the domination of Church by State under the nineteenth century Tsardom. Bulgakov suggested that since in Khomiakov's lifetime, the Church, as a society, was a department of the Russian State, he was forced to restrict his attention to the purely inner aspects of *sobornost'* – not because of fear of the censors, but because this inner realm of worship and doctrine was the only area under the Church's full command. The two Revolutions of the year 1917, by liberating the Church from State control, had revealed the Church to be a society in its own right and with its own organs of governance, and not simply, then, a divine mystery or a spiritual communion. Indeed, Bulgakov went so far in his criticism of Khomiakov on this point as to say that someone who had only read him and no other writer on the subject would just not understand what the Orthodox Church was.

However, Bulgakov retained three points from the Slavophile ecclesiology. First, he regarded the invisible side of the Church as enormously more important than the visible. He maintained that the Church consists of the dead as well as the living – and also of the Angels insofar as they have a relation to humanity and its history. Bulgakov argued that the Church moreover, can be identified with the eschatological condition of the cosmos. It is the anticipation of the final state of the creation, the creation as brought into conformity with God's ultimate will. Bulgakov defined the Church, therefore, as the fullness of the divine 'sophia' – his term for the God-world relationship. The result of this extremely high ecclesiology of – essentially – the invisible Church was that Bulgakov felt bound to regard the actual visible Church as a somewhat unsatisfactory presentation within space and time of the eternal Church of predestined men and Angels.

Secondly, Bulgakov kept Khomiakov's idea that the Church is a union of communes. He regarded the idea of the Church as a single worldwide institution of a unitary kind as itself leasing inevitably to papalism, since a worldwide body must needs possess a worldwide head. Bulgakov, therefore, saw the invisible Church as manifested first and foremost in local Churches. Only subsequently, when these local Churches recognise each other and come to establish ecclesial relations with each other, is the sophianic or eternal Church expressed in the single historic Church conceived as a global unity.

Thirdly, Bulgakov preserved Khomiakov's idea that in the Church there can be no such thing as power, coercion, legal restraint or penalty. The relations of the Church's members express the divine *Sophia*, and the divine *Sophia* expresses the relations of Father, Son and Spirit in God. Since it is unthinkable that there could be forced subordination in the relations of communion of the divine persons, so it is equally unthinkable that there could be forced subordination in the Church. The marks of the Church's life for Bulgakov, as for Khomiakov, are essentially freedom and love.

Thus Bulgakov's ecclesiology takes away with one hand what it has just given with the other. It criticises Khomiakov for not understanding that the Church is a visible hierarchical society. Yet it maintains that the Church is primarily an invisible eschatological reality, that it is essentially a number of local Churches and only very secondarily a single worldwide body, and that relations of power or subordination are foreign to it.

Eucharistic ecclesiology emerged, I believe, as an attempt by the Orthodox to make sense of the confused picture produced by combining Slavophilism with the post-1917 revival of their own traditional idea of the Church as a fellowship of right-believing and right-worshipping Christians furnished with all the institutional means that a society needs for unity and self-direction.

And so we come at last to Afanas'ev.[10] He was born in 1893 in Odessa, in the Ukraine, from a Church-going but not a priestly family. After school, he began medical studies, switched to mathematics, but then found university life disrupted altogether by the outbreak of the First World War, the overthrow of the monarchy in the liberal Revolution of February 1917, the Bolshevik Revolution of the subsequent October, and the ensuing Civil War in which Afanas'ev enlisted on the side of the Whites. After the final victory of Trotsky's Red Army in 1919 Afanas'ev fled to Serbia where he resumed his university studies at Belgrade, this time in theology. This was not, however, because he wished to be a priest. He began very much as a lay theologian like Khomiakov. He was ordained only when in his late 40s, on the outbreak of the Second World War, by which time he had moved to Paris to join the staff of the Institut Saint-Serge.

Afanas'ev's early writings – his doctoral thesis – concerned the relation between the Roman imperial power and the Church in the patristic period. He argued, in writings in both Russian and Serbian hard to track down in the West, that the ecumenical councils were basically a Roman imperial institution. Although the local churches of the early Christian world had accepted their doctrinal decisions as a reflection of the churches' own faith, the conciliar institution itself was not, nor could it be, an intrinsic component of the Church Christ founded.[11]

But if the episcopate in council does not provide the Church with her human foundation, then what does? Clearly, as an Orthodox, Afanas'ev could not opt for the Papacy instead. What he did, in his essay, 'Dve idei vselenskoi Tserkvi' ('Two Ideas of the Church Universal'),[12] was to suggest that the universal Church had no need of any human foundation, since it had no existence apart from that of the local churches which composed it, and *their* existence was founded on their central liturgical action, the Eucharist. This eucharistic ecclesiology, whose first clear spokesman he took to be Ignatius of Antioch, was further described by Afanas'ev in two books: *Trapeza Gospodnya* ('The Table of the Lord'), published in 1952, and the posthumous *Tserkov' Dukha Sviatogo* ('The Church of one Holy Spirit') of 1971.[13]

What, then, is eucharistic ecclesiology? Its key, as its name suggests, lies in the doctrine of the Eucharist. Afanas'ev claimed that, for the New Testament, the doctrine of the Church cannot be separated from that of the Eucharist. More strongly still, the doctrines of the Church are simply an extension or re-expression of the doctrine of the Eucharist. To take the most obvious example: Paul's account of the Church as the Body of Christ in his Corinthian correspondence can be seen as a prolongation of his view of the Eucharist. By sharing the one bread and one cup, we who are many become one body in Christ; that is, by participating in Christ's eucharistic body, in the liturgical assembly, we become his mystical body, the Church.

But how does this idea solve the central problems of post-1917 Russian ecclesiology, namely the simultaneous rejection and acceptance of Slavophilism? On the one hand, eucharistic ecclesiology provides a way of speaking about the Church as a visible hierarchical society – the weak spot of the distinctive pre-1917 Russian ecclesiology. In meeting to celebrate the Eucharist, the Church becomes visible. At the same time, since every Eucharist must have a president or celebrant who acts *in persona Christi*, the visible Church is an hierarchical Church. Thus the Eucharist and the bishop, as primary president of the Church in a given place, become the twin means whereby the Church as a divine mystery takes on concrete, visible, social hierarchical form in history. In this way, eucharistic ecclesiology satisfies the needs identified by Bulgakov in his early criticism of the Slavophiles.

On the other hand, defining the Church in terms of the Eucharist enabled Afanas'ev to justify those elements of Slavophilism which he wished to preserve. First, since the Eucharist is eschatological, an anticipation of the feast of heaven, carried out to celebrate the death of the Lord until he comes again, the

Church built on the Eucharist must also be those things, that is, heavenly and eschatological, more than earthly and of this age. Secondly, since it would be ridiculous to suggest that the entire empirical Church could come together to make Eucharist, even a Eucharist celebrated by the pope, it is clear that the Church's fundamental form must be the *local* Church. Afanas'ev believed that the worldwide eucharistic congresses of the Catholic Church, presided over as these were by a papal legate, constituted a kind of wild attempt to apply an instinctively felt eucharistic ecclesiology to the papal 'monarchy'. Finally, Afanas'ev had to come to grips with the notion that in the Church there cannot be law or power or relations of subordination and superordination. How did he do this? Essentially, he tried to deal with the issue in two stages.

In the first place, he argued that, since the Church is built on the Eucharist, and the Eucharist expresses sacramentally the service or self-giving of the Son of God, the ministry which flows from the Eucharist must have the same character. Thus the bishop, or the different ministers which emerged from the differentiation of the bishop's rôle, and chiefly that of the presbyter, can do nothing which contradicts the nature of the Eucharist from which they themselves – on his view – emerge. To act coercively, to act by means of law, or by appeal to power, would contradict the Eucharist. In the second place, Afanas'ev argued that, although no local Church – not even one endowed with an ancient primacy like Alexandria or Constantinople – can rightly order another local church to change its doctrine or its practice, they can refuse to 'receive' the doctrine or practice of an erring Church. They can, in Afanas'ev's key term 'witness' against such a Church, and in the last resort this witness can involve breaking off eucharistic communion with its members. But this, or so Afanas'ev argues, is not an act of the canon law, an act of power-relations. Rather is it an act of confessing faith and corrective love, which the erring church is free to take notice of or not, as it chooses.

This idea of witness might have led Afanas'ev to a more positive estimate of the main common institution of the universal Church, the ecumenical council. He could have gone on to say that local churches may come together to witness in common to orthodoxy and orthopraxy, such witness being, by definition, final and complete. But he never took this step, and remained quite hostile to the conciliar event. Influenced by his early research into the Roman imperial models followed in part by early Church councils, he continued to believe that the Council was a largely alien importation into Christianity, an attempt to administer the Church as though it were a kind of State.

Curiously enough, Afanas'ev became much more favourable to the Papacy than to the phenomenon of the Councils. In an essay published in French in 1960, he spelled out his view that the ministry of the local Roman Church and bishop 'preside in love' – a citation from the letters of Ignatius of Antioch – in the greater liturgical assembly of the Churches at large.[14] The Papacy or so he came by the early 1960s to think, should be perfectly acceptable to the Orthodox so long as it operated in the way that his own ecclesiology had suggested. In other words, its primacy would have to be a primacy of witness and of reception (together with its corollary, non-reception), of the truth and value of what was taking place in other local Churches – and not a primacy of power, that could be expressed in the terms of canon law.

Afanas'ev's ideas on the Papacy and, more generally, on primacy, which can of course take regional as well as universal form, have not met with general acceptance among Orthodox ecclesiologists.[15] The Afanas'evan account of the Papacy goes, it is felt, too far, whereas the Russian theologian's view of primacy in general goes not far enough. Yet the basic idea of eucharistic ecclesiology has proved enormously influential in all sections of the Orthodox world, so much so that even the historical sources in patristic and mediaeval Eastern theology are now being read in its light. This is neatly illustrated in two modern studies by theologically minded historians. The Catholic liturgical historian Hans-Joachim Schulz wrote:

> Such a (eucharistic) ecclesiology makes strikingly clear how the central action of the liturgical life, the celebration of the Eucharist ... provides the clearest possible theological manifestation of the basic structures of the Church as a community of faith and as a community governed by its shepherds, and at the same time repeatedly brings these structures to their fulfilment in the most intense way possible ...[16]

while Meyendorff had this to say:

> In Eastern Christendom, the Eucharistic liturgy, more than anything else, is identified with the reality of the Church itself, for its manifests both the humiliation of God in assuming mortal flesh, and the mysterious presence among men of the eschatological kingdom. It points at these central realities of the faith not through concepts but through symbols and signs intelligible to the entire worshipping congregation. This centrality of the Eucharist is actually the real key to the Byzantine understanding of the Church, both hierarchical and corporate; the Church is universal, but truly realised only in the local eucharistic assembly, at which a group of sinful men and women becomes fully the 'people of God'.[17]

What one may question is, of course, whether an ecclesiology so resolutely particularist, and some would say (in tendency) congregationalist, is capable of contributing much *either* to overcoming the jurisdictional disputes in Orthodoxy by fostering a greater sense of the unity of Orthodox everywhere, *or* to developing a spirit of universal solidarity such as the Christian Church will certainly need, in the face of such powers as materialistic consumerism, nationalism, secular humanism and a renascent Islam if it is to make much mark on the world of the future.

VIII
George Florovsky and the Idea of Tradition

George Florovsky was born near Odessa on 28 August 1893. His father was a priest: a school chaplain and schoolmaster who would later become rector of the Odessa Seminary and cathedral dean. Florovsky's mother was the daughter of a priest who had been professor of the biblical languages at the same seminary. Such marriages between clerical families were common. Typical of the clerical *soslovie*, 'estate', they were more subject than other marriages to the Church's jurisdiction, its rules and customs. As Dr Lewis Shaw has pointed out, in a masterly and regrettably as yet unpublished study of Florovsky to which I am indebted for this overview of his life and work, the young George Vasilieivič seems to have acquired attitudes of duty, service and self-denial from his family's long history of service to the Church.[1]

Florovsky went from the seminary school into one of Odessa's State gymnasia, where he received a classical education based on German models. Though such schools were obliged by the Ministry of Education and the Holy Synod to include at any rate a minimal number of patristic texts (Russia was of course a confessionally Orthodox State), Florovsky's early academic training followed a conventional, rationalistic German curriculum, which took up a post-Enlightenment view of the classical antecedents of Christian culture. With this foundation laid, he moved on to the philosophy department at Odessa University.

Intellectually, Florovsky's interests were eclectic. His first published work took the form of an experimental study 'On the

Mechanism of Reflex Salivary Secretion' (his own teachers included a pupil of Pavlov),[2] but he also won a medal for essays on logical inference and 'The Myth of Amphitryon in Ancient and Modern Drama' which involved him in both classical philology and comparative literature. Apparently, the contemporary Germano-Russian pedagogic scheme would have included all these disciplines under the broad heading of 'philosophy'.

The essay in logic shows Florovsky under the influence of the Marburg School of neo-Kantianism, and the early writings of Edmund Husserl, the founder of phenomenology. Florovsky's own position at this time was that the universe is a coherent system, of a kind whose pre-determination thought can, to a large degree, lay bare. But in the later years of the First World War Florovsky began to edge away from all forms of Idealist thinking. In a review of new studies of Solov'ev, which can be regarded as his earliest theological or at least religio-philosophical essay, Florovsky sought to demonstrate that the origins of the Slavophile ideal of integral knowledge lie not so much in the philosophy of Schelling as in the contemplative mysticism of the Russian monastic Fathers.

In 1920, Florovsky became Lecturer in Philosophy at Odessa University. His chief interests lay in philosophical psychology and the philosophy of history; it would seem that the inter-action of the two generated one of his key themes, the primacy of freedom in history. He was hardly able to begin teaching however, when his family (still in 1920) fled from Russian territory so as to escape the horrors of the civil war in the Ukraine. They settled in the Bulgarian capital, Sofia, where Florovsky joined a group of young scholars and writers who called themselves 'The Eurasians' – meaning thereby to contrast their approach with that of both Westernisers and Slavophiles. The Eurasians emphasised the rôle of the fourteenth century Mongol invasions in the building, in Russia, of a multi-ethnic State. Unlike many of the intelligentsia, they were not anti-Christian, and indeed found in Orthodoxy a unitive principle beyond any particular pro-Western or Slavophile commitment.

Florovsky himself was not especially interested in the Asiatic current, stressing rather, as his views on what was valuable in Solov'ev would suggest, the contribution of the Byzantine church. Eurasianism appealed to him as an effort to interpret history, both finding meaning within history and providing significance for history. This concern with the meaning of history underlies most of his mature theological work.

Increasingly, and in a way not unlike that of Christopher Dawson in the Catholic West,[3] Florovsky stressed the importance of religion in the making of culture, while the rest of the group gave the lion's share of its energies to political activity, of a left-wing kind. Florovsky responded by an essay entitled 'The Cunning of Reason', in which he defined Christian truth as that which liberates the human being from the constraints of both self and society, in the fellowship of the Church. He maintained that, in the crisis of culture described by Oswald Spengler as 'the decline of the West', Europeans were taking *en masse* to monism, theosophy and even Buddhism owing to a loss of confidence in the empty formulae of Protestant Scholasticism (in Germany) and the 'juridical dogmatics' of Roman Catholicism (in the Mediterranean lands).[4] And yet, so Florovsky continued, even when rebelling against rationalism, Western European thought seems unable to go beyond the concept of gnosis – a religious knowledge – and reach the genuine freedom of religious existence, or life. Husserl's phenomenology now appeared to him as no more than a pan-logism: a new mutation of Hegel's system.

For his own part, he would have preferred to see people adopt the slogan 'Back to Fichte', rather than 'Back to Hegel', since at least Fichte had placed at the head of his system the freedom of the 'I', not the nature of the thing. In this early essay, Florovsky already announced certain characteristic themes of his later theological writing, and notably the belief that redemption consists in the affirmation of the personal principle over against the human tendency to see man as a 'thing', determined by causes external to himself, and to act accordingly.

In 1926, after a period in the émigré Russian academy at Prague (where he took the degree of master of philosophy) and marriage (to a girl born to a Russian family in Finland), Florovsky settled in Paris, at the Institut Saint-Serge, where he was made professor of patristics and systematic theology; and in 1932 ordained to the Orthodox priesthood.

We have already studied the ensuing 'sophiological crisis' in which, over against Bulgakov, Florovsky played a major part. His encyclopaedic but impassioned history of theology in Russia, published originally in 1937 – and later, 1987, in an English translation⁵ – was meant to make clear his own position, with the utmost clarity, *vis-à-vis* Bulgakov and his supporters, whose thought, to Florovsky's mind, revealed all that was worst in the Russian Orthodox intellectual tradition, and above all its tendency to follow after strange gods – whether Roman Catholic, Protestant, or, most fatefully of all, those of philosophical Idealism. Borrowing a key-term from Spengler, Florovsky lamented that the Russian tradition, after the Middle Ages, had suffered a 'pseudo-morphosis' – Spengler's word for what happens when a young culture is squeezed out of shape by another older culture which gains an excessive domination over it.

To make up for these deficiencies, Florovsky proposed – rather as contemporary Catholics were beginning to do in the West – a 'return to the sources', in his case the primary sources of the Russian tradition: namely, the Christian Hellenism of the Fathers of the Greek Church. It was the Fathers' combination of intellectual concentration and ascetic spirituality which, on the foundation of the gospel, had created, Florovsky believed, the concept of *personhood*, so necessary to right living and the proper description of what existence demands. So far as the West was concerned, Florovsky was willing and even eager to broach what he termed a 'responsible' encounter, for it was modern Western scholarship which had enabled the recovery of so much of the patristic witness. Florovsky stressed, however, that only the interior memory of the Orthodox Church can activate the true, but silent, testimony those texts give. For this reason, he concluded, the renaissance of Orthodoxy is a necessary precondition for the solution of the ecumenical problem.[6] After *The Ways of Russian Theology*, therefore, Florovsky's output took the form, consistently enough, of, first, studies of the patristic and early Byzantine tradition, and, secondly, essays on a huge variety of topics in doctrine and Church history.

Although Florovsky was extremely well received by those Anglicans and Protestants whom he sought out, during the 1930s and 1940s in pursuit of this programme, his position at Saint-Serge became ever more difficult. In the summer of 1939, the outbreak of the Second World War found him in Yugoslavia, where he was obliged to spend the years 1939 to 1945. After this uncomfortable experience, he moved, in 1948, to the United States where he would remain in various capacities – working both in Orthodox seminaries and the great universities of Columbia, Harvard and Princeton – until his death in 1979.

Basically, Florovsky sought the revitalisation of Greek Christian theology, seen as the intelligent articulation of lived Orthodox religious experience. His theological work consisted in the setting forth of what he called the 'code' which serves the 'ecclesial mind' in its self-expression in the Church's literary classics – that is, the writings of the Fathers, and in her Liturgy. What was this 'code', this underlying structure? For Florovsky, patristic thought fused Greek cosmology with Israel's confession of a revelation granted to a community conscious of itself as travelling through history. Shaw sums up[7] the contents of Florovsky's dogmatics in this way: his theology is concerned, essentially, with the 'nisus' or direction of creation, insofar as that emerges in the exercise of freedom in salvation history – the key to which is provided by eschatology. Creation, salvation history, eschatology, all approached with the theme of freedom in mind: these are the pillars of Florovsky's thought. What Florovsky wanted was a coherent Christian vision of history, not new speculative theologoumena, which were Bulgakov's central concern.[8] Florovsky considered that, beneath all patristic thought, there lay a synthesis of a distinctive kind. Its two intertwining features were: first, the primacy of will, freedom, personality, in all divine-human interaction, and, secondly, the story of the creation as the transformation of history in Christ.

Florovsky's repudiation of speculation, as the great crime of sophiologists, was not perhaps entirely candid. As Shaw, whom I follow here, has argued: both speculated, but on different subject matters.[9] Whereas the Sophiologists were preoccupied by the nature of the triune God, Florovsky was absorbed by the shape of history. A Florensky might seek the unitive principle underlying knowledge; Florovsky looked for the principle underlying the development of history. He did not wish to risk dissipating the centrality of Christ's role by a possibly fruitless Trinitarian speculation which was not at the heart of the original patristic synthesis. For Florovsky, a metaphysical starting-point to Christian theology was anathema. Influenced by St Maximus the Confessor, he stressed the salvific significance of time, tensed as it is between the beginning, *archê* and the end, *telos*. God is not a logical reality but a meta-logical one, and as such is present in decisive, historical *acts*. In taking Christology to be the centre of patristic discussion, Florovsky found his own preferred themes of personality and freedom under-scored by revelation itself. At one level, what Christ assumed was the character of a culture hero, or champion, who redemptively renews the cultures of history by baptising them into his own ordeal, the Passion, and its outcome, the Resurrection.

Florovsky's stress on freedom does not in any way signify an apotheosis for egalitarian individualism. The pilgrimage to *theôsis*, divinisation, passes along the way of *askêsis*, disciplined self-denial. This journey takes place in the openness of creaturely freedom, but on it we bear each other's burdens as Christ's likeness is formed within us. In Florovsky's scheme of salvation, the task of created freedom is to co-operate with grace in the regenerating of humanity into a new creation. By baptism, the will is cleansed, purified, in a catharisis which will be fully revealed only in the general Resurrection. Meanwhile, the values achieved in Christian existence, the fruits of baptismal regeneration, will be carried forward into the Age to Come. This happens through the high priesthood exercised by Christ, for in that priesthood he gives eternal value to our efforts under grace, until humanity reaches at last the everlasting Sabbath of the End of time.

Criticisms of Florovsky's Project

Since his death, Florovsky's 'programme' has met with considerable criticism. There are two basic objections. First, despite his protestations to the contrary, his project belongs within the more general phenomenon of nineteenth century German-language Philhellenism, whose final philosophical expression was the Graecophilia of Friedrich Nietzsche. If true, this situates his work within a distinctively Western, post-Enlightenment attitude to the Greek 'moment', which has, in itself, nothing to do with the patristic tradition. 'Election', after all, refers theologically to the vocation of universal servanthood ascribed by Scripture and Tradition to Israel and the Church. It gives no justification for cultural chauvinism of any kind.

In the 1970s, for instance, Florovsky had renewed his call for a return to the Greek Christian classics, and for a recognition that to be a Christian is to be a Hellene. This he did at an important meeting at Aarhus, in Denmark between the Eastern Orthodox and the Oriental Non-Chalcedonian Orthodox (the Monophysites). On that occasion, while denying any cultural triumphalism, and emphasising that the Fathers were also Syrian and Latin, he did not enlighten his hearers as to how such non-Greek Fathers could be incorporated into the Christian Hellenic framework, other than by making the quite general assertion that the mind of the Church – *to ekklêsiastikon phronêma* – found them worthy of parity with their Greek equivalents.[10] The question obviously remains as to how the 'mind of the Church' manifested itself to the non-Greek Fathers within the constitutive experiences of their own cultures.

Florovsky's intention, however, was not ungenerous. The Byzantine polity represented in his eyes the best sort of urbanity, cosmopolitanism and universalism.[11] Hellenism had been converted by the Holy Spirit. A culture metamorphosed through divinisation by grace had made of Orthodoxy the spiritual reflection of this universality, the supra-nationality of Byzantium.

A somewhat different line of criticism, secondly, is that Florovsky assumed in the Fathers a consensus of a monolithic kind. His adoption of St John Damascene's dictum that a Father does not fight against the Fathers, since 'all of them were communicants in a single Holy Spirit', enabled him to leave in the shadow the tensions, or even occasional oppositions, among them. Yet, despite his Parisian lectures on the Fathers of the early to the Byzantine centuries, Florovsky was not concerned to trace the history of patristic thought for its own sake. His aim was, rather, to disengage the fundamental principles underlying that thought, principles which could then be taken forward into his own neo-patristic synthesis. Not that he regarded the latter as an exposition of his personal thinking. It was, in his eyes, nothing but faithfulness to Orthodoxy itself. Be that as it may, his presentation of Orthodox life and thought as a grace-borne reaching out towards the God of deification was certainly in tune with, and helped set the tone for, a great deal of modern Orthodox dogmatics.

Florovsky on Tradition

By way of preamble to an account of Florovsky's doctrine of tradition, we can note that, in contemporary Christianity, the concept of tradition is found in, basically, three distinct forms. First, in Protestantism, the Church's tradition is seen as concerned with *adiaphora*: things not strictly necessary for a grasp of saving faith. On this view, whatever *is* necessary for such faith must be found in Scripture, which functions, then, as the primary norm of believing. Secondary criteria, such as the Creeds which tradition hands down, are not thereby ruled out; they are, however, definitely subordinate to the standard of faith, which is the Bible. Secondly, in Catholicism, Scripture and tradition are regarded as complementary aspects of the transmitted revelation. Scripture needs tradition as the medium without whose aid it can neither be received nor understood; tradition needs Scripture as its own primary articulated content. Quite irrespective of whether a 'two-source' theory of revelation is explicitly invoked, some kind of duality is always affirmed. Thirdly, in Orthodoxy, tradition includes Scripture, and it is to tradition, first and foremost, that the Christian looks for truth. In Lossky, for instance, tradition is the total realm where the Holy Spirit transmits revelation, the 'silence' within whose nurturing space the Word is received.[12]

All Churches to some extent define themselves by mutual correlation and contrast. So far as Orthodoxy is concerned, we can say that the concept of tradition, as found in contemporary Orthodox theology, is a particular interpretation of the fundamental theology of earlier centuries. The 'global' view of tradition largely espoused by Orthodox theologians today is, in part, an attack on what are considered the excessively text-oriented or officer-oriented, Churches of the West: Protestantism and Catholicism, respectively.

Although all of Florovsky's mature work is an exploration of tradition, his fullest *ex professo* statement on this subject comes in the essay 'The Catholicity of the Church', reprinted in the first volume of his *Collected Works*.[13] Though the study of tradition is generally regarded in Catholic theology as an aspect of fundamental or foundational theology (since tradition is itself an aspect of revelation), Florovsky deals with it as though it were a dimension of ecclesiology, the study of the Church. This is by no means unreasonable. All theology falls under what has been termed an 'ecclesiological *a priori*': adhesion to the Church is a prior condition of any adequate practice of Christian thinking. Since it is the Church alone which brings us into contact with the intrinsic significance of the event of Jesus Christ, Christian theology can be carried out only in the sphere of the Church, as a reflection on her common faith. Thus tradition can be treated either as the central topic in fundamental theology, where we are concerned to establish the bases of revelation-in-transmission, or as the central topic in ecclesiology, where we are trying to express the essential nature of the Christian community which has received that revelation, and, in receiving it, passes it onwards.

Florovsky's account of tradition belongs with a very high doctrine of the Church. For the author of this essay, the victory of Christ at Easter and Pentecost *consists in* the creation of the Church. The Holy Spirit, descending on the Church at Pentecost, brings about, in principle or in nucleus, the sanctification – the divinisation – of mankind. For Florovsky, the formula, 'Outside the Church there is no salvation' can only be tautologous. It must be true by definition – since salvation *is* the Church. There the two natures, divine and human, remain united just as they do at salvation's source, in the single person of the Church's Lord. The Church is, therefore, 'theanthropic': she is the place where Godmanhood is realised. On the foundation, then, of this high ecclesiology, worked out in terms both of Incarnation and of Antonement, Florovsky goes on to outline his view of how the Church is 'catholic'. He lays to one side the notion that catholicity denotes something quantitative: the Church's missionary extension to all races and cultures. As he writes:

> The universality of the Church is the consequence or manifestation but not the cause or the foundation of its catholicity.[14]

Rather does catholicity derive from what he terms an 'inner wholeness or integrity' in the Church's life. Florovsky points out that, for a Church Father like Cyril of Jerusalem, we find, alongside the geographic concept of catholicity another, and more profound, perspective. For Cyril, the Church is catholic because she teaches Christian doctrine *katholikôs*: fully or completely. Only with the Donatist crisis in the North African Church of the fifth century did this, the premier meaning of catholicity, become marginalised by the sheer force of an urgent appeal to the 'judgment of the whole world', namely, the circle of the Churches in their geographical diffusion. And if this history of the concept be thought excessively Western, Florovsky adds for good measure that in the East, by a development uncannily similar in one crucial respect, catholicity became identified with ecumenicity. In other words, on the later Eastern view, the Church is catholic because her representatives gather from everywhere to meet in council – a position which mirrors that of the post-Donatist West in its concentration on the outer aspect of catholicity, whereas Florovsky wishes to direct our gaze, first of all, to the inner heart of the matter.

The Church, remarks Florovsky, is 'catholic' all through – in her smallest part, in each and every event of her sacramental life – thanks to her union with Christ and with the Holy Spirit. The work of the Spirit and the Son in the Church is to render her catholic by in some sense (shortly to be expounded) abrogating the distinction *both* between individual human persons *and* between the individual generations of human history. And while Florovsky's theology of tradition is, as we shall see, chiefly concerned with this second aspect of achieved catholicity, a word may be offered here about the first also, for the sake of completeness.

According to Florovsky, the work of the Son and the Spirit in the Church brings about what he terms an 'ontological blending of persons'. People cease to be exclusive and 'impenetrable' when they define themselves as belonging to the communion of the Church. In communion, *koinônia*, we accept the other as our own other self. Florovsky is at pains to stress that this must not be confused with collectivism, which means the disparagement and attempted destruction of individual personhood. Instead, as redeemed individuals we come to 'enclose the many in our own self'. Thus each Christian, if he or she consent to become truly a man or woman of the Church, undergoes a 'catholic transfiguration of personality', and becomes a kind of living image of the Holy Trinity, which it at once irreducibly single and plural.

Florovsky is not so naive as to suppose that all members of the
Church see themselves as essentially related to other people in
this profound sense. But this is only to admit that not all actually
reach the level of true catholicity that everyone is called to attain.
These in whom this process has reached its term are the doctors
or Fathers of the Church. This is why, in their witness to faith,
we hear not simply their personal profession but also the self-
testimony of faith itself. Or, in Florovsky's words, the Fathers, of
whatever epoch,

> speak to us from the Church's catholic completeness, from the
> completeness of a life full of grace.[15]

And this brings him to the second aspect of catholicity: its power
to abolish (in a sense yet to be explained) the difference between
historic generations. Thanks to grace, the experience of the
Church in all generations is gathered into what Florovsky calls a
'time-conquering unity'. And here (at last!) he invokes the word
'tradition'.

> To learn from tradition, or, still better, to learn in tradition, is to
> learn from the fullness of this time-conquering experience of the
> Church, an experience which every member of the Church may learn
> to know and possess according to the measure of his spiritual
> humanity – in other words, according to the measure of his catholic
> development.[16]

Florovsky insists that tradition is not discovered by way of
consulting large quantities of ancient texts. It is not 'archaeological'. Authentic tradition does not yield itself, in fact, to deter-
mination by any outward test, such as, for example, the attempt
to identify a 'consensus of the Fathers' using the historical-
critical method for a study of their writings, and other remains.
How then do we locate tradition? Florovsky replies:

> The Church alone is the living witness of tradition, and only from
> inside, from within the Church, can tradition be felt and accepted as
> a certainty.[17]

Florovsky does not, however, leave this statement free-standing as a piece of sheer ecclesiastical self-assertion. He explains it theologically by arguing that tradition is nothing other than the distinctive testifying, in post-Pentecostal history, of the Holy Spirit. Just as the Word Incarnate preached the good news of the Father's love and mercy in the time of the first disciples, so ever afterwards the Spirit has preached the good news of Jesus Christ in the time of the Church. The way in which the Spirit preaches is not, of course, by himself uttering human words. He preaches, rather, by animating tradition. Here, then, we have a high doctrine of tradition to parallel Florovsky's high Christological (and pneumatological) doctrine of the Church.

Curiously, Florovsky does not employ this high doctrine of tradition for exclusively conservative purposes. He does not say that, because the Church's tradition is inspired by the Spirit, our Christian life and thinking should be, in all essentials, turned towards the past. He declares that loyalty to tradition

> means not only concord with the past, but in a certain sense freedom from the past.[18]

These words are striking but they are not wholly unexpected. Florovsky's denial that tradition has any external criterion already points in this direction. There follow a justly famous passage:

> Tradition is not only a protective, conservative principle; it is primarily the principle of growth and regeneration. Tradition is not a principle striving to restore the past, using the past as a criterion for the present. Such a concept of tradition is rejected by history itself and by the consciousness of the Church. Tradition is authority to teach, authority to bear witness to the truth. The Church bears witness to the truth not by reminiscence or from the words of others, but from its own living, unceasing experience, from its catholic fullness ... Tradition is a charismatic, not an historical principle.[19]

In the name of this charismatic principle, Florovsky proceeds to cast a critical eye over Orthodoxy's two main rivals in the

Christian universe: the churches of the Reformation, and Rome. Looking first to Protestantism, Florovsky argues that Scripture cannot be self-sufficient: not because the written Word of God is in some way defective, but because it lays no such claim to autarchy. The Bible is, he writes, a 'God-inspired *eikôn* of the truth, but not the truth itself'. Thus, in classical Reformation teaching

> the liberty of the Church is shackled by an abstract biblical standard for the sake of setting free individual consciousness from the spiritual demands enforced by the experience of the Church. This is a denial of catholicity, a destruction of Catholic consciousness.[20]

And citing the somewhat eccentric Anglican author, W. R. Inge, Dean of St Paul's Cathedral, London, from 1911 to 1934, Florovsky calls the Protestant Reformation a 'return to the Gospel in the spirit of the Koran'. To declare Scripture self-sufficient is, in practice, to subject it to the interpretation of the individual scholar, since the Bible has thus become cut off from its true context, the living experience of the Church. Yet surely, one may interject, to subordinate Scripture to Christian experience is itself to exalt subjectivity over the Word of God? Florovsky anticipates this objection, and counters it. The nub of the objection, he remarks, lies in the accusation that the Orthodox care nothing for the original meaning of Scripture, as something given, embedded, in all its objectivity, in history. He replies:

> We must not think that all we have said denies history. On the contrary, history is recognised in all its sacred realism. As contrasted with outward historical testimony, we put forward no subjective religious experience, no solitary mystical consciousness, not the experience of separate believers, but the integral, living experience of the catholic Church: catholic experience and Church life. And this experience includes also historical memory. It is full of history. But this memory is not only a reminiscence and a remembrance of some bygone events. Rather it is a vision of what is, and of what has been, accomplished, a vision of the mystical conquest of time, of the catholicity of the whole of time.[21]

In the Church's corporate experience, the architectonics of the sacred history, the gift of revelation and its perpetuation through time, become available to individual human subjects, who can discern the contours of God's self-disclosure in no other way.

If the text-oriented approach to revealed truth typical of the Reformed churches is thus harshly dealt with at Florovsky's hands, he does not spare his criticism of Roman Catholicism, for its officer- or institution-centred approach. For Florovsky, the majority vote of bishops in a general council, or the consensus of the faithful, is no infallible guarantee of Christian truth. These things are to be judged by the truth; they are not themselves its judges.

> Catholic experience can be expressed even by the few, even by single confessors of faith, and this is quite sufficient. Strictly speaking, to be able to recognise and express catholic truth we need no ecumenical, universal assembly and vote; we even need no 'ecumenical council'. The sacred dignity of the council lies not in the number of members representing their churches. A large 'general' council may prove itself to be a 'council of robbers' [here Florovsky has in mind the Second Council of Ephesus, 449, declared a *latrocinium* two years later at Chalcedon] or even of apostates. And the *ecclesia sparsa* [the scattered Church] often convicts it of its nullity by silent opposition. *Numerus episcoperum* [the counting of bishops] does not solve the question. The historical and practical methods of recognising sacred and catholic tradition can be many; that of assembling ecumenical councils is but one of them, and not the only one.[22]

And Florovsky maintains that the views of the Fathers or doctors of the Church may often have greater spiritual value and decisiveness than the definitions of councils. Such opinions, he goes on, do not need to be verified by any supposed 'universal content'. They are themselves the criterion for evaluating the judgments of others: to this the Church testifies in silent reception. And so decisive value resides in inner catholicity, not in empirical universality.

In Florovsky's remarks here we may detect a certain dislike of the conciliar phenomenon as such. Ever since Florence there has been, in some Orthodox circles, distrust of councils. Thus for instance in the fifteenth century we find Metropolitan Jonas of Moscow arguing that it is heretical to say that there can be further councils beyond the Seven. We have seen how, in the modern period, Florovsky's colleague at Saint-Serge, Nikolai Afanas'ev, held, more radically still, that the very principle of ecumenical councils was forced on the Church by the Roman emperors, against the grain of the apostolic tradition which is one of witness, not legal authority. Florovsky's marked preference for the inner, over against the outer, in matters of catholicity is not, however, in keeping with the character of Christianity as an incarnational religion. There is no reason why the Holy Spirit cannot use the institutional arrangements of human beings as well as the non-institutional, since he transcends both – and is capable, therefore, of absolute immediacy to each of them. Office and charism are not mutually exclusive terms. Not only in Catholicism but in Orthodoxy too, office in the Church is only possible because it is charismatic.

Conclusion

Such strictures on Catholicism, seen as standing over against Orthodoxy, were inevitable once Florovsky had decided to take his stand on the developed Byzantine experience. The true Church exists within the deep recesses of Byzantium, harmoniously uniting the twin poles of empire and desert, culture and asceticism. As Shaw puts it:

> Central to this visionary, culture-transforming 'synthesis' or 'code' was his notion of Tradition (*paradôsis*), which is the grace-given experience of the Church, through the sacramental indwelling of the Spirit in the ecclesial *oikonomia*. Suspicious of contemporaneous disciplines of scriptural scholarship, Florovsky was compelled to appeal to the 'Living Voice' or 'Living Tradition' of the Church – *paradôsis*, as identified or sensed by the *ekklêsiastikon phronêma* ('ecclesial mind') – as a means of bearing down that which was 'unOrthodox'. His theology was polemical. The 'ecclesial mind'

of the Church, *paradôsis* and *katholikotês* ('catholicity') as determined by him – with constant recourse to the 'metahistorical'
ecclesial foundations, *kêrygma* and dogma – were therefore the
essential and determinative factors in whatever he actually wrote
and taught.[23]

IX
Alexander Schmemann and Liturgical Theology

Alexander Schmemann was born in Estonia in 1921. Although his family was Russian-speaking, and identified itself with Russia, his father's stock were, as his surname suggests, Baltic Germans. The family left Estonia for France in the course of the later 1920s, and Paris, the centre *par excellence* of the Russian diaspora, would be Schmemann's home until 1951 when he abandoned Europe for the United States. In the 1930s, Paris had a Russian community numbering some tens of thousands, and a child could enjoy, should his parents so wish, an entirely Russian education of the *ancien régime* kind. Schmemann's schooling was initially of this sort. He spent several years as a 'cadet' in a Russian military school at Versailles, prior to transferring to a *gimnaziya*, high school, whence, however, he proceeded to a French *lycée* and finally to the University of Paris. Although the Russian schools provided a traditional religious education, it was not there that he discovered Orthodoxy as a living reality but in the liturgical life of the Russian cathedral in the Rue Daru, where he served as an altar boy and later as a sub-deacon. During the Second World War, when he also married Juliana Osorguine, herself a child of a Church-oriented Russian family and at the time a classics student at the Sorbonne, Schmemann studied at the Institut Saint-Serge, at the time still dominated by the figure of Sergei Bulgakov. Though respectful of Bulgakov, Schmemann was not attracted by his sophiology. Schmemann gravitated towards another member of the Institute's staff, A. V. Kartashev, himself a distinguished respresentative of the pre-Revolution theological establishment in the old Russia. Church history was, then, to be the primary sphere in which Schmemann's mind would move, and his candidate thesis took, indeed, as its subject the theocratic element in mediaeval Byzantine society. At the end of the war, Schmemann took on the post of lecturer in Church history at Saint-Serge, first as a layman, and then as a priest, following his ordination in 1946 by the Russian exarch of the patriarch of Constantinople, Archbishop Vladimir Tikhonitsky.

Two more influences conspired to ensure that the particular form taken by Schmemann's Church historical interests would be *liturgiological*. First, he took as his spiritual father Archimandrite Cyprian Kern, lecturer in patristics at Saint-Serge and priest of the parish of SS Constantine and Helena at Clamart. Kern's own great love was the Liturgy and its theological meaning;[1] his liturgical taste, so Meyendorff assures us, left its mark on Schmemann's own sensibility.[2] Secondly, Schmemann was influenced by the eucharistic ecclesiology of Nikolai Afanas'ev, then lecturer in canon law at the same school. Of his strictly Church-historical interests, Meyendorff writes:

> His discussion of Byzantine theocracy, and his readings in Church History in general – as well as his initial dissertation topic [on the Council of Florence, an abandoned project] – come from his concern with the *survival* of the Church, as Church, during the centuries of an ambiguous alliance with the State, and the survival of Orthodoxy in its mediaeval confrontation with Rome.[3]

In Meyendorff's view, Schmemann lacked the necessary patience for a meticulous examination of the Church's past: the 'existential today' was, for him, what really mattered. And despite his interest in the zealous defence of Byzantine particularism at Florence (he would publish a treatise by Mark of Ephesus, that great anti-unionist, on the Resurrection), he learned, in the course of the later 1940s and 1950s, from such Catholic theologians of *ressourcement* as Jean Daniélou and Père Louis Bouyer. These men much influenced his idea of liturgical theology, of the

Christian meaning of time, of the full significance of the Paschal mystery of Christ. Or, as Meyendorff, once again, puts it:

> If their legacy was somewhat lost within the turmoil of post-conciliar Roman Catholicism, their ideas produced much fruit in the organically-liturgical and ecclesiologically-consistent world of Orthodoxy through the brilliant and always effective witness of Fr Schmemann.[4]

Schmemann's move from France to America was determined in part by his frustration with the backward-lookingness of many of his colleagues, concerned as these were with keeping alive the Russian tradition in exile rather than in establishing a territorial, French-speaking Church in their new *patrie*. He was also influenced by the decision of his old mentor, George Florovsky, to abandon Saint-Serge for the United States. In 1955, however, Florovsky would leave the fledgling St Vladimir's Seminary: in 1962, when it moved from the cramped accommodation of a house on Broadway and 121st Street, New York, to its present site in the more rurified environment of Crestwood, New York State, Schmemann became Dean of the burgeoning faculty there, a post which he held until his death in 1983. As dean, Schmemann was concerned to provide priests and theologians for a wider Orthodoxy than simply the Russian jurisdiction, and he played a major part in the effort to secure an autocephalous Orthodox Church in America, a campaign successfully concluded in 1970, when the Patriarch Alexis (Simansky) of Moscow signed the 'Tomos of Autocephaly' granting self-government to the Russian congregations in that country, the nucleus, or so it was hoped, of an eventual pan-Orthodox American Church embracing the clergy and faithful of all jurisdictions. Alexander Schmemann died in 1983.

Worshipping the Lord in the Beauty of Holiness

This chapter will concentrate on what was undoubtedly Schmemann's principal theological contribution: his studies of Christian worship, and above all, of the meaning and implications of the Byzantine liturgy in its origins and historic development for a grasp of what that worship may be.

The richness of the texts, gestures and to some extent music of the Byzantine liturgy would be generously conceded by all familiar with them. In comparison with the Roman rite, or any Western liturgical form, it is more exuberant, more dramatic. In practice, this Byzantine liturgy is now identical with the liturgy of Orthodoxy, since over the centuries, the Orthodox ousted the native non-Byzantine Oriental rites from those parts of the Near and Middle East where they were once the norm. Thus, for instance, the Orthodox patriarchate of Alexandria does not celebrate the Coptic liturgy, nor does the Orthodox patriarchate of Antioch worship with any variant of the Syrian liturgical family. In effect, with the exception of one or two experiments in Western-rite Orthodoxy (chiefly in France and North America), the Orthodox liturgy *is* the Byzantine liturgy *tout court*.

In modern times, Orthodox apologists frequently appeal to the undoubted splendours of their rite so as to suggest that the understanding of liturgy as such differs in the Eastern and Western churches. They claim, in effect, that the contrast between the sobriety of the Western liturgy and the poetic expansiveness of the Byzantine, is not simply a matter of style or culture. Two differing concepts of what it is to have a liturgy are involved. Generally, the Orthodox place little emphasis, in such apologetic contexts, on the didactic or educational rôle of the Liturgy. True, Scriptural passages are read out there; patristic and post-patristic texts of considerable theological weight are sung or announced; a homily is usually given, even if at the end and often, at least in the Greek tradition, by a layman. But even here the main purpose is not instruction. The task of the Liturgy is, rather, doxological: it invites us to give glory to God, the readings and sermon remaining within this same all-important perspective. On this view, the outward signs of the Liturgy are attempts to give expression to the divine Glory; our response to that Glory is the act of glorification: in other words, our recognising the Glory, and praising it. The splendid ritual setting of Orthodox worship should not be seen as a matter of aesthetics in the narrow sense. It is not just that, when worshipping God, we should use the best materials we can. The frescoes and icons, the vestments and vessels, the chant, the exalted quality of the texts, all this is meant to disclose something of the Glory of Father, Son and Holy Spirit, using created beauty to manifest the Uncreated. The worshipping community responds to the divine Glory in its midst by further ritual action: acclamations of praise and petition, bowing, making the sign of the Cross, prostration. Orthodoxy is ritualistic because it believes worship to be above all doxology.

Furthermore, Orthodox spokesmen speak of the liturgical act as possessed of truly cosmic proportions. Not only the Pantocrator himself, but also the Angels, the invisible Church and the divine Wisdom as embodied in all creation make up the assembly (*sobor*) of the worshipping Church.

Such commentators may draw attention to the character of the place in which the Liturgy is enacted: a microcosm of the entire spiritual world, with both space and time gathered up, concentrated, by the Liturgy itself. Indeed, as the Byzantine church-building developed, this tendency to regard the church as the spiritual universe in miniature became ever more pronounced, as iconographic schemes of church decoration testify. In Schmemann's work – writing as a professional liturgiologist (by analysis of the historic forms of the Liturgy) and as a theologian of the Liturgy (a student of the Christian significance of those historic forms) – these commonplaces of Orthodox reflection are, however, displaced as we shall see, by rather different concerns.

Schmemann's Programme for 'Liturgical Theology'

The proper place to begin would seem to be Schmemann's own *Introduction to Liturgical Theology*, translated from the Russian in 1966, and dedicated to the memory of Saint-Serge's professor of patristics, himself the author of a distinguished study of the

Eucharist, Archimandrite Cyprian Kern. Schmemann opens by situating his own study against the background of some pre-decessors. He berates the Orthodox Scholastics of nineteenth century Russia for accepting what he regards as a typically Western dichotomy between theology and worship. Those Russian schoolmen, influenced as they were by Latin theological forms, barely adverted to the texts of the Liturgy in their theological work. While not denying the status of the Liturgy as a *locus theologicus*

> the whole spirit of their system and method excluded a living interest in liturgics, in a search for those elements in the Church's liturgy which could operate as an independent and indeed theological 'standard of measurement' in the task of expounding the Church's faith.[5]

For them, sadly, 'liturgics' was scarcely more than the study of rubrics, a 'practical' or 'supplementary' discipline concerned with the technical execution of the rites, not the exploration of theology's heartlands. Schmemann is less harsh when dealing with the historical theologians of the same period. Though their work was, in a wide sense, archaeological, such scholars as N. F. Krasnoseltsev and A. A. Dimitrievsky, by helping chart the genesis and subsequent history of the liturgical forms, laid the necessary foundations for any enquiry into the theological meaning of the Liturgy as a whole, and in its component parts. In fact, Schmemann ascribes the rise of a truly theological interest in the liturgy to the recovery of a theandric sense of the mystery of the Church – her divine-human character, her life as the body of Christ.

In itself, the rise of such a liturgical theology belongs equally to Orthodoxy, Catholicism and indeed Protestantism, in its more classic variants. It had become clear, in liturgically-minded circles in the West of the inter-War years, that

> without such theological 'reflection' the liturgical revival was threatened either by an excessive submission to the 'demands of the

day', to the radical nature of certain 'missionary' and 'pastoral' movements quite prepared to drop old forms without a second thought, or, on the other hand, by a peculiar archaeologism which considers the restoration of worship in its 'primitive purity' as the panacea for all contemporary ills.[6]

And while the lion's share of liturgical-theological research went, inevitably, to Western students, such Occidentals – and here Schmemann cites more especially Dom Oliver Rousseau, monk of Chevetogne – found themselves appealing more and more to the witness of Orthodoxy in the attempt to restore those emphases and categories to some degree lost in the Church of the West. Calling the liturgical revival an 'Orthodox' movement in a non-Orthodox context, Schmemann found a twofold basis for the making of a fully Orthodox liturgical theology: the researches of the West, and the uninterruptedness of the liturgical tradition in the Orthodox Church.

On the basis of these reflections, Schmemann felt able to construct a definition of what liturgical theology is. It is a theological account both of worship and of the entire liturgical tradition of the Church. Schmemann distinguished between three levels, or stages, of enquiry which this enterprise involved. First, which concepts or categories have the potential to express the nature of the Church's liturgical experience? Secondly, how may these ideas be connected with the ampler system of concepts used by theology in its exposition of her faith? Thirdly, how may the discrete data of liturgical experience be presented as a connected whole? Such a coherent totality could only be, in the last analysis, that 'rule of prayer', indwelling the Church, which determines her 'rule of faith': *lex orandi, lex credendi.* And in this regard, Schmemann stresses, over against an atomistic appeal to liturgical proof-texts in dogmatic theology, what he calls the 'liturgical co-efficient' of each individual element, be it text, chant, gesture. By this phrase he means 'that significance which, apart from its own immediate content, each acquires as a result of its place in the general sequence or order of worship'. Only so can liturgics be of more than arbitrary or occasional use in Orthodox dogmatics.

In his opening preamble, Schmemann makes a number of subsidiary statements which fill out this definition, and at the same time enable us to grasp what is distinctive in his approach. He insists that the forms of the Byzantine Liturgy are not, whatever some Orthodox may say, 'a set of age-old and unchangeable regulations', and also that the variation between the rubrical directions of the Greek and Slavonic *typica* (liturgical rule-books) shows that *in principle* Orthodoxy does not require uniformity in worship. Later, he will go so far to say that, since these *typica* retain in their titles a reference to their geographical origins (the *Ordo* of St Sava monastery, for the Slavs; the *Ordo* of the Great Church of Constantinople, for the Greeks), they were originally

> the exposition of local rules, the description of how the Church's liturgical tradition was observed under given conditions in a given period.[7]

Nor does Schmemann's willingness to subvert attitudes to the Liturgy widespread among contemporary Orthodox stop there. He deplores the emergence of a distinction between, on the one hand, truly corporate worship, and, on the other 'private' offices, designed to meet individual needs (and notably celebrations of baptism, chrismation, marriage, funerals, and other rites for the departed).

> The purpose of worship is to constitute the Church, precisely to bring what is 'private' into the new life, to transform it into what belongs to the Church, i.e. is shared with all in Christ. In addition, its purpose is always to express the Church as the unity of that body whose head is Christ. And, finally, its purpose is that we should always 'with one mouth and one heart', serve God, since it was only such worship which God commanded the Church to offer.[8]

By the same token, Schmemann regrets the tendency to speak

of the Eucharist as simply one among the sacraments of the Church, albeit the most important. The Eucharist is, rather, the Church's 'eternal actualisation as the Body of Christ, united in Christ by the Holy Spirit'. It can only be, then, the source and goal of the Church's liturgical activity at large – despite the evident chronological sense in treating the sacraments of initiation (baptism and chrismation) prior to the Eucharist itself. Schmemann's own theology of the Holy Eucharist is found, above all, in his first book, *Tainstva kreščeniia*, 'The Sacrament (or Mystery) of the Kingdom', as expanded into his last (posthumously published) work, *Evkharistiia*. Here we find Schmemann organising a study of eucharistic theology in terms of a number of themes drawn from the progressive unfolding of the Byzantine rite, the 'shape of the Liturgy' as he calls it in a phrase taken from the great Anglican liturgiologist Dom Gregory Dix. So we have the Eucharist as, respectively, the sacrament of the assembly; of the Kingdom; of 'entrance'; of the Word; of the faithful; of offering; of unity; of 'anaphora'; of thanksgiving; of remembrance; of the Holy Spirit, and, lastly, of communion.[9]

This extremely rich and wide-ranging theological meditation on the ritual unfolding of the Byzantine Mass would constitute Schmemann's single most substantial contribution to realising his own programme for an Orthodox liturgical theology as set forth in his Introduction. There he expressed the view that liturgical theology could do worse than adopt a five-art scheme for the exposition of its subject-matter: first, by way of preamble, an account of the Church's *Ordo* – the basic structure of Liturgy at large; secondly, a study of the sacraments of initiation – baptism (to which he devoted his *Of Water and the Spirit*,)[10] and chrismation; thirdly, an exposition of the true centre of the liturgical life, the Holy Eucharist; fourthly, an explanation of the 'Liturgy of time', the daily, weekly and yearly cycles of prayer – his *Great Lent* would consider one of the most crucial of the latter:[11] and fifthly something on the 'Liturgy of the sanctification of life', a portmanteau term which covers, in Schmemann's usage, not only the sacraments of marriage, penitence and the healing of the sick, but also the non-sacramental rites concerned, in Orthodox tradition, with birth and death.

Schmemann's reformist ambitions were not by any means restricted, however, to the provision of a more theologically adequate structure for liturgical theory in the Orthodox Church. He also entered a number of caveats, expressed, often enough, quite acerbically, on the shortcomings of modern Orthodox liturgical consciousness and life. He did not hesitate to speak of a 'liturgical crisis' in the Church – not so much in the sense of particular defects in the customary manner of celebration as in that of a pervasive 'liturgism' which makes of worship an object of the love of the faithful, and almost the sole content of Church life. Though without worship there is no Church, Christ did not establish a society for the observance of worship but in a way of salvation, a new life, in which worship plays an irreplaceable part. The wider transformative aim of the divine saving plan was Schmemann's subject in a not too felicitously entitled study, *The World as Sacrament*.[12] Schmemann felt able to call worship the purpose of the Church – but only on condition that we see worship as the fullest expression, and most notable fulfilment, of her nature – of her unity and charity, her knowledge of and communion with God. In Orthodox practice, however, *tserkovnost'*, love for the Church, is in danger of degenerating into love for the church building and its rites, while, by a perverse paradox, the Liturgy itself is predominantly explained in terms of a Christological, rather than ecclesial, symbolism: the Little Entrance (when the priest comes out to read the Gospel) taken as image of Christ coming forth to preach, the Great Entrance (when the eucharistic Gifts are brought to the altar for consecration) as Christ going to his sacrifice. As Schmemann asked, rhetorically:

> Whoever sees that in this action she is not depicting the life of Christ before the congregation, but is manifesting, creating and fulfilling *herself* as the Body of Christ?[13]

Moreover, making worship an end in itself has the effect of

secularising, even 'profaning', the other activities of the Church. The parish becomes an essentially lay organisation, concerned for the provision of what worship demands (a priest, the fabric of the building, and so forth), while the hierarchy are pushed out of not only administration but even teaching, since these spheres are, unlike worship, 'unsanctified'.

Finally, and here Schmemann comes to what will be the leit-motif of his essay collection, *Church, World, Mission*, if worship ceases to be the expression of the true being of the Church, then by the same token it can no longer manifest the Church *vis-à-vis* the world, as the self-disclosure of her mission and transfiguring purpose.[14] I shall return to Schmemann's desiderata for a liturgical renewal in Orthodoxy by way of conclusion.

Schmemann and the Shape of the Liturgy

If it is characteristic of modern liturgical renewal to downplay, to the Church's grave loss, the anthropological need for continuity in religious symbolic action, it is nonetheless equally typical, and a compensating strength, that it emphasises, the theological need for an intelligible shape to the Liturgy. The primary concern of Schmemann's *Introduction to Liturgical Theology* is with the nature of the *Ordo*, the basic structure which underlies, and alone makes sense of, the multifarious rites, texts, gestures. For Schmemann, the vagaries of current liturgical practice already raise the question of the *Ordo*, for several features common to the *typica* (and hence, it would seem, proper to the *Ordo*) are ignored by contemporary Orthodox: for instance, the provision for the celebration of the Eucharist in the evening on certain days, and the prohibition on any prayer of absolution outside the sacrament of Repentance. Indeed, Schmemann identifies two widespread ways of evading the *Ordo*'s demands. One, which he describes as 'legalistic' and 'formalist', consists in accepting, and even vehemently insisting upon, the very letter of the *Ordo* yet getting round it in practice by a variety of devices, such as reducing the *kathisma*, the appointed psalms, to a few verses.

The other strategy, which Schmemann calls 'essentially, indifference to the *Ordo* or structure of worship as such', involves treating it as a kind of back-room resource: only the more popular items are selected and then celebrated with maximum impressiveness.

Yet the whole tradition of the Church witnesses to the rôle of the *Ordo* as absolutely central: the notions of order and structure, of rite, are contained in that of her worship itself. As, in Paul's phrase, a 'reasonable service', *logikê latreia*, that worship can neither be a dead letter to be followed blindly, nor ancient custom revivified only insofar as it corresponds to modern sensibilities. No: the meaning of the Church's life must be sought in the *Ordo*, insofar as it defines the general pattern of her worship. The search for the *Ordo* is

> the search for or identification of that element of the *typicon* which is presupposed by its whole content, rather than contained by it; in short, its general 'philosophy'.[15]

For Schmemann one does not have to search far to become aware that the *Ordo*'s two principal elements are the Eucharist and the 'Liturgy of time' – the daily, weekly, and yearly cycles (even though the first of these cycles is largely disused in modern churches). The sacramental Eucharist and the 'non-sacramental' Liturgy of time do not just co-exist here: rather does their connexion constitute the *Ordo* in its most fundamental form. On the one hand, the time of the Eucharist's celebration appears irrelevant, since in the sacrificial Supper is manifested a past event (the Passover of the Lord) in all its supra-temporal reality and effectiveness. On the other hand, all celebrations of the Eucharist are in fact placed in some relation to time: most obviously within the weekly cycle, where Sunday is the day of the Eucharist *par excellence*. The modern liturgical movement errs, in Schmemann's opinion, whenever it tries either so to emphasise the Eucharist that all else becomes a matter of indifference, or (as with the German Benedictine Odo Casel's *Mysterientheologie*)[16] to make all worship an expression of the Mystery of Christ, thus placing other rites and prayers on the Eucharist's own exalted level. But this only increases the desirability of an investigation of the origin and the development of the *Ordo*.

As to the *origins* of Christian worship, Schmemann cannot avoid taking up a position *vis-à-vis* the scholarly debate on that subject which had occupied Western scholars for some decades. An influential theory (supported by, among others the distinguished French students of Christian antiquity Louis Duchesne and Pierre Batiffol) maintains that, in the age before the Council of Nicaea, the Eucharist was the Church's sole act of public worship, other prayers, connected with the hours of the day (and night) being no more than private devotions. The fourth century saw, by contrast, a liturgical revolution whereby, through the influence of the growing monastic movement, such private prayers became part and parcel of the official cult. With the accumulation of evidence, this theory became harder to sustain, but was revived on a different basis by Gregory Dix. For Dix, the ante-Nicene community could not have regarded any other act than the Eucharist as her proper worship, since only the Eucharist corresponded to that exclusively eschatological understanding of her life which was the hallmark of the primitive Church. As Schmemann sums up Dix's position:

> There could be no liturgy rooted in time, having reference to the times and hours of human life, because the Church herself regarded herself as a departure out of time, as the renunciation of that world which lives wholly in time and is subordinated to it and measured by it.[17]

Against this, countervailing witnesses, also from England, can be brought to the stand. Such men as P. Freeman and C. W. Dugmore considered that the structure of Christian worship originates, rather, in the worship of Judaism, and notably in that of the synagogue services, which were nothing if not a sanctification of time.

Schmemann himself proposes to resolve the question by stepping back, and taking a broader look at the relation between Judaism and primitive Christianity at large. The worship of the early Christians was at once participation in the old, and the presence of the cult of the new, and in this, worship simply reflects the wider position of the 'New Israel' *vis-à-vis* the synagogue:

> Just as the Scriptures of the Old Testament found their 'key' in the apostolic preaching of the Word, in the kerygma of the messianic community, so the 'old' cult needed to be fulfilled in the new, and only in and through it did it receive its significance . . .[18]

And yet, since everything to which the ancient cult testified – the revelation of the Old Testament concerning God, creation, man, sin, salvation – is presupposed by the New, the New has meaning only on the condition that the Old is preserved. The 'liturgical dualism' of Jewish Christianity reproduces in the medium of worship the inter-relation of Old and New Covenants which defines the very Gospel itself. Nor did Gentile Christianity fail to perceive the importance of this connexion: when Israel after the flesh locked the doors of the synagogues against the Christians, the synagogue worship survived in the Eucharistic synaxis (the Liturgy of the Word).

But how then was the eschatology of the early Church (in, above all, the Eucharist) combined with the idea of the sanctification of time drawn from Hebrew worship? Schmemann points out that 'time' for the Old Testament is hardly non-eschatological in significance. Morning, evening, day, the sabbath, the feasts: all these reminded the Israelite of the coming great 'Day of the Lord'.

> This is the liturgy of time; but not natural or cyclical time, not that time which is, so to speak, 'immanent' in the world, determining and containing it within its own self-sufficient, cyclical rhythm. It is time that is eschatologically transparent, time within which and over which the living God of Abraham, Isaac and Jacob is constantly

acting, and which discovers its real meaning in the Kingdom of
Yahweh...'[9]

Christianity did not differ from Judaism in its theology of time,
but in its conception of the events whereby this time is spiritually
measured: for now time acquires a special intensity as the time of
the Church, when the salvation given by the Messiah is accomplished. The Eucharist manifests the Church as the new *aiôn*, for
it is the presence of the Lord who was raised and who raises in
his turn, and as such it is a participation in the final Kingdom. As
the epiphany in this age of the Age to Come, the Eucharist
cannot abolish the Liturgy of time: for, should that come to pass,
time would really be emptied of significance, and become merely
a series of intervals between Eucharistic celebrations. The new
cult required for its real fulfilment inclusion in the rhythm of
time. It needed combination with the Liturgy of time in order to
be applied to time, as the sacrament which consecrates Christians
to their mission of showing forth in the world the *parousia* of the
Lord. And *this* is what we see unfolding in pre-Nicene liturgical
practice. Contrary to what a wholly world-renouncing cult
would indicate, the Eucharist is celebrated on a fixed day, and
that day is located in reference to the Jewish sabbath: Sunday, the
prima sabbati, at once the first day and the eighth; the day of the
beginning of creation, for Christ restores creation after sin, and
the day of victory over the forces of evil, the beginning of the
new Age. And this 'theology of Sunday', indebted to the French
patristic scholar Jean Daniélou, gives Schmemann the confidence
to assert that the daily hours of prayer attested by such pre-
Nicene writers as Origen, Tertullian, Hippolytus were not
merely private devotions (these writers, indeed, agree on the
desirability of common assembly as the setting for prayer) but
acts of the Church as such. The universal acceptance of Evening
Prayer and Morning Prayer as liturgical services, presupposing
an assembly of the Church in its various orders, as found in all
the traditions of the Great Church, confirms that they belonged,
before the monastic movement, to the *lex orandi*. Nor, after the

weekly and daily cycles, was the *yearly* cycle of the sanctification of time absent from early Christianity. The festivals of Passover (Easter) and Pentecost were preserved not from inertia, but as the biblical and liturgical promises of Christian faith in the inauguration of a new time within the old. It is easy to see how Schmemann's account of liturgical origins here fits in beautifully with his presentation of the aim of the Liturgy: the manifestation of the Church's nature for the salvation of the world.

Schmemann on the Growth of Orthodox Worship

How, then, did this primitive *Ordo* develop? Very schematically, Schmemann speaks in terms of (a) four processes – the development of Church ceremonial, and its architectural setting; the appearance of new festal cycles and other complications to the Liturgy's temporal structure; the growth of hymnody; and the evolution of the sanctoral cycle, the veneration of the saints and their relics, and he sees these processes as working themselves out through (b) three main periods – the luxuriant flowering of the fourth and fifth centuries; the gradual stabilisation of forms in the sixth to eighth centuries; and the final completion of the Byzantine 'type' of worship, which he traces to the ninth century. Schmemann stresses the continuity of the post-Constantinian developments with the pre-Constantinian age. Even though the peace of the Church provided, essentially, freedom of cult, no heterogeneous change in the nature of Christian worship was thus effected. Churches pre-existed Constantine, and ceremonial development is already clear from the 'Apostolic Constitutions'. The Theophany cycle (Christmas and Epiphany) has roots in the pre-Constantinian period. The new cycles and services did not destroy the prior daily and weekly cycles. And the cult of the saints is directly related to the celebration of their *natalia* or heavenly birthdays, already practised in the second century.

For Schmemann, the main positive change which overcame

the liturgy with Constantine was the Church's new capacity to manifest her affirmatory attitude towards the world in its cosmic sweep: previously inhibited by awareness of the pagan – and thus in considerable part demonic – character of her environment. At the same time, the new missionary possibilities opened up by the Edict of Milan led to a change in liturgical piety – Schmemann's phrase for the particular *psychological* way in which the cult was accepted, 'its experience within the religious mind, its refraction within the consciousness of the believer'. Whereas in the pre-Nicene period, that 'co-efficient of refraction', as Schmemann, (with his penchant for mathematical analogies) calls liturgical piety, was eschatological and ecclesiological – an awareness of the newness of the Church as the fullness of what was promised to Israel, now it changes its inflection, becoming more 'mysteriological' in character. The meeting of Church and world took place 'on the ground of cult', which thus became a vital instrument in the 'churching' of the masses. Schmemann stresses, however, that, although Christianity was radically distinguished from the mystery religions of antiquity by the fact that it was a saving *faith*, and faith moreover in the significance of genuine historical *fact*, nonetheless this new liturgical piety did not necessarily entail a distorting metamorphosis of what had gone before – for the cult had always enjoyed a place of unparalleled importance as the revelation of the eschatological fullness of the Kingdom, an anticipation of the 'Day of the Lord'.

Various consequences followed. The church-building, earlier the *domus ecclesiae*, the house which made possible the eucharistic assembly, now became a church-sanctuary where the Lord's Table was united with the tomb of a saint (later, the placing of relics in the altar) – thus conjoining, as André Grabar showed in his *Martyrium*,[20] the *hêroôn*, the temple-memorial of a hero at the place of his burial or theophany, with the *basilica*, the place for public assembly and State cultus. Alongside this goes the growth of interest in sacred topography, in Palestine, the East at large, and Rome. And in Constantine's own city, Constantinople, the building of a church in the centre of a city indicated its setting within the old idea of the temple as the mystical core of the city, sanctifying its life and rendering it *sub auspiciis deorum*.[21]

The 'inner solemnity' of the simple gestures of early cult, as recorded in, say, Justin Martyr are now externalised, chiefly through borrowing ceremonial features from the Imperial court ritual of the Hellenistic monarchs, more 'admissible' for the Church as a source than were the pagan liturgies *comme tel*. Again, the celebration of particular events in the history of salvation, which Dix ascribed to the post-Constantinian Church's 'reconciliation with time', its introduction of sacred history into the rhythms of natural life, and Dom Bernard Botte to the influence of the Trinitarian and Christological controversies of the age, Schmemann attributes rather to this same shift in liturgical piety. Whereas the early Christian cult was synthetic, in that remembrance was directed to the saving character of the whole work of Christ (easily seen as focused in the special celebration of Easter), later piety was concerned to dramatise discrete events within that continuum, to re-live them psychologically and religiously. He finds it no coincidence that it was Jerusalem, and the Holy Land in general, which became perhaps the first centre of this 'representational cult'.

Yet we shall not be surprised to find that Schmemann's history includes its meed of criticism, sometimes acerbic, of later developments.

In the Byzantine epoch the emphasis was gradually transferred from the assembly of the Church to the exclusive and actually self-sufficient significance of the clergy as celebrants of the mystery. The Sacrament was celebrated on behalf of the people, for their sanctification – but the Sacrament ceased to be experienced as the very actualisation of the people as the Church.[22]

And if the clearest sign of that change was the transferring of the title 'holy doors' from those of the church to the iconostasis, and the accompanying prohibition on the laity entering therein, earlier ritual changes had anticipated this, while the displacement of the ecclesiological understanding of the liturgical action by a Christological one, and the shift from a corporate to an individual understanding of Eucharistic reception, sealed this process. In these and similiar criticisms Schmemann is much influenced by the comments of his older colleague, Nikolai Afanas'ev.

From these perhaps unduly negative remarks Schmemann passes to the brighter subject of monasticism. For Schmemann, monasticism cannot itself be understood as a liturgical movement. Early monasticism, that is, possessed no special liturgical ideology:

> The cult of the Church remained the one lawful cult of monasticism, and the monastic cult was never suspect in the eyes of the Church.[23]

Indeed, to begin with, monasticism did not even regard itself as a special 'part' of the Church: in its first, eremitical, moment the question hardly arose, and in its second, coenobitical period, monastic groups were more likely to regard themselves as a renewal of the apostolic community than as a special institute. What was new in monasticism was, rather, its emphasis on prayer as a life in its own right and, within this, on the chanting of the Psalms. Though devotional rules and an *ordo* of prayer appeared early in monasticism, they developed not as an order of worship but within a pedagogical system intended to guide the monk towards spiritual freedom. Monasticism, as, following Louis Bouyer's study of Athanasian Egypt, Schmemann presents things, was essentially a reaction against the (ethical and psychological) 'secularisation' of the Church. In the post-Constantinian epoch:

> The Church remained more than ever in the centre of the world, but now as its protection and sanction, as its judge and law, as the source of its sanctification and salvation, and not as the revelation of the Kingdom 'coming in power' and bestowing in this world (whose form is passing away) communion in the 'age to come' and the 'Day of the Lord'.[24]

According to Schmemann – and here surely he exaggerates – in the monastic *ordo*, times and hours for prayer have no significance except inasmuch as they enable the whole of life to be filled by prayer. When part of this devotional rule was inserted into the liturgical *ordo*, as with Compline, it remained essentially 'non-liturgical': thus Compline (in the Byzantine East) can be sung 'in the cell', it does not presuppose a ministerially ordered assembly, nor does it have a definite theme, as do Vespers and Matins. The monastic attitude whereby the Hours were seen primarily as ascetical actions, underlies, according to Schmemann, the indifference with which modern Orthodox can transfer Vespers to the morning or Matins the evening; it also, in his view, modified Eucharistic attitudes, encouraging the notion that the Eucharistic rite was an opportunity to receive 'spiritual succour', an instrument of piety.

And so the characteristically Byzantine 'synthesis' was prepared. In Byzantium, the *oikoumenê* was blended with the monastic affirmation of salvation as ascetic withdrawal: monks became publicly accredited Christian maximalists, and as a result their *ordo* eventually provided the general form of the Byzantine *typicon* itself. And, as Greek succeeded Coptic as the primary cultural carrier of the ascetic movement, a mystical understanding of monasticism became dominant, and linked up with the mysteriological piety characteristic of the post-Constantinian church. The Byzantine synthesis was the fruit of this hybridisation. Parish and monastic worship fused – by the ninth century – so that, leaving aside any elements added to the *typicon* after that date we are left with three basic strata: the Judaeo-Christian foundations of the cult; the new liturgical piety of the post-Nicene parish church; and monasticism.

Schmemann's brilliant reconstruction of the origin and development of the *Ordo* thus enables him to trace virtually every element in Byzantine worship to its source. To the *first* stratum, the Judaeo-Christian level, belong the most primitive elements of Vespers and Matins: the chanting of psalms and hymns, which goes back to the time of the synagogue. The 'secret' prayers, as now read by the celebrant during the recitation of the Psalter can also be related to the *tephilla*, the intercessory prayers of synagogue worship. Paul speaks of psalms, hymns and spiritual songs, and, following such Western liturgical *periti* as Anton Baumstark and Egon Welleçz, Schmemann identifies the 'hymns' with a variety of Old Testament canticles and the *Nunc Dimittis*, and the 'songs' with such melismatic chants as the alleluia. Schmemann stresses the fully liturgical character of these services (in the *Didascalia* and the *Apostolic Constitutions* celebrated by people and officiant), and is happy with Dugmore's proposal that, given their strong resemblance to the fore-Mass, they may have formed the first part of the Eucharist on the days of its celebration, and on other days constituted offices of their own.

Schmemann also ascribes to the Jewish-Christian stratum the Eastern celebration of Mass on Saturdays, the observance of Wednesdays and Fridays as fast-days (found at Qumran, and given a new meaning by reference to Christ's betrayal and death); the annual cycle of Easter and Pentecost, and possibly also that of the Epiphany (since otherwise Jewish Christianity would have preserved two eschatological feasts, Passover and Pentecost, but not the third, Tabernacles).

In the *second* stratum Schmemann locates the phenomenon of chanting as a major factor in worship and also that of dramatic ritual. (Chanting here stands in contrast to reading, and concerns *troparia*, *kontakia*, versicles and so forth.) Such hymnography is indebted to both Hellenistic and Syriac models. As Schmemann puts it:

> The position of chanting in Byzantine worship was determined by two 'co-ordinates'. Its place in the structure of worship, what we have been calling its liturgical function, may be traced to the ceremonial, 'festal' concept of cult, characteristic of Hellenic liturgical piety, while its content and poetic form may be traced back to the early Christian, biblical and 'Semitic' tradition.[25]

By 'dramatic ritual' Schmemann has in mind, in the first place, the system of entrances and exits, and other processions typical of the Byzantine liturgy. Other features of the characteristically post-Constantinian 'parish' contribution would be: first, the multiplication of festivals, partly the result of the need to replace pagan feast-days and partly thanks to stress on specific disputed doctrines (and on this Schmemann speaks sharply, considering that in Byzantine Orthodoxy the liturgical year dissolved into an atomised series of feast-days); and, secondly, the extraordinary growth in the veneration of the saints, to the point where the *Menaion*, the monthly sanctoral, inundated the *Oktoichos*, the book of the weekly cycle.

So far as the *third* monastic contribution is concerned, Schmemann stresses the reading of psalms in sequence, as also the parallel phenomenon of the *lectio continua* of Scripture. Also relevant here are: the 'principle of prolongation', that is, the repetition of certain brief prayers; the use of bowing as an expression of contrition and receptivity; the ascetic concept of fasting, and a related view of Holy Communion, and the consequent gauging of frequency and infrequency of reception in terms of the individual's spiritual state; the decision of his spiritual director; the discipline of the monastery, and so forth.

In brief, the confluence of the Christian city and the monastic desert, in creating in Byzantium a Christianity at once mysteric and ascetic, determined the final form which the Orthodox liturgy would take. Following the lead of the pre-Revolutionary Russian liturgical historian M. Skaballanovič, Schmemann plumps for Jerusalem as the site where the final merger took place.

A main centre of historical-mysteriological worship (compare the Catechetical Instructions of St Cyril) it was also a home of monks, both in the city and in the Palestinian desert beyond, where, according to Cassian, the monastic hours were similar to those of the secular churches. Early on, however, the synthesis was accepted at Constantinople, where the practice of the Studite monastery gave it a new twist. Beginning with the 'Triumph of Orthodoxy' at the close of the Iconoclast crisis, the two inter-related *typica* are crystallised, and by the twelfth century the *Ordo* is barely distinguishable from that used by the Byzantine rite Church today.

Schmemann's Agenda for Liturgical Renewal

Where contemporary Orthodoxy is concerned, Schmemann stresses that this 'synthesis' should be determining for the future chiefly in terms of the Church's original *lex orandi* – rather than the liturgical psychology at once mystery-oriented and ascetic, with which later generations suffused subjectively the *Ordo*'s objectivity. What should this mean? In other words, what are the points which, in Schmemann's view, an authentic Liturgical Movement in the modern period, should stress?

First, the rhythm of fast and Eucharist, essential to a sound eschatology. For Schmemann, the Eucharist should not be celebrated every day, as in the West it is not on Holy Saturday, and only in truncated form on Good Friday. Many days should be fast days, as they were in the West until the Codex of popes Pius X and Benedict XV, and, to a lesser extent until the Second Vatican Council.

Next, the daily cycle should be allowed its proper weight as what Schmemann terms

> a kind of constant contemplation of the world and the time within which the Church dwells, and of those ways of evaluating the world and its time which were manifested by the Parousia of the Lord.[26]

Thirdly, a liturgical reform must manifest the unity of the liturgical year in the celebration of Easter. Fourthly, worship must come across as the corporate act, and corporate fulfilment, of the Church. Fifthly, it must be seen as the disclosure of the deepest significance of the conciliar confession of dogmatic faith. In worship, doctrine must come to life.

A Concluding Question

To what extent have these demands been fulfilled by the liturgical movement in the Western Church? To what extent can that movement act as a model for the liturgical self-reform of Orthodoxy? And to what extent, by contrast, can the twentieth century liturgical reform, in its actual realisation be regarded as a warning lesson about the dangers which lie in the path of reconstructing on theoretical principles an organic tradition of worship? The answers that can be given to these questions will no doubt create a dividing-line *among* Orthodox and Catholics as much as *between* them. But their pertinence is undeniable.

X
Panagiotis Nellas and Anthropology

Panagiotis Nellas was born in 1936 and studied theology at the University of Athens, though later he did post-graduate work in France and, briefly, in Rome. A lay theologian, unmarried, he taught not in a university faculty but in an Athenian high school. This was not from any lack of ability for higher things, for, as Bishop Kallistos Ware commented on the early death of Nellas, at the age of fifty:

> It is a tragic loss to Greek theology, for, along with Christos Yannaras, his contemporary and friend from student years, Panagiotis Nellas was perhaps the most gifted and original religious thinker of the 'middle' generation at work in Greece today, and at the time of his sudden death he was at the height of his creative activity.[1]

We may assume that his decision to teach adolescents had an apostolic inspiration; Nellas was also connected with the revival of monastic life on Mount Athos, and frequently stayed at the monastery of Stavronikita there. The lion's share of one of his main works, *Zôon theoumenon* – 'The Deified Animal', my principal subject in this chapter – was written in that setting.

Most of Nellas's work was devoted to the fourteenth century Byzantine theologian Nikolas Kabasilas, recently canonised by the Church of Greece. His prolegomena to the study of Kabasilas appeared in 1969,[2] and this was followed in 1975 by a more detailed monograph.[3]

What Nellas called Kabasilas's 'Christocentric anthropology' is a major part of what will be my concern in expounding Nellas's own theology in this chapter.

Much of his theological activity involved eliciting the contributions of others in collaborative ways. In 1968 Nellas launched a series, *Epi tas Pêgas*, 'To the Sources', which was modelled on the French series *Sources Chrétiennes*, but on a much smaller scale. He himself contributed to the first volume, a set of homilies on the Mother of God by Kabasilas. Each volume contains an original Greek text, with a modern Greek translation and introduction and notes. Bishop Kallistos Ware remarks:

> His aim in this, as in almost all his theological work, was to relate patristic thought to the modern world, to render the Fathers intelligible and relevant to reflective Christians of our own day who are not specialists in theology, to make the Father speak as our contemporaries.[4]

In the service of this project, Nellas founded in 1982 the review *Synaxi*, which brought together a wide variety of contributors dealing with not only theology and Church affairs, but also art and literature, politics and culture. At his death in 1986 he left behind two unpublished manuscripts, one on, once again, Kabasilas, and the other on Maximus the Confessor.

The Animal Whom God Would Deify

In the preface to *Zôon theoumenon*, Nellas explains that the purpose of this, his most systematic theological work, despite his dislike of the term 'system', is the revival of patristic anthropology for his own contemporaries. The phrase 'The Deified Animal' aptly sums up, he feels, the common patristic approach to the doctrine of man, even though he admits that there is not one single patristic anthropology but many. Still, something can be said about what is common in the Fathers' approach. That common doctrine is the theme of his book. Its initial statement, in the preface, bears the citation:

Participating as the Fathers did in the common search of mankind for the true nature and meaning of existent things, they accepted that man is a 'rational animal' or a 'political animal', and they would not have doubted that man is 'what he eats' or 'what he produces' or 'what he feels'; but they added that his true greatness is to be found not in these things but in the fact that he is 'called to be a god'. They stressed that man realises his true existence in the measure in which he is raised up towards God and is united with him ...[5]

And Nellas goes on

At the same time, they have described in depth and in detail what man's nature is like when it maintains its bond with God and what happens when it breaks this bond, how its various psychosomatic functions work in either case, and what perception of its existence it has when united with God or separated from him.[6]

'The Deified Animal' opens, rightly enough, by pointing out that the basic foundation of Christian anthropology lies in the doctrine of man as in the image of God. Although the image theme had philosophical antecedents, it was decisively shaped by the biblical revelation, first in Genesis and the Wisdom tradition but then in the New Testament where its Christological content gives to anthropology new dimensions. In line with his opposition to an extremely confident conceptual theology, Nellas prefaces his account of patristic anthropology by Gregory of Nyssa's statement that human nature is 'not open to contemplation'. Since God is incomprehensible, his image in man must be also.[7] This for Nellas is why we cannot find in the Fathers a definitive formulation of what it is about human nature that makes it the divine image. The vital point is not so much the particular patristic applications of the term 'image' as the simple fact that the Fathers took the expression 'in the image' as the crucial tool in their anthropological enquiries.

Basically, according to Nellas, the patristic anthropology of man as made in the image of God derives from the teaching of St Paul for whom, as the hymn in the opening chapter of the Letter to the Colossians makes clear, the image of God *par excellence* is

Christ, the first-born of all creation and head of the body, the Church.[8] The same term 'image', *eikôn*, also appears in Paul's teaching elsewhere, in First Corinthians and the Letter to the Ephesians, where it is used to make the point that man, in order to be made whole, must put on the image of Christ, the heavenly man, and thus attain to the measure of the stature of the fullness of Christ, that we may no longer be children.[9] Thus for Paul man's growth to full stature coincides with his, what Nellas terms, his 'christification'.

More specifically, what the Fathers did was to unite the Pauline theme of Christ as the image of God with the Genesis motif of man as *in* the image of God. And so in Irenaeus, Clement, Origen, Athanasius, Gregory of Nyssa, Christ is the image of God, man the image of Christ: man is the image of the image. The importance of this for Nellas is that it helps us to define the three most important points in anthropology: first, the *structure* of man; secondly, the *destiny* of man; thirdly, the *origin* of man.

First, the Christological *structure* of man. Although the dogmatic manuals in use in the Greek Church, like that of Trembelas, attempt to localise man's being in the image in his rationality, it is, for Nellas, more correct to say that

man is rational because he was created in the image of Christ, who is the hypostatic Logos of the Father.[10]

Such a claim could find sufficient support in Athanasius, and notably in his *De incarnatione*, chapter 3. Similarly, Nellas argues that man is creative because he is the image of the Logos through whom all things were made, resting this time on a text from Clement of Alexandria's *Pedagogus* (II. 10). Again, man is sovereign over the other species because Christ is the almighty Lord and King and man is made to Christ's image – here Nellas appeals to a text from Gregory of Nyssa's *On the Creation of Man* which does not, however, itself explicitly include a Christological reference, maintaining rather that our nature is an image of the

Nature which rules over all things. The same Cappadocian Father provides Nellas with his patristic authority for maintaining that man is free because he is the image of him who is absolute self-determination, a reference to the *De virginitate*, while Theodore of Mopsuestia, more rarely cited by the Orthodox because of the strictures on his theology levelled by the Second Council of Constantinople of 552, provides the basis for Nellas's claim that man is responsible for the creation since his archetype, Christ, is the recapitulator and Saviour of all men. So the structure of the human being, patterned as it is on that of the Logos, Christ, involves rationality, creativity, sovereignty, freedom and cosmic responsibleness.

Before leaving this topic of the structure of man, Nellas makes two final claims. First, man's body-soul unity, which links together matter and spirit, reflects the unity of divinity and humanity in the Word Incarnate, or, as Nellas puts it, the 'unconfused union of uncreated divinity and created contingency'.[11] Actually, such a comparison is, historically speaking, more Monophysite than Chalcedonian, which is perhaps why Nellas goes on to qualify it, with reference to an anonymous Byzantine treatise on the divine image in man, printed in Migne's *Patrologia Graeca* volume 89. According to this unknown author, just as Christ, the Word Incarnate, acts theandrically, in both divine and human natures, so man works psychosomatically, through both soul and body. Secondly, and lastly where Nellas's remarks on the structure of man are concerned, there is the fact that man is simultaneously person and nature, or, better, a person who reveals nature and renders nature concrete: thus echoing the being of the Son of God who constitutes a distinct personal hypostasis of the one indivisible substance common to Father, Son and Holy Spirit.

So far, however, or so Nellas claims, his account has remained at the level of a static or anatomical analysis. Nothing he has said expresses explicitly, at any rate, the dynamic impetus found within man's being, his being turned towards a *destiny*. And this is the point which he now addresses. As he writes:

In fact, man, having been created 'in the image' of the infinite God, is called by his own nature – and this is precisely the sense of 'in the image' from this point of view – to transcend the limited boundaries of creation and to become infinite.[12]

One wonders here whether Nellas is really reflecting the positions of Scripture and the Fathers or whether, on the contrary, a certain 'titanism' is not distorting here his view of anthropology – of the kind associated in the modern epoch with the *Uebermensch* of Nietzsche, himself not without a certain influence, as we have already noted, on Florovsky's theology. Be this as it may, Nellas goes on to speak of how, called thus to transcend his own limits, man's destiny is to thrust forward towards the totality of knowledge, to supremacy over the cosmos, and to a complete realisation of justice and peace, which reflects at once the moral communion of the Holy Trinity and that mode of life of man's archetype, the Logos, in whose image he has been formed and in which image alone he can find his peace and rest. But beyond all of these vocations – noetic, cosmic and socio-political, the supreme transcendence to which man is destined is that of God himself, the uncreated Creator for whom, for the sharing of whose life, he was made.

After these disquisitions on the structure and destiny of man, Nellas comes to deal with his *origin*. One might have thought that, logically, this should precede the other two, but in Nellas's view the question of man's distinctive ontological stature is only decisively raised by the thesis, put forward in an account of his structure and destiny, of man's divine orientation and goal. As he puts it:

> As the truth of the material creation and its potentialities are revealed and realized in man, so too the truth of created man and his potentialities are revealed and realized in the uncreated God. With this it becomes evident that the reason why man remains and will remain a mystery to science is the fact that what lies at his core, by reason of his very structure, is a theological being which falls outside the scope of science.[13]

For man to in some way resemble God and to incline towards God he must have in his origin some element of the divine. What is this element? For the developed Byzantine tradition, as interpreted by Nellas, while the gulf between created nature and the uncreated nature is absolute and infinite, the equally infinite goodness of God has bridged it. The initial foundation of that bridging process is the divine energies, distinct, on the Palamite doctrine, from the divine *ousia*. The energies of God, supporting as these do the created order and guiding it to its perfection, acquire in man a specific created vehicle, and a specific direction. That vehicle is human freedom, and that direction the union of man with the divine Logos. This is for Nellas the deepest meaning of the phrase 'in the image'. The late eighteenth century Athonite monk, St Nikodimos of the Holy Mountain, basing himself on Palamas, and, behind Palamas, on John Damascene, taught, Nellas reports, that in God there exists three modes of union and communion: according to substance; according to hypostasis; and according to energy. Only the Trinitarian persons are united according to *substance*. The *hypostatic* union was effected by the Logos when he assumed flesh. But union according to *energy* was bestowed on man with his creation in the divine image. This energetic union, brought about in Adam, prepared for the hypostatic union which, by comparison with the energetic union, alone is complete and perfect, immutable, indestructible, since in Christ the divine and the human natures possess the same person. And yet despite the Fall the aim conveyed by the original energetic union was not abolished, since God does not repent of his own counsels. It continued to be the essential purpose of the training of the Jewish people, and the content and goal of all sacred history. Nellas concludes, therefore:

It thus becomes clear that the essence of man is not found in the matter from which he was created but in the archetype on the basis of which he was formed and towards which he tends. It is precisely for this reason that, in the patristic treatment of the theme of the origin of man, the theory of evolution does not create a problem – just as for the believer the form of the wood from which an icon has been made does not create a problem. Science may well have an obligation to study the 'matter' from which man was formed, but every serious scientist knows that it is impossible for him to undertake a thorough investigation, using the objective scientific method, of the 'archetype' on the basis of which man was formed. As the truth of an icon lies in the person it represents, so the truth of man lies in his archetype. And this is precisely because the archetype is that which organises, seals and gives shape to matter, and which simultaneously attracts it towards itself. The archetype constitutes the ontological content of the phrase 'in the image'.[14]

Man's ontology is then fundamentally 'iconic', but here Nellas hastens to pick up again the threads of his earlier patristic interpretation by affirming that the archetype of man is not simply the Logos, but the Logos incarnate.

It is *Jesus Christ* whom man's iconic ontology reflects.[15] The fact that when Adam was made Christ as the *incarnate* Word did not exist is, for Nellas, neither here nor there. In God's supra-temporal reality, Christ was always and already the 'first-born of all creation'. The truth that Adam was, then, created in the image of Christ, yields another truth of specially marked significance. Created in Christ's image, Adam's vocation was, evidently, so to grow in purity and the love of God that God would come to dwell with him, that the Word would enter into hypostatic union with humanity and thus appear in history as the Christ. And taking his stand on texts of Maximus the Confessor, Palamas and Kabasilas, Nellas concludes that

> the fact that God formed man [in the image] means, in the last analysis, that he formed him in this way so that he might tend of his own nature, by the very fact that he is man, towards the Image.[16]

From this, Nellas makes some other important inferences.

First, the incarnation of the Word of God was not just a consequence of the Devil's victory over man, for the union of the divine and human natures fulfilled the everlasting counsel of

God. This appears to be indistinguishable from the celebrated thesis put forward in the Latin West by Rupert of Deutz and then, more fully, by Duns Scotus. Nellas, however, claims that the patristic teaching along these lines found in, say Maximus the Confessor, is not 'internally related' to Scotus's question, and maintains that the position of Scotus remains but a possible theological opinion in the Orthodox East. The difference is that, so as to preserve the gratuitousness of the Incarnation, Nellas wants to avoid all notion that God's glory required the sending of the Son, or that the Son's mission was necessary if the creation were to achieve its own full development precisely as creation.

Secondly, since man before the Fall was man before Christ he was at that time but an imperfect and incomplete child, still in need of salvation. As Nellas accepts, this notion of Adam as child, though the teaching of Irenaeus, is somewhat isolated, perhaps, in the patristic corpus as a whole.

But he goes on from there to state a point which has wider patristic support. In his own words:

> Human nature could not have been completed simply by its tendency; it had to attain union with the Archetype. Since Christ is 'the head of the Body, the Church', a fact which means in patristic thought that Christ is the head of true humanity, as long as human nature had not yet received the hypostatis of the Logos it was in some way without real hypostasis – it lacked real 'subsistence'. It was like an unmarried woman – unfruitful and as Paul says 'without a head'. The realisation of man as a truly completed, 'saved' being took place with the birth of Christ. Real men 'were born when Christ came into this life and was born'. For this reason Basil the Great calls the day of Christ's birth truly and not metaphorically the birthday of mankind.[17]

Thirdly, then, the Incarnation, and the work of the Word Incarnate, are not exhausted by redemption from sin. Christ accomplishes man's salvation not only in a negative way, freeing him from the consequences of sin, but also in a positive way by bringing to completion his iconic being. Salvation is, accordingly, wider than redemption; it is deification.

Fourthly, the anthropological meaning of such deification is in fact Christification. When Paul urges the faithful to attain to mature manhood, in the measure of the stature of the fullness of Christ, and to acquire Christ's mind and Christ's heart, he is not simply speaking piously or sentimentally, nor he is thinking only of ethical improvement.

Fifthly, the struggle of the Fathers with the heresies of the ancient Church had as its aim, in Nellas's view, the preservation of the ultimate goal and real meaning of life in Christ. The struggle for orthodoxy was implicitly anthropological. For example, Arianism, by teaching that Christ is a creature, inevitably limited life in Christ to the created order. Nestorianism, by teaching that the human and divine natures are contiguous but not really united ended by maintaining that man can approach the infinite but not penetrate it. Monophysitism by regarding man's salvation as his absorption into God found itself preaching man's effective annihilation – and so on.

To these entirely valid points, Nellas appends some rather more controversial remarks which have to do with the criticisms of Western-type theology common to the more original Greek theologians, as of the spread of that theology through, above all, the work of the Athens school. Nellas questions whether the theses he has just set forth are anything like typical of later Western Christianity, that is, of the Latin Church from the twelfth century onwards. There came to be in the mediaeval West, he holds, and later, in nineteenth century Greece, a different theological and anthropological outlook from the one he has just described, one with soteriological and ecclesiological connotations markedly at variance with those of Orthodoxy proper. More positively, however, he notes that the theme of deification has re-surfaced even where it was in abeyance. But he insists that it must not remain at the level of spiritual theology, merely, but become the foundational category of all theological anthropology. To be true man, man must live theocentrically, and when he does so he realises himself by reaching out into infinity; he attains his true fulfilment by extending into eternity.

These claims provide the essential skeleton of Nellas's own theological anthropology which, in the rest of *Deification in Christ* he clothes in the flesh and blood of greater concreteness by deploying a large range of texts, biblical, patristic, Byzantine and liturgical – as befits, after all, a theologian of *ressourcement*. I hope, however, that enough has been said here to trace for the reader the main lines of his thought, and to exhibit its attractive character – simultaneously humane, theocentric and, above all, Christological as it is. Nellas's programme of re-thinking anthropology in Christological, indeed, Christo*centric*, terms, is markedly reminiscent, in the modern Catholic context, of the work of Hans Urs von Balthasar, while his attempt to relate by a kind of extended pastoral theology all dimensions of human life to this centre – such phenomena as, for example, marriage, politics, culture and art – renders his project not unlike that of the Roman pope contemporary with the publication of *Zôon theoumenon*, John Paul II.

XI
Christos Yannaras and Theological Ethics

Christos Yannaras was born in Athens in 1935 and studied both in Greece, at the theological faculty of Thessalonica University, and abroad, at Bonn and at the Sorbonne. Author of some twenty books, and a frequent contributor to the better Athenian newspapers, he is currently Professor of Philosophy at the Panteios Institute in Athens.

Yannaras holds together the vocations of theologian and philosopher, while being at the same time highly sensitive to the witness of literature and art. In the largest sense, the aim of his writing is to relate the patristic tradition of the Orthodox Church to contemporary issues, though he sees the latter to some considerable extent through the lens provided by philosophical Existentialism. For Yannaras, as Bishop Kallistos Ware has remarked, concern for the *person*, as the locus where being or nature is apprehended, constitutes the link binding patristic theology and existentialism together.[1] In the theological ethics of Yannaras, play is made with the dual meaning of the word *êthos*: ethics, morality, is nothing but the expression of the proper ethos of persons.

What this might mean is spelled out in the opening chapter of *The Freedom of Morality*. Here Yannaras defines his distinctive approach by distinguishing it from the other accounts of general ethics currently available. For him, these fall into two basic categories. In the first, ethics is a system of norms laid down by authority, whether divine in a religious context or simply transcendental in a secular one, where authority is represented by the impersonal principle of State power. In the second, ethics, taken as the ground rules for social inter-action, is conceived in purely conventional terms. On broadly utilitarian grounds, human beings in society accept certain rules for behaviour or principles for evaluating individual character, and seek to modify or refine them as time goes on, using philosophy or the human sciences to study the manifestations of social behaviour. What both these notions of general ethics have in common, so Yannaras maintains, is their separating of human morality from man's existential truth and what he terms, with a deliberate allusion to patristic Christology and Trinitarian doctrine, man's 'hypostatic identity'. Actually, the manner in which Yannaras asserts that human personhood forms the foundation of all inner subjectivity as well as all outer activity seems to owe more to *Kant* than to any Church Father. As he writes, by way of rhetorical question:

> Does human individuality have an ontological hypostasis, a hypostasis of life and freedom beyond space and time? Does it have a unique, distinctive and unrepeatable identity which is prior to character and behaviour, and which determine them? Or is it a transient by-product of biological, psychological and historical conditions by which it is necessarily determined, so that 'improvement' in character and behaviour is all we can achieve by resorting to a utilitarian code of law?[2]

Assuming the answer 'Yes' to all these questions, Yannaras goes on to define morality as 'an existential event'. To be moral is to realise a fullness of existence or life, to be immoral is to fail to realise this, and, in so doing, to distort one's true hypostasis. Such a view of general ethics has the merit, in the context of theology, that it at once allows morality its linkage with the notion of salvation. Salvation is continuous with morality, in that man's potential for existence, for a life beyond space, time, and conventional relationships is achieved by salvation with a completeness which morality can only partly or provisionally anticipate.

In the Orthodox tradition, then, as Yannaras interprets it, ethics begins with the ontological question, What is being, and what does it mean for man to be? But for the Church there can be no answer to these questions, so Yannaras continues, which prescinds from divine revelation. In saying this, he denies (quite rightly!) the possibility of an autonomous philosophical enquiry into ethics in the Christian context; for Yannaras, ethics is theological-philosophical, or it is sub-Christian. Yannaras sets out his ethics, as Maritain and Gilson, in the Western Catholic context, set out their metaphysics, by beginning from the disclosure of the divine name in Exodus 3 as 'I am He who Is'. In this divine word, the truth of existence, or the reality of being, is identified with God's personal hypostasis: 'I'. And here Yannaras can cite to good effect a passage of Gregory Palamas's *In Defence of the Holy Hesychasts*:

> When speaking to Moses, God did not say, 'I am essence'; for he who is, is not from the essence, but the essence is from he who is. He who is has comprehended within himself all being.[3]

Or, in Yannaras's terms: being issues not from essence, which would render it an ontological necessity, but from the person of the Father who in the freedom of his love 'hypostatises' being into a Trinitarian communion, begetting the Son, spirating the Holy Spirit. Yannaras calls the unity in communion of the three divine persons 'God's mode of being', and he identifies this with the ethos of the divine life. The effect is, he remarks, to single out *love* as the ontological category *par excellence*.

In order to apply this in a derived sense to human living, Yannaras invokes the biblical doctrine of man's creation in God's image, to his likeness. Yannaras's reading of this doctrine follows from what has already been thus briefly stated about the mystery of God himself. Man can be said to be created in the image of the Holy Trinity because he is naturally one in essence but personally in many hypostases. Yannaras writes:

> All men have a common nature or essence, but this has no existence
> except as personal distinctiveness, as freedom and transcendence of
> their own natural pre-determinations and natural necessity. The
> person is the hypostasis of the human essence or nature. He sums up
> in his existence the universality of human nature, but at the same
> time surpasses it, because his mode of existence is freedom and
> distinctiveness.[4]

The Creator's love, which alone gives substance to being, makes
human being an existential event of personal communion and
relationship. Man was created to become a partaker in the freedom
of love which is true life. Though all creation derives from God's
will and energy, man is the only creature to whom God has given
substance in the mode of personal existence, being as a *prosôpon*,
literally a 'facing towards' something, and this means above all,
for Yannaras, a being referred to, or related to, that fullness of
communion and relationship which is God. Like Maritain and
Gilson, but with a rather different end in view, Yannaras
contrasts here the person with the mere individual. The person is
not an individual, a segment or sub-division of human nature as
a whole; he or she represents, rather, the possibility of summing
up the whole in a distinctiveness of relationship, by an act of self-
transcendence. This makes persons unique, and such uniqueness
is the defining characteristic of man's personal mode of being. So
Yannaras distances himself in no uncertain terms from the long-
standing search in Christian theology for some attribute of the
soul, of man's nature as spirit, which will correspond to the
biblical image of God and form its basis, a privileged point of
contact between God and human nature. Or rather Yannaras re-
interprets the aspects of the soul thus commonly identified in
terms of his own personalism. As he puts it:

> Rationality, free will and dominion define the image of God in man
> because they relate, not to the 'spiritual' nature of man, but to the
> ways in which the person is distinguished from the nature and
> constitutes in itself a hypostasis of a life unshackled by any natural
> predetermination. Man is rational, and has free will and dominion in

creation because he is a personal being, and not because he is a 'spirit'.[5]

But in that case, how did the misunderstanding of these powers as general qualities of the soul arise? The answer Yannaras gives to this question shows that he does not regard that misunderstanding as a crude one, but, quite the contrary, as of a subtle kind. He writes:

> We do not know these human capacities as generic, objective properties: that is simply how thought converts them into independent and discrete concepts. We know them as something absolutely different in every distinctive personality. They are, to be sure, potentialities or energies of human nature in general, and possessed by every human being; but they always reveal the uniqueness of a person. They have no existence other than as manifestations of personal distinctiveness.[6]

The true foundation of the image is then the hypostatic character of human nature, the *personalised* mode of being of both body and soul. Because this is so, the image of God in man is preserved even in the tragedy of human freedom, even after the Fall. Morality for Yannaras is indeed the way in which man relates to the adventure of his freedom. If on the one hand ethics reveals what man *is*, as the image of God, it also shows what he can *become*, via this 'adventure of freedom', namely, a being transformed in God's likeness.

Having thus set forth the bases of his theological ethics, Yannaras at once turns to deal with the foundation of the moral *problem*: the Fall of man, and human sinfulness, which is for him, primarily, existential failure. Yannaras does not linger over questions about the historicity of the original human pair but embarks at once on an exploration of what the primordial human Fall can be said to involve. The Fall of man takes place, he tells us

> when he freely renounces his possibility of participating in true life, in personal relationship and loving communion – the only possibility for man to *be* as a hypostasis of personal distinctiveness.[7]

In falling, the human being rejects personal communion with God, falling back instead onto his own nature for which he claims autonomy and self-sufficiency. The result of the Fall is not just immorality but an existential lie, or rather, in being immorality it is an ontological fiction. Human nature partakes in true life only insofar as it transcends itself in man's hypostatic mode of being. In seeking natural autonomy, man becomes self-alienated, and Yannaras graphically describes the further consequences of this estrangement. As he explains, in the sinful condition

> [man's] personal existence is not destroyed, because it is precisely this that presupposes his freedom to experience existential alienation. But his personal distinctiveness ceases to sum up the possibilities of human nature in the existential fact of a relationship and communion which transcends nature and frees existence from natural necessity. Personal distinctiveness is confined within nature, as an individual autonomy which confronts the autonomy of others, thus fragmenting nature. Human nature is fragmented into individual wills expressing the individual being's need and effort to survive in his natural self-sufficiency: existence is identified with the instinctive, natural need for independent survival. The natural needs of the individual being, such as nourishment, self-perpetuation and self-preservation, become an end in themselves: they dominate man, and end up as 'passions', causes of anguish and the utmost pain, and ultimately the cause of death.[8]

According to Yannaras, this explains the uniqueness of the original Fall: the first fragmentation of nature is decisive for all human beings who live afterwards. The freedom of the human person has degenerated into a merely individual will, set against other individual wills, and one moreover in antithetical separation from nature, leading man to experience his own being as contradictory, as in Paul's account of such inner disintegration in chapter 7 of the Letter to the Romans. While not using the term 'original sin', which is rare, indeed avoided, in most Orthodox theology as a typically Latin Augustinianism, Yannaras clearly has his own version of the doctrine which that phrase encapsulates. After the Fall, each new human being is born into the world subject to his own individual nature's need to survive in existential autonomy. And this way of putting things leads Yannaras to make his own statements of the atheistic Existentialist Jean-Paul Sartre. In *L'Etre et le Néant*, Sartre had written, 'My original fall is the existence of the other', and on this Yannaras comments:

> The 'other' is always an affirmation of the inescapable fragmentation of our nature. Every 'other' is an immediate, empirical testimony to the person's inability to overcome the dynamic impulse towards the fragmentation of human nature into individual autonomous units: the 'other' is my condemnation to be the bearer of an individual or natural will for survival. For this will is not the product of freedom, but an impulse, an instinct and a need: it is the subjection of personal distinctiveness to the natural demand for the survival of the species. This demand is a torment to us, since it can be fulfilled only as an antagonistic confrontation with the existential autonomy of other individuals.[9]

This is why, as Sartre also declares, in his play *Huit Clos*, 'Hell is other people', for other people torment me with the revelation that I am condemned for ever to my individual autonomy. Yet, according to Yannaras, the Orthodox novelist Fyodor Dostoevsky had understood this more truly when he makes the Starets Zosima, in *The Brothers Karamazov*, define Hell as 'the torment of not loving'. Because what other people provide is not the cause of my hell but its occasion: its *cause* is to be found in my own 'incarceration in the egocentric autonomy of my individuality'. That is why the deepest Hell is occasioned by God, not in an act of judgment but simply in his own existing as the One whose loving goodness calls me to true life. Most provocative of all, however, is the fact that Yannaras also takes up in an appreciative way the nihilistic philosopher Friedrich Nietzsche's statement that authentic human identity lies 'beyond good and evil': one of the most controversial aphorisms used to describe the *Uebermensch*, the 'Super-man', in Nietzsche's *Thus Spake Zarathustra*. However, Yannaras means by this phrase, in his own transferred context, something quite innocuous. Namely, that the Church's ethics have to do not so much with evaluative categories as with ontological realities: in other words, Orthodox ethics depend on soteriology and notably the belief that fresh resources of being, enabling the regeneration of man and the transformation of his activity, are now graciously made available by the Saviour. As Yannaras explains:

> This existential change in the human nature 'altered' by the Fall is beyond the capacities of fallen man. It is fundamentally the work of the head of a new humanity: the work of the second Adam, Christ, who in his own person summed up and recreated human nature as a whole, the mode of man's existence. It is existential reality of the 'new creation' of his body, the Church.[10]

According to Yannaras, the 'moral crisis' of the contemporary West is not at all a rejection of authentic Christian ethics, but only of spurious degenerate forms of the latter – and more specifically a sub-Christian legalism of behavioural canons, and a pseudo-Christian idealism or angelism consisting in a commitment to 'values'. Both of these are, he maintains, travesties of genuine theological ethics, on which he writes:

> There are no abstract theoretical principles or conventional legal 'axioms' in the ethics of the Church, no impersonal imperatives. The foundation of this ethic is the human person; and person means constant risk, freedom from all objectification, and the dynamics of death and resurrection.[11]

These ethics are, accordingly, an ethics of repentance, of the Paschal passage from death to life. In his ethics, therefore, sin is needful – because sin is our recognition of death, of the separation of our hypostasis from its own true life. Only through conscious experience of such death can man approach the revelation of life, the possibility of rising with Christ. Indeed, Yannaras goes so far as to say that the real substance of the Gospel is the transformation of sin into repentance, or, in his favoured terms, of existential failure into fullness of life.[12] The absolutely crucial event in the history of ethics, in this perspective, is the Incarnation – when the human nature which had become existentially autonomous through Adam's rebellion was hypostatically united with God. The person of Christ becomes, with a reference to St John's passion narrative

> the axis around whom 'the children of God that were scattered abroad are gathered together', so that previously autonomous individuals form a unity of personal co-inherence and love.[13]

Sharing in what Yannaras calls the 'existential unity of the communion of saints' or, alternatively, the 'theanthropic body of Christ', comes about through repentance, which he defines as 'a change in our mode of existence', brought on when, negatively, man ceases to trust in his own individuality and, positively, entrusts his life to God in Christ through the Church. Such repentance brings about an altogether new cast of mind and sensibility – quite irrespective of any fresh moral achievement. On the one hand, the Christian knows that Christ, the Mother of God and the saints love him despite the fact that he is a sinner; on the other, his subjection to the passions enables him to become aware of the various kinds of tyranny exercised by his natural will. In the Church, sin becomes the starting-point for man to experience the miracle of his salvation by Christ – a point which Yannaras backs up with some telling quotations from the desert Fathers.

The most fundamental ethical conviction of Yannaras is, then, that Gospel morality refers to a real, existential transfiguration of human nature, and not to a 'deontology' which would leave man's nature unchanged in its basic capacities or lack of them. With the coming together of divine and human natures in the Word Incarnate, and the harmonising of the natural wills of God and man in his person, fallen human nature is freed from its self-imposed bondage in the chains of mortal individuality. Christ's theanthropic existence hypostatises the mortal being of man, forming thereby a new creation, a new humanity which exists in communion with the Father, now that it has been assumed, 'mortal and bloodstained', by the hypostatic love of the Son. The regeneration of human individuals requires only their assent to Christ's ecstatic love for them, or what Yannaras calls

> an effort, however small, to reject one's individual self-sufficiency, to resist its impulses and to will to live as one loving and loved.[14]

Not that Yannaras is an ethical minimalist: on the contrary he speaks of the whole of Orthodox asceticism as life in conformity to this ethos: in its various practices it is, he writes,

> the endeavour which confirms man's freedom and his decision to reject the rebellion of his individual will and to imitate the obedience of the second Adam.[15]

What he denies is that such an ethos, or the attempt to live conformably with it, can be expressed in legal terms, or in terms of the virtues – the two chief notions around which *Catholic* moral theology, be it noted, in its main schools of thinking has revolved. This denial at once encounters problems, and notably the prominence enjoyed by the concept of law in the Old Testament, as well as the special rôle of virtue of charity in the New. Yannaras replies that the aim of faithfulness to the Law in the Old Testament was the manifestation of God's covenant with his people – not a matter of individual justification. As in *Exodus* the Law is given to Moses with the divine Name, so, in Yannaras's exegesis the Israelite law, unlike, by implication, any other, was a call to the people of Israel to receive and mediate the reality of God, by communion and relationship with him. So Yannaras can accept the statement of the Matthaean Christ that he has come not to put an end to the Law but to fulfil it, arguing that the 'new commandment' of the Gospel is none other than the person of Christ, the perfect image of God, carried about by every believer who remains true to the Law of love which engrafts him into Christ's body, the Church. It is just that centrality of the Law of love in the New Testament revelation which according to Yannaras, ensures that we cannot think of charity as *one* of the virtues, even the most important of them. Yannaras, taking his cue from the First Letter of John, identifies love with the restoration of the divine image and so with man's return to true existence, authentic life: 'For love is of God, and every one that loves is born of God, and knows God'. Indeed, Yannaras's interpretation of the injunction to 'lose one's life' in order to save it moves beyond a rejection of the person with individualised nature and the biological and psychological self-defence of the ego to a Lutheran-sounding attack on the idea of inherent justification. Losing one's life means also, for him,

> renouncing individual attainments, objective recognition of virtue and the sense of merit, which are the mainstays of our resistance to the need for communion with God and trust in him.[16]

But here his real target is what Yannaras calls the 'established ethics of secularised Christianity'. The belief that one is living up to one's moral obligations suffices to cut off from the true existence disclosed in the hypostasis of Christ. Such an ethics misses the point of the salvation brought by Christ whose essence is *koinônia*, and which affects, via the Orthodox canons on feasting and fasting, even such things as how we take food, now transformed into a *common* experience of the use of good things. For Yannaras, the supreme paradigms of theological ethics are the 'fools for Christ', such 'holy fools' being a recognised category of Orthodox sanctity. The fools are vessels of grace in that they refuse any objective recognition of virtue or piety knowing that this separates man both from God through self-satisfaction and from his fellow men, because they dare not expose to him their need and weakness. Yannaras interprets the 'shocking freedom' of the fools in paschal terms: their death to conventional forms was a resurrection into a life of hypostatic distinctiveness in the love which knows no bounds or barriers.

Thus the holy fools are the 'classics' of Orthodox ethics, while the Liturgy, and above all the Eucharist, is the climax of ethical living. In the eucharistic Liturgy, life returns, as Yannaras puts it

> to its hypostatic source as thanksgiving, *eucharistia*, as a loving response which sums up existence, the world, and the beauty of the world, in personal distinctiveness and freedom.[17]

The Eucharist unifies the life of persons in the community of Christ's theanthropic nature, and thus restores the ethos proper to man as the image of God. It returns to man's being or mode of existence the fullness of the personal communion of the Holy Trinity; it manifests the character of ethical perfection in man, which is at once existential and theological. The morality of the Church is, therefore, a *liturgical morality*. The Liturgy is not simply an expression of religious worship. It is the core and the sum of the Church's life and truth, of her faith and ethics. As Yannaras writes in his introduction to Orthodox Theology, *Elements of Faith*:

> Initiation into the truth of the Church is participation in her way of life, in a festive gathering of the faithful, in the visible actualization and revelation of the new humanity which has conquered death.[18]

And Yannaras stresses in this connexion the *cosmic* dimension of the Liturgy, on the grounds that the inner principle of the world is found only in the eucharistic relationship between creation and Creator. As he writes, and this closing quotation will prepare us for the last topic of this study, eschatology, the theology of the End:

> The Church's Eucharist is a cosmic liturgy: it sums up the life of the world and the inner principle of the world in the 'principle' of man, in the human word glorifying God, the word which is made flesh in man's life. This is Christ's word for obedience to the Father's will, the 'yes' of the Son's assent. The Eucharist is man's assent to the assumption of his nature by Christ, an assent which unifies the principle, the 'word' of all created nature, in the 'yes' of Christ's

obedience. Man is the celebrant of the eucharistic nature of the world: the restoration of life as communion, communion of the persons within human nature, as a communion of participation in the life of the world. And its sums up the oneness of the life of created things in a movement, an impulse which is eucharistic and loving, turning back towards God.[19]

XII
Paul Evdokimov and Eschatology

Pavel Nikolayevič Evdokimov was born in 1900 in St Petersburg. In 1907 his father, an army officer who had gained some celebrity by calming insurgent troops after the Revolution of 1904–5, was assassinated by a private soldier belonging to an extreme Left-wing terrorist grouping. With his twelve year old brother, the little Paul made his way into central Russia to re-join his mother and pay his last respects to his father's body.

Olivier Clément, the French Orthodox lay-theologian, suggests that this scene gave Evdokimov two of his great theological themes, the sacrificial love of the Father and that *sourire du Père*, 'smile of the Father', which we shall have all eternity to contemplate:

> True psycho-analysis does not reduce the mystery. It shows how, throughout our entire destiny, the mystery draws us to itself.[1]

Paul's mother, a woman from the old aristocracy, was interested in theology, and even wrote some though she never published it. However, she did initiate Paul into his life of faith, a faith of which his second wife, a Japanese, was to say after his death: 'He believed just as one breathes.'

Similarly, Clément remarks:

> He belonged to that spiritual race for whom God is much more real than the world, or rather for which the world has no other reality than that of being theophanic.[2]

Evdokimov was sent, after his father's death, to the Cadets' training college of the imperial Russian army, but during the holidays his mother took him off to monasteries, whose guest-houses were often, in the old Russia, thronged with visitors of both sexes: one gets a good idea of this from the early chapters of Dostoevsky's *The Brothers Karamazov*. At the moment when the October Revolution burst on Russia, the family were at Kiev. Paul's reaction was to begin studying theology at the Kiev Academy. This notwithstanding, he was mobilised by the White Army and served as a combatant for two years. His definitive view of those terrible events was, however, that at its roots the Revolution was a phenomenon of the spiritual order which could only be both overcome and assumed by a spiritual renaissance.

And so Evdokimov, like the Russian theologians we have studied earlier in this book, became an exile. The experience may have proved more constitutive for him than for them. A Catholic student of Evdokimov's work has suggested that he took exile as a key for grasping the human situation as a whole, and especially in its relation to past and future. The 'universalising' of that experience, suggests G. Vendrame, furnished him with

a formal horizon for the understanding of the mystery of man as that existent in continual search for its identity, which, in that search, constructs itself anthropologically, religiously, ecclesially.[3]

Like so many Russian exiles, Evdokimov passed by way of Constantinople to Paris where he paid for his philosophical and theological education by a variety of manual jobs, ranging from taxi-driving to cleaning railway carriages. A scholarship salvaged the situation, and enabled him to study full time at the newly founded Institut Saint-Serge where his meetings with Bulgakov and Berdyaev were decisive. Bulgakov developed Evdokimov's 'instinct for Orthodoxy' by making him read the Fathers, live the Liturgy and discover the world of the icon.

But it was Berdyaev who awakened in him his more distinctive ideas – the tragic freedom of man, and its possible resolution: response to God through a Spirit-enabled loving creativity. In

1927, he married a Franco-Russian girl from the Midi and settled in the south of France. It seems to have been one of those *ménages* where the husband acts as mother and the wife works. While his wife taught Italian for a living, Evdokimov prepared his doctoral thesis, which took as its subject Dostoevsky and the problem of evil. In this study, Evdokimov portrayed Dostoevsky in the light of Russian religious philosophy as the prophet of a Christianity renewed by the experience of atheism. In this work Evdokimov asks, If the world *is* a theophany – something he personally had believed from childhood, and found confirmed in Bulgakov's sophiology, then what is the significance of the appalling evil which we see in history? He finds the answer to his own question in the *kenôsis* of the Son of God, a *kenôsis* whose aim is to place before human freedom the ultimate choice: self-deification or the God-man.[4]

In 1944, Evdokimov published his second book *Le Marriage, sacrement de l'amour*, which drew its title from John Chrysostom but much of its content from German Romanticism. Alas, in 1945, Evdokimov's wife was to die of cancer. Meanwhile, during the war, Evdokimov had been working with the resistance movement CIMADE (*Comité inter-mouvements pour l'acceuil des évacués*) to save Jews from the unwelcome attentions of the German occupying force and the anti-Semitic Vichy government of Marshal Pétain. With the ending of the war, this work for displaced persons became, apart from his writings, his real life work. He integrated it with his theological vision by means of an Old Testament text:

The stranger who dwells with you will be for you a compatriot and you will love him as yourself,[5]

and gave a Christological interpretation to the refugees, whether from central and Eastern Europe, or, as later, from the Third World, whom he helped. Apart from directing the Maison d'Acceuil (at Serrès and then Massy), Evdokimov also taught at Saint-Serge as well as working for both the World Council of

Churches and the Ecumenical Institute founded by the Constantinople patriarchate at Bossy on Lake Geneva.

In 1954 Evdokimov re-married, and although *les secondes noces* are looked upon by the Orthodox Church as distinctly imperfect, this one appeared, in Clément's words, to have 'liberated the force of creation' in the new husband.[6] A positive stream of books began to cascade forth, and with them, his influence became notable for the first time in Catholic circles too. In 1964, he became the representative of the Institut Saint-Serge among the ecumenical observers at Vatican II, and Clément discerns Evdokimov's mark here and there in the text of *Gaudium et Spes*. In 1967, when the Institut Catholique de Paris produced a pup, the Institut Supérieur d'Etudes Oecuméniques, Evdokimov was called to teach there. In 1968, the University of Thessalonica, ever alert to unusual Orthodox minds with potential impact on the Churches of the West, gave him its doctorate *honoris causa*. Evdokimov died in 1970.

Evdokimov's Eschatology

Let us turn then to our principal interest in Evdokimov – which is the considerable rôle of eschatology in his presentation of Orthodox theology as a whole. In his teaching, this rôle belongs with the general revival of the eschatology theme in the Christian theology of this century. In the periods of the Reformation and Counter-Reformation, eschatology was chiefly an individualist affair, concerned with the destiny of each person, and relegated to something of an appendix to theology as a whole, as in the treatise *De novissimis*, 'on the Last Things'. In the twentieth century, by contrast, not only has corporate, as distinct from individual, eschatology made a comeback, but, better still, individual and corporate eschatological elements are frequently re-integrated with each other, and thus regain their proper balance and proportion. Just as the individual Christian, from his baptism to his death, is poised between Christ's first coming and his *Parousia*, so the world too is now in an interim period between those extraordinary events, or meta-events. During this in-between time, the Church works, under the Holy Spirit, to transform the world into the likeness of Christ. As history moves on, the Last Things make their advance: the profane is conse-crated until the Kingdom of God be established in fullness.

When Evdokimov arrived in France, this retrieving of eschato-logical awareness was just getting under way in Western theology. In Catholicism, it was indebted in part to the move-ment of *ressourcement*; to the concern for biblical theology which revived the themes of judgment and apocalypse; to the interest in the Fathers which led to the discovery of the notion of *epektasis*, prominent in Gregory of Nyssa and Maximus the Confessor – the unending 'reaching forth' of the soul towards transcendence; and to the liturgical revival, where people recovered the original meaning of the celebration of Advent in the Western liturgies, and the future orientation of the Eucharist as a proleptic presence of the final Kingdom. But, in addition, the French Catholic revival also owed its renewed eschatological awareness to its ecumenical contacts – contacts with German and Swiss Pro-testantism, where Karl Barth, Rudolf Bultmann and Oscar Cullmann were all (admittedly, in extremely different and scar-cely compatible ways) 'eschatological theologians', and to the presence on French soil of the Russian Orthodox diaspora.

All of these diverse influences would be catalysed by the Second World War, so that the most prominent French eschato-logists came to prominence in the years immediately following that war. And these were: Jean Daniélou and Louis Bouyer. And here I touch on a point closely relevant to Evdokimov. The revival of eschatology in the West was not just a *livresque* affair: academic, bookish. Just as the collapse of the old European order in the First World War, and notably that of the Second Reich with its proud Protestant tradition of learning, inspired Barth to write his commentary on the Letter to the Romans, so the horrors of the Third Reich catalysed Barth's French, and Catho-lic, equivalents. All optimism about human progress being set aside, what can give a firm foundation to hope in the light of

Dachau and Auschwitz, and, indeed, with the dropping of the atom bomb on Nagasaki and Hiroshima? Similarly, in Russian Orthodoxy, the strongly accented eschatological consciousness of twentieth century theologians derived from the experiences of the 1917 Revolution, the Civil War and exile. Having seen a human world of meanings collapse one could the more readily conceive of, and imagine, the passing away of the world-order as a whole. Having experienced what the English fantasist J. R. R. Tolkien called a 'pareschaton', one could never forget the New Testament disclosure of the eschaton to come.

What then is Evdokimov's fundamental attitude to eschatology? It is important to note that his eschatological vision is not, as is sometimes the case, based on a pessimistic assessment of creation and history. He called his basic posture, indeed, 'eschatological affirmation', as distinct from, and counterposed to, 'eschatological negation'. The Christian, he thought, affirms the world, but in such a way as to open the world to what lies beyond itself, namely paradise, eternity. Our appreciation of man's historical activity must, he believed, be fundamentally positive, since all culture originates from the divine command to 'cultivate' – to share in God's creative power. And yet, in order for culture to fulfil its mission and actualise its own authentic nature, it needs to be made aware that it is not an end in itself. It cannot develop into the infinite, and, if it be closed within its own limits, it will create only insoluble problems. According to Evdokimov, sooner or later, philosophy, art and social life are brought up short at their own boundaries or limits. When that point is reached, a choice must be made. Either culture will attempt (fruitlessly) to turn the finite into the infinite, or else it will recognise the infinite – God – for what he is.

It is at this juncture that Christian faith is called upon to reveal the eschatological face of culture. This is, as Evdokimov presents it, a somewhat paradoxical task, for, on the one hand, Christian faith promotes culture in this world, and yet, on the other, by virtue of its own eschatological dimension invites culture to transcend itself, and so to cease to be, at least as an immanent, this worldly activity. In Evdokimov's preferred vocabulary, culture must pass from a state of being a matter of symbols to a condition of reality. In the latter, philosophers, artists and social reformers – the bearers, in Evdokimov's eyes, of the three main constituents of culture – draw not on any human resources but on the royal and universal priesthood given to believers in baptism. Through this new resource, they then proceed to transform culture into what Evdokimov calls *un lieu théophanique* – a 'theophanic place', where the divine reality of the Kingdom manifests itself in the works of culture and culture becomes accordingly doxology, the praise and glorification of God. Thus, under the influence of grace, culture tends to become Liturgy, a revelation of the transfigured form of the *logos*, or intrinsic meaning, of things. As he wrote in an essay:

> Culture, in its essence, is a search in history for what is outside its limits. It becomes the expression of the Kingdom through the things of this world. Every judgment on culture is made by referring to the presence of God within it, a presence which is simultaneously a sign and an expectation. In the same way, the historical coming of Christ in the Church requires us to live in expectation of the Christ of glory still to come, and the Eucharist, too, is both an affirmation of the end of everything that is transient, and at the same time in this very affirmation is the radiance of eternal life.[7]

Or, as he puts it more simply, in his *L'Art de l'Icône*, 'earthly culture is the icon of the heavenly Kingdom'.[8]

From this perspective, Evdokimov's interest in actual icons – in iconography, the designing of icons, and in iconology, their interpretation – does not represent primarily a concern for liturgical or sacred art for its own sake. Although Evdokimov was troubled by the state of aesthetics – as of all aspects of human culture in the modern West, he saw the icon as, above all, a paradigm of an eschatologically transformed human work. As the Vietnamese Cistercian Father Peter Phan, the chief authority on Evdokimov's theology of culture, has put it:

An icon for Evdokimov is at the same time a theological vision, a sacramental, an expression of authentic art, a product of asceticism and mystical communion, an eloquent witness to transcendence and incarnation, a prophetic harbinger of the eschatological transfiguration of the universe.[9]

More widely, then, Evdokimov's eschatological vision of human culture appears to be based on five principles.

First, there is a principle of theological anthropology at work here. Man is God's image, though an image which, through the Fall, is reduced to what Evdokimov calls 'ontological silence'. Nevertheless, that image, though dumb, is still there in its objective reality, and is re-awakened, in fact, by salvation which liberates the dynamic quality of the image, namely, its tendency to become the full likeness of God. Man's aim in history, for Evdokimov, is to achieve the eschatological likeness to which he was called from the beginning.

Secondly, underlying Evdokimov's eschatology there is a Christological principle. The *imago Dei* is not simply man's own constitutive principle. It also discloses a truth about God: and this is that God desires to be man. In Christ, at least as Evdokimov understands the Chalcedonian definition, the two sides of the image human and divine, reach their culmination. God becomes 'homoform' and man 'deiform'. Thus Christ is the supreme realisation and the absolute norm of all human culture. In the aftermath of the Incarnation, man is called on to create a unity without confusion between, on the one hand, the divine element in society – that is, the Church – and, on the other hand, the human element – the world with its culture. And just as the human was, at the Incarnation, assumed by the divine, without losing its own integrity, so too culture will be assumed by the Kingdom.

Thirdly, Evdokimov has a pneumatological principle. The Christification of history is actually achieved by the Holy Spirit who brings culture to its eschatological fulfilment. Evdokimov refers to the Spirit in this connexion as the 'Iconographer of

Beauty', who, as the 'Finger of the Father', retouches all the images of human culture produced by those men and women who have opted for the true Infinite, and makes of cultural forms the 'icon of the Kingdom'.

Fourthly, Evdokimov's work turns on a liturgical or ecclesiological principle. The Church is a perpetual Pentecost, and so is essentially eschatological, something most clearly expressed in the sacraments, and notably in the Eucharist. There the Church, as he writes in *L'Orthodoxie*, 'metabolises cosmic matter into the Bread of the Kingdom'.[10] It is this messianic meal which allows the Church to see herself as the inauguration of eschatology and the anticipation of the expected *Parousia*. By this communion of holy gifts (one meaning of the *communio sanctorum* of the Creed), in nuptial encounter with the Lord and in the diversity of the flames of Pentecost, each human hypostasis, called as he or she is to give a unique face to human nature in Christ, finds a grounding in the communion of saints (the other meaning of the Creed's *sanctorum communio*). For Evdokimov, consequently, the Eucharist transcends all opposition between the individual and the collective. Eucharistic existence is a life in common where personal diversity and ontological unity are complementary aspects of a single mystery, in the image of the Holy Trinity.

Lastly, Evdokimov has an ascetic principle. Since man and nature are both fallen, culture, which is man's cultivation of nature, is also infected. The human heart is, as Evdokimov's study of Dostoevsky had suggested, fertile in giving birth both to evil and to good, and that split in the heart has its effect throughout culture – above all, in the disintegration of the original unity of truth, goodness and beauty. The only remedy for this inner alienation in man, nature and culture, is what Evdokimov calls the 'eschatological maximalism' of monastic *askêsis*. Culture, that is, must travel the same path as the monks of the desert. It must become aware of its own alienation and ambiguity, just as the early ascetics concentrated on that self-understanding which made them aware of their own evil thoughts. In the Eastern Church, so Evdokimov points out, everyone must practise an 'interior monasticism', submissive to all the demands of the Gospel, whose fulfilling, in the service of God and man will keep the Christian in joyful expectation of the glorious *Parousia* to come.[11] The desert Fathers, whom the French Dominican student of the ancient world, A. J. Festugière, saw as embodying a clash between culture and holiness, Evdokimov regards as icons of a culture renewed by the Gospel – though they stand, admittedly, at a negative moment in its dialectical coming-to-be. As 'God's rebels', they proclaim the end of profane history, and the coming of a new City inhabited by new men.[12] By their confrontation with the 'deifugal' passions, with 'every obscure element of evil', the great ascetics take down into the depths of the divided self the divine therapy, the cure of death by eternal life.[13] Then, just as the soul rises little by little through asceticism to final *theôsis* or deification by grace, so culture, though the 'baptism' of *askêsis*, breaks through to its eschatological dimension and achieves its destiny – namely to be a cosmic liturgy, a prelude to the worship of heaven.

Evdokimov tries to apply these five principles to various aspects of reality, ranging from the philosophy of religion through the practice of art to the institution of marriage. His eschatological vision also allows him to relate with each other the various theological disciplines, so that dogmatics, morals and spirituality all appear as organically interconnected. Though Evdokimov had no intention of creating a theological system, in one sense he has done so through the sheer force of his eschatological vision.

On the other hand, Evdokimov's idiom is far from what we normally expect of the systematic theologian. He achieves his ends by means of densely poetic language, filled – some would say over-filled, over-loaded – with biblical, liturgical and literary references which do not always make for clarity of argument. One either loves Evdokimov or chokes on him. And just as he met with the warm admiring approval of the Orthodox of Thessalonica, so at St Vladimir's, New York, he was never forgiven for his fierce opposition to the neo-patristic revival of

Florovsky which took as its programme the removal from the texture of Orthodox theological discourse everything that was not the pure milk of Christian Hellenism, the message, and the medium, of the Greek Fathers.

Eastern Christendom knows its share of *odium theologicum*; the reconciliation of charity and truth is itself an eschatological undertaking.

Conclusion

If, as I write now, in 1994, the prospects for ecumenical *rapprochement* between the Catholic and Orthodox Churches seem bleaker than at any time since the Second Vatican Council (1962–65), there remains at least the effort of common charity – a part of which will consist in the joyful 'reception' of the evangelical truths found in the thought, spirituality and worship of either side. In this study caveats have been offered at certain points where the thinking of Eastern Orthodox Christians, or, at any rate, of influential theologians among them, seems to me to depart from the interpretation of the Gospel found in the tradition of Catholicism. But more striking has been the extent to which the work of Orthodox dogmaticians in the twentieth century concurs with that of the best – the most ecclesially recognised – divines of the Catholic Church in the same period. By a twofold movement of 'going back to the sources' and reverent speculation, scribes of the Kingdom can bring out of the ecumenical treasure-house gifts new and old. If there is light from the East there is also, and complementarily, a *lumen occidentale* also. For in the last analysis the light of theology is the radiance of the glory which shone out in the Face of Jesus Christ, the Church's common Lord.

Notes

Chapter I: *Introduction*

1. A. Schmemann, *The Historical Road of Eastern Orthodoxy* (Et London 1963).
2. M. Rinvolucri, *Anatomy of a Church* (Et London 1966).
3. [K.] T. Ware, *The Orthodox Church* (Harmondsworth 1963).
4. J. Meyendorff, *The Orthodox Church* (Et London 1962).
5. A. Nichols, *Rome and the Eastern Churches: A Study in Schism* (Edinburgh 1992). (As it is, I am grateful to the publishers of this title, T. & T. Clark, for permitting some reprinting in pp. 4–10 below.)
6. Since writing this book, I have discovered Karl Christian Felmy's splendid study, *Die orthodoxe Theologie der Gegenwart. Eine Einführung* (Darmstadt 1990).
7. Canon 34 of the self-styled 'Apostolic Collection', a book of canons which stands first in all Orthodox canon law collections.
8. A. A. Bogolepov, *Toward an American Orthodox Church: The Establishment of an Autocephalous Orthodox Church* (New York 1963).
9. C. A. Frazee, *The Orthodox Church and Independent Greece, 1851–1852* (Cambridge 1969).
10. For a beautifully evocative account see P. Hammond, *The Waters of Marah: The Present State of the Greek Church* (London 1956).
11. Y. A. Kourvetaris and B. A. Dobratz, *A Profile of Modern Greece in Search of Identity* (Oxford 1987), p. 163: 'Owing to secularization, industrialization, urbanization and political change, the influence of the Orthodox Church is declining in Greece. This is evident not only from the problems of recruiting clergy but also from church attendance which is higher in small towns and villages than in large cities.' During the years 1981–89 under the PASOK (Pan-Hellenic Socialist Movement) government a separation of Church and State was mooted.
12. For early twentieth-century Greek theology, and the founding of

these schools, see F. Gavin, *Some Aspects of Contemporary Greek Orthodox Thought* (London 1923). For a survey of the more recent period see the English translation of the article by A. Koumantos, 'An Outline of the Present Theological Situation in Greece', *Sobornost* 6, 9 (1974), pp. 663–70. The differentiation of these faculties into pastoral and scientific departments complicates the situation somewhat; and currently, the differences between the two schools are less marked.

13. P. Trembelas, *Dogmatikê tês Orthodoxou Katholikês Ekklêsias* (Athens 1959–61). This first edition was subsequently translated into French and published as *Dogmatique de l'Église Orthodoxe Catholique* (Chevetogne-Bruges 1966–68). A second Athenian edition was published in 1978 from which all citations in this chapter are taken.

14. L. Ott, *Grundriss der katholischen Dogmatik* (Freiburg 1970).

15. P. Trembelas, *Dogmatikê tês Orthodoxou Katholikês Ekklêsias* (Athens 1959–61; 2nd edn 1978), p. 2.

16. C. Yannaras, *De l'absence et de l'inconnaissance de Dieu d'après les écrits aréopagitiques et Martin Heidegger* (Paris 1971); and *To prosôpo kai ho erôs. Theologiko dokimio ontologias* (Athens 1976).

17. C. Yannaras, 'Orthodoxy and the West', in A. J. Philippon (ed.), *Orthodoxy, Life and Freedom. Essays in Honour of Archbishop Iakovos* (San Bernardino, Calif., 1973, reprinted 1980), see also Yannaras' *Timioi me tên Orthodoxia. Neoellenika theologika dokima* (Athens 1968).

18. C. Yannaras, *Hê eleutheria tou êthous. Dokimes yia mia orthodoxê theôrêsê tês Ethikês* (Athens 1970). Published in English translation as *The Freedom of Morality* (Crestwood, NY., 1984).

19. C. Read, *Religion, Revolution and the Russian Intelligentsia, 1900–1912* (London 1979).

20. A. Kniazeff, *L'Institut Saint-Serge de Paris. De l'Academie d'autrefois au rayonnement d'aujourd'hui* (Paris 1974).

21. *Philokalia The Complete Text* (London 1979–)

22. Florovsky's writings in various languages were published in English as the *Collected Works* (Vaduz, Liechtenstein, 1987).

23. For an account of the seminary manuals commissioned by Patriarch Justinian in 1949–51 see A. Johansen, *Theological Study in the Rumanian Orthodox Church under Communist Rule* (London 1961). They have been largely superseded by the superior work of a younger generation, led by Dimitru Staniloae.

24. D. Staniloae, *L'Eglise orthodoxe roumaine. De la théologie orthodoxe roumaine des origines à nos jours* (Bucharest 1974), pp. 211–84. Staniloae's

chief work is the three volume *Teologia dogmatica ortodoxa* (Bucharest 1978).
25.   For relations with the West, see E. D. Tappe, 'The Rumanian Orthodox Church and the West', in D. Baker (ed.), *The Orthodox Churches and the West, Studies in Church History*, Volume XIII (Oxford 1976), pp. 277–92.
26.   M. A. Fahey, 'Orthodox Ecumenism and Theology, 1978–1983', *Theological Studies* 44 (1983), p. 637.
27.   A. A. Bogolepov, *Toward an American Orthodox Church: The Establishment of an Autocephalous Orthodox Church* (New York 1963). And see P. Trembelas, *The Autocephaly of the Metropolia in America* (Brookline, Mass., 1973).
28.   For an overview of the prevailing climate, see A. Johansen, *Theological Study in the Russian and Bulgarian Orthodox Churches under Communist Rule* (London 1963).
29.   Serbian ecclesiology is, however, notably affected by the movement of zealously nationalist neo-mediaevalism called *Svetosavlje*. See T. Bremer, *Ekklesiale Struktur und Ekklesiologie in der Serbischen Orthodoxen Kirche im 19. und 20. Jahrhundert* (Würzburg 1992).

Chapter II: *Vladimir Lossky and Apophatic Theology*

1.   This piece of research was only completed just before Lossky's death, in 1958, and was published posthumously, with a preface by Étienne Gilson, in 1960. See V. Lossky, *Théologie négative et connaissance de Dieu chez Maître Eckhart* (Paris 1960).
2.   V. Lossky, 'Otvitsatelnoe bogoslovie v uchenii Dionisiya Areopagita', *Seminarium Kondakovianum* III (Prague 1929), pp. 135–44. This article took as its subject the precise relation of Denys to negative theology. It was translated into French in the *Revue des Sciences Philosophiques et Théologiques*, XXVIII (Paris 1936), p. 204ff.
3.   V. Lossky, *Spor o Sofii. Dokladnaya Zapiska Prot. S. Bulgakova i Smisl' Ukaza Moskovskoi Patriarchii* (Paris 1936). This book ('The Question About Wisdom') was not published in French or English.
4.   R. D. Williams, 'The Theology of Vladimir Nikolaievich Lossky. An Exposition and Critique' (Ph.D thesis, Oxford 1975), pp. 12–13, with a reference to *Spor o Sofii*, pp. 18–19.

5.   Anon., 'In memoriam Vladimir Lossky, 1903–1958', *Contacts* 31 (1979), p. 118.

6.   V. Lossky, *Essai sur la théologie mystique de l'Église d'Orient* (Paris 1943).

7.   Lossky's private journal, 'Sept jours sur les routes de la France', was never published. However, its bearing on Lossky's development is summarised in R. D. Williams, 'The Theology of Vladimir Nikolaievich Lossky. An Exposition and Critique' (Ph.D thesis, Oxford 1975), pp. 14–21.

8.   See especially, V. Lossky, 'Le problème de la *Vision face à face* et la Tradition patristique de Byzance', in K. Aland and F. L. Cross (eds), *Studia Patristica* II (Berlin 1957). The problem of the apparent denial by many Greek, and even Latin, Fathers of the *visio facialis* taught by the late mediaeval Catholic Church had already exercised the Iberian Scholastics of the sixteenth century, and notably Gabriel Vasquez. Lossky's approach is eirenic: the 'unity of the Christian tradition rich in diverse theological perspectives', must not be confused with the 'doctrinal uniformity of a systematised teaching'. In particular, Lossky appealed, in mitigation of the seeming contradiction of Latin West and Byzantine East, to for instance, the difference between the *visio Dei secundum essentiam* of Scholastic theology, on the one hand, and the theological epistemology of the Eunomians where claims to knowledge of the divine *ousia* had an unacceptable meaning, on the other. In the latter, the question of the face-to-face vision was not directly posed: conceptual knowability – of the Father – was what was in question. Also relevant were the different meanings which the notion of light as revealing of Divinity could have in different theologians. It was not necessarily a *mere* light, as opposed to the Godhead, but could be the very Glory of the divine being itself – over against the Messalian opposition of a sensible light to an (Origenist) intellectual one.

9.   V. Lossky, 'Introduction', in L. Ouspensky, *Der Sinn der Ikonen* (Bern 1952). This was translated into English the same year and published as *The Art of the Icon* (Boston, Mass., 1952).

10.   According to Olivier Clément, at the time of his death Lossky was planning a comparative study of Palamism and the Rhineland mystics. This would have shown how the fundamental intuitions of Western mystical theology were Orthodox – yet frustrated by *Filioquism*. Through awareness of the reality of Uncreated Grace, participated by them, the Western mystics saw the vision of God as an existential

communion, but were unable to found this insight in either theology or ecclesiology. Hence, in Lossky's eyes, their path led ineluctably, via the *Theologia Deutsch*, to Martin Luther. See O. Clément, 'Vladimir Lossky: un théologien de la personne et du Saint-Esprit. Mémorial Vladimir Lossky', *Messager de l'Exarchat russe en Occident* 30–31 (1959), pp. 204–5.

11.   Lossky's eschatology lectures were published posthumously as *La Vision de Dieu* (Neuchâtel 1962). So, too, were a group of essays on soteriology, which came out as *À l'image et à la ressemblance de Dieu* (Paris 1967). Contributions on other dogmatic themes were printed, under the general title, 'Theologie dogmatique', in the *Messager de l'Exarchat du Patriarch russe en Europe occidental* 46–50 (1964–65). These were later translated into English and published as *Orthodox Theology: An Introduction* (Crestwood, NY., 1978).

12.   V. Lossky, *Essai sur la théologie mystique de l'Eglise d'Orient* (Paris 1943). Published in English translation as *The Mystical Theology of the Eastern Church* (London 1957).

13.   Cited by R. D. Williams, 'The *Via Negativa* and the Foundations of Theology: an introduction to the Thought of V. N. Lossky', in S. Sykes (ed.), *New Studies in Theology* I (London 1980), pp. 95–118.

14.   Ibid.

15.   V. Lossky, *The Mystical Theology of the Eastern Church* (London 1957), p. 8.

16.   Ibid., pp. 8–9.

17.   J. Mouroux, *L'Expérience chrétienne: Introduction à une théologie* (Paris 1952). Published in English translation as *The Christian Experience: Introduction to a Theology* (London 1955).

18.   B. Zenkovsky singles out as a typifying feature of Russian philosophy before the Revolution that it remained closely linked to religious culture. Indeed, Zenkovsky can offer a definition of philosophy, from the Russian perspective, in these terms: 'Where we find a search for unity of the spiritual life through the medium of its rationalisation – *there* we have philosophy.' See B. Zenkovsky, *Historie de la philosophie russe* (Paris 1952–54), Vol. I, p. 8. And, for the views of Solov'ev, see in particular, J. Sutton, *The Religious Philosophy of Vladimir Solovyov. Towards a Reassessment* (London 1988).

19.   V. Lossky, *The Mystical Theology of the Eastern Church* (London 1957), pp. 8–9.

20.   But see E. Oikonomos, *Bibel und Bibelwissenschaft in der Orthodoxen Kirche* (Stuttgart 1976).

21. V. Lossky, *The Mystical Theology of the Eastern Church* (London 1957), p. 11.

22. V. Lossky, 'L'Apophase et la theologie trinitaire' in *À l'image et à la ressemblance de Dieu* (Paris 1967). Published in English translation as *In the Image and Likeness of God* (New York 1974), p. 15.

23. Ibid., p. 28.

24. R. D. Williams, 'The *Via Negativa* and the Foundations of Theology: an introduction to the Thought of V. N. Lossky', in S. Sykes (ed.), *New Studies in Theology* I (London 1980), p. 98.

25. This insistence on the explicitly Trinitarian character of genuine apophasis, in the context of a characteristically Cappadocian stress on the complete equality of the persons, is, as Williams has pointed out, the grounds of Lossky's considerable reserve on the topic of early Alexandrian theology. See R. D. Williams, 'The *Via Negativa* and the Foundations of Theology: an introduction to the Thought of V. N. Lossky', in S. Sykes (ed.), *New Studies in Theology* I (London 1980), p. 102: 'The significant fourth century development which precludes the Cappadocians from regarding God as an intellectual monad is [for Lossky] the maturation of Trinitarian theology, the final agreement that between the *homoousion* and pure Arianism there was no middle way. Clement's solution [in treating the Father, and, especially the 'depths' of his hypostasis as the only true locus of transcendence] thus ceases to be an option; and Origen's attempts to modify this by speaking of a vision of the Father "in" and "with" the Logos, while continuing to treat "the Father" as "co-terminous with the divine simplicity", is equally inadmissible. Once it is firmly established that the three persons of the Godhead are in all respects equal, there can be no doubt that "to see God is to contemplate the Trinity" . . . '. See also an internal citation of V. Lossky, *The Vision of God* (London 1963), p. 68. But on this entire question, compare Garrigues with Williams; see J.–M. Garrigues, 'Theologie et monarchie. L'entrée dans le mystère du "sein du Père" comme ligne directrice de la théologie apophatique dans la tradition orientale', *Istina* 15 (4) (1970), pp. 435–65.

26. W. Kasper, *The God of Jesus Christ* (Et New York 1991), p. 261.

27. In his preface to Lossky's study of Eckhart, Gilson states that Lossky – rightly – identified the heart of Eckhart's teaching as a doctrine of the ineffability of God. See V. Lossky, *Théologie négative et connaissance de Dieu chez Maître Eckhart* (Paris 1960), p. 10. And, a few pages later (p. 13) Lossky himself can write *à propos* of Eckhart's

teaching on the *nomen innominabile* : 'What else is indeed a negative way save a quest where one sees oneself obliged successively to reject all that can be found and named – denying finally the very quest itself, inasmuch as it still implied the idea of that which is being sought.'

28.   Indeed, one of the criticisms made of Palamism by Western theologians is that it seems excessively cataphatic! It takes an analogy drawn from the created world and applies it to God in an effort to understand what lies beyond all earthly comparison.

Chapter III: *John Meyendorff and neo-Palamism*

1.   J. Meyendorff, *Gregoire Palamas. Défense des saints hésychastes* (Louvain 1959).

2.   J. Meyendorff, *Introduction à l'Étude de saint Grégoire Palamas* (Paris 1959). Published in English translation as, *A Study of Gregory Palamas* (London 1962). See also, J. Meyendorff, *Saint Grégoire Palamas et la mystique orthodoxe* (Paris 1959).

3.   J. Meyendorff, *Byzantine Theology: Historical Trends and Doctrinal Themes* (Crestwood, NY., 1974; 2nd edn New York 1979). See also, J. Meyendorff, *Le Christ dans la théologie byzantine* (Paris 1969). Published in English translation as, *Christ in Eastern Christian Thought* (Washington 1969).

4.   J. Meyendorff, *Byzantium and the Rise of Russia. A Study of Byzantine-Russian Relations in the Fourteenth Century* (Cambridge 1981).

5.   Ibid., p. 3.

6.   J. Meyendorff, *Imperial Unity and Christian Divisions* (Crestwood, NY., 1989).

7.   For his account of the ecclesiological background to the Catholic-Orthodox schism, see, in addition to the works already cited, *Orthodoxy and Catholicity* (New York 1965).

8.   K. T. Ware notes that, during his time in prison, Palamas sent his works to the Grand Master of the Hospitallers at Rhodes and, some few years later, expounded his views to the papal legate, Paul of Smyrna, during the latter's visit to Constantinople in 1355. See K. T. Ware, 'The Debate about Palamism', *Eastern Churches Review* IX (1977), p. 58. Palamism was not regarded as an obstacle to reunion at Florence, interestingly.

9.   *Homilies* XV.20, with an internal citation of Psalm 24.

10. The connection between *hesuchia* and the invocation of the 'memory of Jesus' had been made as early as John Climacus: see his *Ladder*, 27.

11. For anticipations of the Hesychast understanding of the 'Light of Thabor', see G. Habra, *La Transfiguration selon les Pères grecs* (Paris 1973).

12. 'Palamite' theologians would include such masters as Lossky, Florovsky, Evdokimov, Staniloae, Yannaras, and Olivier Clément.

13. Yet in the eighteenth century, when scholars on Mount Athos collected and edited spiritual writings in the *Philokalia*, they did not conceal the differences between the early Greek Fathers – St Maximus Confessor with his more developed theology, Symeon the New Theologian and the thirteenth and fourteenth century Hesychasts whose methods of prayer Palamas defended. According to George Every, they regarded these differences as analogous to those found in the spiritual development of the individual 'who comes to deeper insight through many tribulations'. See G. Every, 'The Study of Eastern Orthodoxy: Hesychasm', *Religion* IX.1 (1979), p. 76.

14. M. Jugie, 'Palamisme', *Dictionnaire de Théologie Catholique* XI (1932), cols. 1735–1818. For earlier negative references to Palamism by seventeenth century Catholics and nineteenth century Anglicans, see K. T. Ware, 'The Debate about Palamism', *Eastern Churches Review* IX (1977), p. 45.

15. J. Meyendorff, *Byzantine Theology. Historical Trends and Doctrinal Themes* (Crestwood, NY., 1974; 2nd edn New York 1979), p. 2.

16. Ibid., p.3.

17. Ibid.

18. Ibid., pp. 8–9. See also K. T. Ware, 'The Debate about Palamism', *Eastern Churches Review* IX (1977), p. 46. Relevant here is Ware's statement that there is room in theology for 'antinomy', seen as ' . . . the affirmation of two contrasting or opposed truths which cannot be reconciled on the level of the discursive reason although a reconciliation is possible on the higher level of contemplative experience.'

19. J. Meyendorff, *Byzantine Theology. Historical Trends and Doctrinal Themes* (Crestwood, NY 1974; 2nd edn New York 1979), p. 9.

20. J. Meyendorff, *A Study of Gregory Palamas* (London 1962), p. 154.

21. 2 Pet 1:4.

22. Cf. J. Meyendorff, *Byzantine Theology. Historical Trends and Doctrinal Themes* (Crestwood, NY., 1974; 2nd edn New York 1979), p. 9. Meyendorff's affirmation is that Byzantine gnoseology, with its claim

that a direct experience of God is possible for man, is ' . . . precisely founded upon a sacramental, and therefore hierarchically structured ecclesiology, which gives a christological and pneumatological basis to personal experience, and presupposes that Christian theology must always be consistent with the apostolic and patrisitic witness.' Some Western Christians would prefer to interpret this communion in terms of intention – as will or love – but, as Gabriel Patacsi has pointed out, '. . . every "intentional" union presupposes already a prior "entitative" union.' See G. Patacsi, 'Palamism before Palamas', *Eastern Churches Review* IX (1977), p. 66: 'All knowledge and love are in fact the fruit of a certain "touching" or of a mutual influence which, without leading to confusion of essences, happens on the level of objective being . . .'.

23. See J. Meyendorff, *Saint Grégoire Palamas et la mystique orthodoxe* (Paris 1959), p. 90. Here, Meyendorff, while admitting our ignorance as to whether Palamas's opponent, Barlaam the Calabrian, had direct acquaintance with the Nominalist philosophy of Ockham, maintains that, nonetheless, it was ' . . . in the name of Nominalism that, from his earliest theological essays, directed against the Latin theology which for him is identified with that of 'Thomas', he rejects the claim of the Latins to 'know' God and to 'demonstrate' the procession of the Holy Spirit from the Son.'

24. Endre von Ivanka, 'Palamismus und Vätertradition', in *L'Église et les églises* II (Chevetogne 1955), pp. 29–46.

25. Yves Congar, *Je crois en l'Esprit-Saint III* (Paris 1980).

26. G. Philips, 'La grâce chez les Orientaux', *Ephemerides Theologicae Lovanienses* XLVIII (1972), pp. 37–50. And two contributions by A. de Halleux, 'Palamisme et Scolastique. Exclusivisme dogmatique ou pluriformité théologique?', *Revue théologique de Louvain* IV (1973), pp. 409–42; and 'Palamisme et tradition', *Irénikon* 48 (1975), pp. 479–93.

27. J.–M. Garrigues, 'L'energie divine et la grâce chez Maxime le Confesseur', *Istina* 19 (1974), pp. 272–96.

28. J.–P. Houdret, 'Palamas et les Cappadociens', *Istina* 19 (1974), pp. 260–71.

29. G. Patacsi, 'Palamism before Palamas', *Eastern Churches Review* IX (1977), p. 66.

30. I. Trethowan, 'Irrationality in Theology and the Palamite Distinction', *Eastern Churches Review* IX (1977), pp. 19–26. See also R. D. Williams, 'The Philosophical Structure of Palamism', *Eastern Churches Review* IX (1977), pp. 27–44.

31.   K. T. Ware, 'The Debate about Palamism', *Eastern Churches Review* IX (1977), p. 46.
32.   M. Jugie, 'Palamisme', *Dictionnaire de Théologie catholique* XI (1932).
33.   S. Guichardan, *Le problème de la simplicité divine en Orient et en Occident au XIVe siècle: Grégoire Palamas, Duns Scotus, Gennadios Scholarios* (Lyons 1933).
34.   J. Meyendorff, 'The Holy Trinity in Palamite Theology', in *Trinitarian Theology East and West* (Brookline, Mass., 1977), pp. 25–43.
35.   Cf. B. Krivocheine, 'Simplicité de la nature et des distinctions en Dieu selon S. Grégoire de Nysse', *Messager de l'Exarchat du Patriarche russe en Occident* XXIII (1975), pp. 133–58. Ware at least accepts the divine simplicity – 'antinomically' affirmed with the Palamite distinction, 'The Debate about Palamism', *Eastern Churches Review* IX (1977), p. 49.
36.   C. Yannaras, 'The Distinction between Essence and Energies and its Importance for Theology', *St Vladimir's Seminary Quarterly* XIX (1975), p. 244.

Chapter IV: *Sergei Bulgakov and Sophiology*

1.   On Bulgakov's life, see W. F. Crum, 'Sergius N. Bulgakov: from Marxism to Sophiology', *Saint Vladimir's Theological Quarterly* 27 (1983), pp. 3–26.
2.   Cited in J. Pain and N. Zernov (ed.), *A Bulgakov Anthology* (London 1976), p. 3.
3.   For Bulgakov's literary output, see K. Naumov (ed.), *Bibliographie des oeuvres de Serge Boulgakov* (Paris 1984).
4.   C. Graves, *The Holy Spirit in the Theology of Sergei Bulgakov* (Geneva 1972), p. 3.
5.   L. Bouyer, 'An Introduction to the Theme of Wisdom and Creation in the Tradition', *Le Messager orthodoxe* 98 (1985), pp. 149–61, and here at p. 141.
6.   P. Florensky, *Stolp i utverzhdenie istiny* (Moscow 1914).
7.   S. N. Bulgakov, *Svet nevechernii: Sozertsania i umozreniia* (Moscow 1917).
8.   S. N. Bulgakov, *Autobiographicheskie Zametki* (Paris 1946).
9.   Bulgakov's books which make up the 'little trilogy' are: *Kupina neopalimaia* (Paris 1927) – 'The Unburnable Bush' on Our Lady; *Drug*

zhenikha (Paris 1927) – 'The Friend of the Bridegroom' on John the Baptist; and *Lestvitsa Jakovlia* (Paris 1929) – 'Jacob's Ladder' on the angels.

10.   The 'great trilogy' is made up as: *Agnets Bozhii* (Paris 1933) – 'The Lamb of God', which is Bulgakov's Christology; *Uteshitel'* (Paris 1936) –'The Comforter', which is his pneumatology; and *Nevesta Agnitsa* (Paris 1946) – 'The Bride of the Lamb', his ecclesiology.

11.   For their interconnexion, see the major study of Bulgakov's pneumatology, C. Graves, *The Holy Spirit in the Theology of Sergei Bulgakov* (Geneva 1972), p. 3.

12.   *Agnets Bozhii* (Paris 1933), p. 122.

13.   C. Graves, *The Holy Spirit in the Theology of Sergei Bulgakov* (Geneva 1972), p. 7.

14.   See C. Lialine, 'Le débat sophiologique', *Irénikon* XIII (1936), pp. 168–205.

15.   For example, *Svet nevechernii* (Moscow 1917), p. 212: Sophia is 'a special fourth hypostasis of another order . . . the beginning of a new creaturely multihypostaticity'.

16.   S. N. Bulgakov, 'Ipostas i ipostasnost' ('Hypostasis and hypostaseity') , *Sbornik Statei, Posviashchenniikh Petru Berngardovichu Struve* (Prague 1925), pp. 353–71.

17.   See Endre von Ivanka (ed.), 'Die Lehre von der göttlichen Weisheit (Sophia-Lehre)', *Handbuch der Ostkirchlichenkunde* (Dusseldorf 1971), pp. 143–56. In this essay, von Ivanka describes sophiology as *neurussiche Gnosis:* a confusion of natural, philosophical knowledge with the supernatural knowledge of faith, plus elements of mysticism both natural and supernatural as well. However, sophiology conceived as an 'artistic and intuitive' approach to the eternal beauty disclosed in the creation is treated more kindly.

18.   S. N. Bulgakov, *O Sofii, Premudrost' Bozhii* (Paris 1935); and, later, *The Wisdom of God. A Brief Summary of Sophiology* (London 1937).

19.   S. N. Bulgakov, *The Wisdom of God. A Brief Summary of Sophiology* (London 1937), p. 18.

20.   B. Newman, 'Sergius Bulgakov and the Theology of Divine Wisdom', *Saint Vladimir's Theological Quarterly* 22 (1978), p. 53.

21.   S. N. Bulgakov, *The Wisdom of God. A Brief Summary of Sophiology* (London 1937), p. 34.

22.   C. Andronikof, 'Préface', K. Naumov (ed.), *Bibliographie des oeuvres de Serge Boulgakov* (Paris 1984), p. 40.

23. C. Andronikof, 'Le problématique sophianique', *Le Messager orthodoxe* 98 (1985), pp. 46–7.

24. L. Zander, *Bog i Mir*, I (Paris 1946), pp. 194–5.

25. S. N. Bulgakov, *Ikon i ikonopochitanie* (Paris 1931), pp. 51–2.

26. Ibid.

27 C. Andronikof, 'Le problématique sophianique', *Le Messager orthodoxe* 98 (1985), p. 56.

28. B. Newman, 'Sergius Bulgakov and the Theology of Divine Wisdom', *Saint Vladimir's Theological Quarterly* 22 (1978), p. 73.

Chapter V: *John Romanides and neo-Photianism*

1. B. de Margerie, *The Christian Trinity in History* (Et, Stillwater, Mass. 1982), p. 161.

2. Ibid., p. 162.

3. Ibid, pp. 165–6. For the address by Paulinus, see J. D. Mansi, *Sacrorum conciliorum nova et amplissima collectio* XIII (Florence 1757–89), cols. 834–45.

4. J. Gill, 'Filioque', *New Catholic Encyclopaedia* 5 (Washington, D.C. 1967), p. 914.

5. H. Denzinger and A. Schonmetzer (eds), *Enchiridion Symbolorum, Definitionum et Declarationum de Rebus Fidei et Morum* (Freiburg 1963), 32nd ed., 850, p. 275.

6. Ibid., 1301, p. 331.

7. J. Romanides, *To protopaterikon hamartêma* ('The Sin of our First Father') (Athens 1957 and, 2nd ed., 1989).

8. J. Romanides, *Rômaiosunê, Romania, Roumelê* (Thessalonica 1975).

9. J. Romanides, *Franks, Romans, Feudalism and Doctrine. The Interplay between Theology and Society* (Brookline, Mass., 1981).

10. Ibid., p. 60. An important element in the reconstruction by Romanides of the aetiology of the *Filioque* dispute here is his presentation of the role of Pope Nicholas I in the Frankish-Byzantine dispute over the infant Bulgarian Church. But J. Meijer, *A Successful Council of Union. A Theological Analysis of the Photian Synod of 879–80* (Thessalonica 1975) concludes that Nicholas was anxious to '*curtail* the influence of the Franks . . . in Bulgaria' (my italics). Meijer claims support for his view in works by J. Karmiris and B. Laourda, two Greek Orthodox writers. See J. Karmiris, 'The Schism of the Roman Church', *Theologia* 21

(1950), p. 415; and B. Laourda, 'Ho patriarchês Photios kai hê epochê sou', *Gregorios ho Palamos* 38 (1955), p. 69.

11.   J. Romanides, *Franks, Romans, Feudalism and Doctrine. The Interplay between Theology and Society* (Brookline, Mass. 1981), p. 62.

12.   Ibid., p. 63.

13.   Ibid., p. 73.

14.   Ibid., p. 76.

15.   J. Romanides, *Dogmatikê kai sumbolikê theologia tês Orthodoxou katholikês Ekklêsias* I (Thessalonika 1973), pp. 10–19.

16.   J. Romanides, *Franks, Romans, Feudalism and Doctrine. The Interplay between Theology and Society* (Brookline, Mass. 1981), p. 95.

17.   Ibid., pp. 94–5.

18.   Ibid., p. 64.

19.   A. Nichols, 'The Reception of St Augustine and his Work in the Byzantine-Slav Tradition', *Angelicum* 64 (1987), pp. 437–52; republished in idem., *Scribe of the Kingdom. Essays on Theology and Culture* (London, 1994), I, pp. 113–26.

20.   For details of the document, and those arising later from the working group, see H. G. Link (ed.), *Apostolic Faith Today. A Handbook for Study* (Geneva 1985), pp. 180–1.

21.   Ibid., p. 183.

22.   Ibid., p. 187.

23.   Ibid., pp. 245–56.

24.   Ibid., p. 249.

25.   Ibid., p. 234.

26.   Ibid., p. 237.

27.   Ibid.

28.   For the harm done by Lossky's speculation on the ecclesiological consequences of the *Filioque*, see H.–M. Legrand's comments in *Revue des Sciences Philosophiques et Théologiques* 56 (1972), pp. 697–700. A balanced view is that of the late Professor Nikos Nissiotis. On the one hand he regarded the Catholic 'distortion' of the primacy as owed to the lack of a pneumatological ecclesiology, while on the other hand recognising a nugget of truth in the view that the East, by Mono-patrism, has absorbed the procession of the Son into that of the Spirit and thus absorbed the visible messianic mission of Christ in his (Roman) vicar by the invisible mission of the Spirit as unifying principle within the Church. See N. Nissiotis, 'The Main Ecclesiological Problem of the Second Vatican Council', *Journal of Ecumenical Studies* 2,

1. Nissiotis believed that, just as the Son, in the Trinity, is the centre of the union between Father and Spirit, so in ecclesiology the communion of sister churches which makes up the universal Church must have a centre of communion. The mission of the Spirit is always exercised under the influence of Christ the Head.

29. For this text, see C. Davey and K. Ware (eds), *Anglican–Orthodox Dialogue, 1920–1976* (London 1977).

30. *The Dublin Agreed Statement, 1984* (London 1985).

31. See R. A. Lowrey, 'The Filioque Clause of the Creed in Recent Ecumenical Dialogue'. In this essay, published by the Pontifical University of St Thomas (Rome 1987), Lowrey cites (p. 50), Paragraph 7 of the *Anglican–Orthodox Joint Doctrinal Discussions. The Filioque Clause. Comments received from the Vatican Secretariat for Promoting Christian Unity*.

32. G. Marchesi, 'La questione del *Filioque* oggi', *CiviltààCattolica* (1982), pp. 533–47.

33. B. de Margerie, *The Christian Trinity in History* (Et, Stillwater, Mass. 1982), pp. 168–74. He makes special reference to the Johannine Apocalypse and notably to Apoc 22:1 – but also to Apoc 1:16 and 19:15.

34. In fact, one rite of the Oriental Catholic Churches has chosen to incorporate it, namely the Greek-Albanian rite in use in Calabria and at the monastery of Grottaferrata. This policy has been established since the first half of the eighteenth century. In 1988, however, the Latin rite bishops of Greece itself, with the consent of the Holy See, removed the clause from the Creed as recited in the Mass. This concession by Rome appears to hold good only when the Roman Liturgy is celebrated in the Greek language within the territorial jurisdiction of the Greek State itself.

Chapter VI: *Panagiotis Trembelas and Orthodox Christology*

1. See D. Staniloae, 'The Christology of the Synods', *Ekklesiastikos Pharos* 56 (1976), pp. 130–7.

2. A fuller account is given in A. Nichols, *Rome and the Eastern Churches* (Edinburgh 1992), pp. 55–73.

3. F.–J. Nieman, *Jesus als Glaubensgrund in der Fundamentaltheologie der Neuzeit. Zur Genealogie einer Traktat* (Innsbrück and Vienna 1983).

4. See A. Nichols, *Byzantine Gospel: Maximus the Confessor in Modern Scholarship* (Edinburgh 1993).

5.   It should be noted however that the Russian theologians of the diaspora, even when applauding the condemnation of the sophianic Christology, can show a strong undercurrent of sympathy for Bulgakov. See, for example, the quasi-official history of the Paris Seminary by Alexei Kniazeff, *L'Institut Saint-Serge de Paris* (Paris 1974). The recognition that Christology cries out for a general Christian picture of the world to undergird and reinforce it (such as we find in Maximus or Thomas) evidently leads to the feeling that those who try to provide one must be treated with kindness when they fail.

6.   P. Trembelas, *Dogmatikê tês Orthodoxou Katholikês Ekklêsias* (Athens 1959–61; 2nd edn 1978).

7.   Ibid., p. 1.

8.   Ibid., p. 7.

9.   Ibid.

10.   Ibid., p. 26.

11.   See K. T. Ware in the *Eastern Churches Review* III, 4 (Autumn 1971), pp. 477–80. Bishop Ware makes the following criticism: 'The whole scheme of the *Dogmatiki*, the order and arrangement of subjects, the treatment of each topic, much of the terminology and categories invoked, bear unmistakably the stamp of the West . . . While the *content* of his book is unwaveringly Orthodox, the *method* is definitely occidental.'

12.   P. Trembelas, *Dogmatikê tês Orthodoxou Katholikês Ekklêsias* (Athens 1959–61; 2nd edn 1978).

13.   Ibid., II, p. 19.

14.   H. L. Martensen, *Den christelige Dogmatik* (Copenhagen 1849. A fourth edition was published in 1883.) Trembelas would presumably have known the German translation, first published at Kiel in 1850 with a fourth edition following at Leipzig in 1897.

15.   P. Trembelas, *Dogmatikê tês Orthodoxou Katholikês Ekklêsias* (Athens 1959–61; 2nd edn 1978), II, p. 82.

16.   Ibid., p. 117.

17.   P. Galtier, 'Les anathématismes de s. Cyrille et le Concile de Chalcédoine', *Recherches de Science Religieuse* 23 (1933), pp. 45–57.

18.   A. Gaudel, 'La théologie de l'*assumptus homo*: histoire et valeur doctrinale', *Revue des Sciences Religieuses* 17 (1937), pp. 64–90, 219–34; 18 (1938), pp. 45–71, 201–17.

19.   For de Basly's work, see J. Kaup, 'Basly, Déodat-Marie', *Lexikon für Theologie und Kirche* 2 (Freiburg 1958 and 1986), cols 47–8. For more

on this intriguing figure see L. Seiller, *La France franciscaine* 20 (1937), in which there is a bibliography, pp. 95–112, together with an appreciation, pp. 167–84.

20. H. Diepen, 'Un Scotisme apocryphe: la christologie du P. Déodat de Basly', *Revue Thomiste* XLIX (1949), pp. 428–92.

21. For more on the whole controversy, see J. McWilliam, 'Patristic Scholarship in the Aftermath of the Modernist Crisis', *Anglican Theological Review* XLVIII, 2 (1986), pp. 106–23.

22. W. Kasper, *Jesus the Christ* (Et London 1976), pp. 243–9.

Chapter VII: *Nikolai Afanas'ev and Ecclesiology*

1. P. K. Christoff, *An Introduction to Nineteenth Century Russian Slavophilism. A Study in Ideas: I – A. S. Xomjakow* (The Hague 1961).

2. For the repercussions of the non-reception of Florence, see B. Schultze, 'A. S. Chomjakow und das Halb-Tausend Jubilaum des Einigungkonzils von Florenz', *Orientalia Christiana Periodica* 3 (1938), pp. 473–96.

3. The theme of P. P. O'Leary, *The Triune Church. A Study in the Ecclesiology of A. S. Xomjakov* (Dublin 1982).

4. The thesis of his *L'Eglise latine et le protestantisme au point de vue de l'Église d'Orient* (Lausanne 1872).

5. P. P. O'Leary, *The Triune Church. A Study in the Ecclesiology of A. S. Xomjakov* (Dublin 1982), pp. 58–82, 112–15, 153–164.

6. P. Duprey, 'La structure synodale de l'Église dans la théologie orientale', *Proche Orient Chrétien* 20 (1970), pp. 1–22.

7. P. K. Christoff, *An Introduction to Nineteenth Century Russian Slavophilism. A Study in Ideas: I – A. S. Xomjakow* (The Hague 1961), p. 94.

8. T. Andreev, 'Moskovskaia dukhovnaia akademiia i Slav'ianofili', *Bogoslovskii Vestnik* 3 (1915), pp. 563–644.

9. S. Swierkosz, *L'Église visible selon Serge Bulgakov. Structure hiérarchique et sacramentelle* (Rome 1980), pp. 17–28.

10. For a much fuller account see A. Nichols, *Theology in the Russian Diaspora. Church, Fathers, Eucharist in Nikolai Afanas'ev, 1893–1966* (Cambridge 1989).

11. N. Afanasijev, *Državna vlast na vaseljenskim saborima* (Skoplje 1927). See also (under the Russian, rather than Serbian, spelling of his surname), N. Afanas'ev, 'Provintsial'nye sobrania Rimskoi imperii i

vselenskie sobori. K voprosu ob uchastii gosudarstvennoi vlasti na vselenskikh soborakh', *Zapiski Russkogo nauchnago instituta v Belgrade* 5 (1931), pp. 25–46.

12.   N. Afanas'ev, 'Dve idei vselenskoi Tserkvi' ('Two Ideas of the Church Universal'), *Put'* 45 (1934), pp. 16–29.

13.   N. Afanas'ev, *Trapeza gospodnia* ('The Lord's Table') (Paris 1952); and *Tserkov' Dukha Sviatogo* ('Church of the Holy Spirit') (Paris 1971). The latter appeared soon after publication in a French translation, *L'Eglise du Saint-Esprit* (Paris 1975).

14.   N. Afanas'ev, 'L'Église qui preside dans l'Amour' in N. Afanas-sieff *et al* , *La primauté de Pierre dans l'Église orthodoxe* (Neuchâtel 1960), pp. 7–64. There is an English translation of the latter – with the name of his (presumably better known) fellow-Russian theologian, J. Meyen-dorff, placed first on the title page – published as *The Primacy of Peter in the Orthodox Church* (London 1963). See especially, pp. 57–110.

15.   K. C. Felmy, 'Petrusamt und Primat in der modernen orthodoxen Theologie', in H. J. Mund (ed.), *Das Petrusamt in der gegenwärtigen theologischen Diskussion* (Paderborn 1976), pp. 85–99.

16.   H.–J. Schulz, *The Byzantine Liturgy* (Et New York 1986), pp. xix–xx.

17.   J. Meyendorff, *Byzantine Theology* (Et London 1974), p. 6.

Chapter VIII: *George Florovsky and the Idea of Tradition*

1.   F. L. Shaw, 'An Introduction to the Study of Georges Florovsky', (Ph.D thesis, Cambridge 1991), p. 24. Shaw's writings on Florovsky's intellectual development via the disciplines of philosophical psychology and the philosophy of history, add considerably to the biographical information otherwise available. See especially T. E. Bird, 'In Memoriam Georges Florovsky, 1893–1979', *Greek Orthodox Theological Review* 24 (1979), pp. 342–50. See also, G. H. Williams 'Georges Vasilievich Florovsky: His American Career, 1948–1965', *Greek Orthodox Theological Review* XI, 1 (1965), pp. 7–107, though this ranges more widely than the title would suggest.

2.   G. Florovsky, 'On the Mechanism of Reflex Salivary Secretion', *Bullétin de l'Académie impériale des Sciences* 2 (1917), pp. 119–36.

3.   C. Dawson, *Religion and the Rise of Western Culture* (London 1950), is the fullest expression of the thesis first stated in Dawson's *Progress and*

Religion (London 1929). On Dawson's work, see C. Scott, *A Historian and his World. A Life of Christopher Dawson, 1889–1970* (London 1984).

4. Florovsky's essay was published in *Ishkod k vostoku* (Sofia 1921), pp. 28–39. The book Florovsky refers to here is is one of the most celebrated of the works of Oswald Spengler, the German analyst of cultural history. See O. Spengler, *Der Untergang des Abendlandes. Umrisse einer Morphologie der Weltgeschichte* (Munich 1920–22).

5. G. Florovsky, *The Ways of Russian Theology* (Et Vaduz 1987).

6. G. Florovsky, 'Westliche Einflüsse in der russischen Theologie', *Kyrios* 2 (1937), pp. 1–22. See, too, G. Florovsky, 'Patristics and Modern Theology', *Procès verbaux du Premier Congrès de théologie orthodoxe* (Athens 1939), pp. 238–42.

7. F. L. Shaw, 'An Introduction to the Study of Georges Florovsky', (Ph.D thesis, Cambridge 1991).

8. See especially G. Florovsky, 'The Predicament of the Christian Historian', in W. Leibrecht (ed.), *Religion and Culture: Essays in Honour of Paul Tillich* (New York 1959), p. 60, where he writes: 'The decisive contribution of the Christian faith to the understanding of history was not in the detection of the radical 'historicity' of man's existence, that is, of his finite relativity, but precisely in *the discovery of perspective in history*, in which man's historical existence acquires relevance and meaning.' (Florovsky's italics.)

9. F. L. Shaw, 'An Introduction to the Study of Georges Florovsky', (Ph.D thesis, Cambridge 1991).

10. G. Florovsky, 'The Christological Dogma and its Terminology (and Discussion Notes)', in P. Gregorios *et al* (eds), *Does Chalcedon Divide or Unite? Towards Convergence in Orthodox Christology* (Geneva 1981), pp. 121–6.

11. This is one of the poles of Florovsky's 'Empire and the Desert: Antinomies of Christian History', *Greek Orthodox Theological Review* III, 2 (1957), pp. 133–59. Further illuminating asides on the imperial idea in Christian thought are found in 'Vladimir Soloviev and Dante: the Problem of Christian Empire', *For Roman Jakobson. Essays on the Occasion of his Sixtieth Birthday* (The Hague 1956), pp. 152–60.

12. L. Ouspensky and V. Lossky, *The Meaning of Icons* (Et Crestwood, NY., 1983), p. 47.

13. G. Florovsky, *Bible, Church, Tradition* (Et Belmont, Mass., 1972, and Vaduz, Liechtenstein, 1987).

14. Ibid., p. 40.

15. Ibid., p. 44.
16. Ibid., p. 46.
17. Ibid.
18. Ibid., p. 47.
19. Ibid.
20. Ibid., p. 48.
21. Ibid., p. 49.
22. Ibid., p. 52.
23. F. L. Shaw, 'An Introduction to the Study of Georges Florovsky', (Ph.D thesis, Cambridge 1991) , pp. 5–6.

Chapter IX: *Alexander Schmemann and Liturgical Theology*

1. J. Meyendorff, 'A Life Worth Living', *St Vladimir's Theological Quarterly* (1984), pp. 3–10, and here at p. 3.
2. Ibid., p. 5.
3, Ibid.
4. Ibid., p. 6.
5. A. Schmemann, *Introduction to Liturgical Theology* (Et London 1966), p. 10.
6. Ibid., pp. 12–13.
7. Ibid., p. 29.
8. Ibid., pp. 19–20.
9. A. Schmemann, *The Eucharist. Sacrament of the Kingdom* (Et Crestwood, NY., 1988).
10. A. Schmemann, *Of Water and the Spirit. A Liturgical Study of Baptism* (Crestwood, NY., 1974).
11. A. Schmemann, *Great Lent* (Crestwood, NY., 1974).
12. A. Schmemann, *The World as Sacrament* (London 1966).
13. A. Schmemann, *Introduction to Liturgical Theology* (Et London 1966), p. 25.
14. A. Schmemann, *Church, World, Mission: Reflections on Orthodoxy in the West* (Crestwood, NY., 1979).
15. A. Schmemann, *Introduction to Liturgical Theology* (Et London 1966), pp. 32–3.
16. On Casel's work, see T. Filthaut, *Die Kontroverse über die Mysterienlehre* (Darendorf 1947).

17. A. Schmemann, *Introduction to Liturgical Theology* (Et London 1966), p. 41.
18. Ibid., pp. 49–50.
19. Ibid., p. 56.
20. A. Grabar, *Recherches sur le culte des reliques et l'art chrétien antique* (Paris 1943–46). Published in two volumes over these years.
21. A. Schmemann, *Introduction to Liturgical Theology* (Et London 1966), p. 92.
22. Ibid., p. 99.
23. Ibid., p. 104.
24. Ibid., p. 106. Schmemann is indebted here to remarks in L. Bouyer, *L'Incarnation et l'Église corps du Christ dans la théologie de saint Athanase* (Paris 1943).
25. A. Schmemann, *Introduction to Liturgical Theology* (Et London 1966), p. 128.
26. Ibid., p. 164.

Chapter X: *Panagiotis Nellas and Anthropology*

1. K. T. Ware, 'Foreword', in P. Nellas, *Deification in Christ. Orthodox Perspectives on the Nature of the Human Person* (Et Crestwood, NY., 1987), pp. 9–10.
2. *Prolegomena eis tên meletin Nikolaou tou Kabasila* (Athens 1968).
3. *I peri dikaioseôs tou anthrôpou didaskalia Nikolaou tou Kabasila* ('The Teaching of Nikolas Kabasilas on Justification: A Contribution to Orthodox Soteriology') (Peiraeos 1975).
4. K. T. Ware, 'Foreword', in P. Nellas, *Deification in Christ. Orthodox Perspectives on the Nature of the Human Person* (Et Crestwood, NY., 1987), p. 11.
5. P. Nellas, *Deification in Christ. Orthodox Perspectives on the Nature of the Human Person* (Et Crestwood, NY., 1987), pp. 15–16.
6. Ibid.
7. Gregory of Nyssa, *On the Creation of Man*, II. Cited in P. Nellas, *Deification in Christ. Orthodox Perspectives on the Nature of the Human Person* (Et Crestwood, NY., 1987), p. 22
8. Col 1:15–18.
9. 1 Cor 15:49; Eph 4:13–14.

10.   P. Nellas, *Deification in Christ. Orthodox Perspectives on the Nature of the Human Person* (Et Crestwood, NY., 1987), p. 25.
11.   Ibid., pp. 26–7.
12.   Ibid., p. 28.
13.   Ibid., p. 30.
14.   Ibid., p. 33.
15.   Ibid., p. 35.
16.   Ibid., p. 36.
17.   Ibid., p. 38, with internal citations of (in order) Col. 1:18; Kabasilas, *Life in Christ*, 2; I Cor 11:1, 3; Kabasilas, *Life in Christ*, 4; and Basil's *On the Nativity of Christ*, 6.

Chapter XI: *Christos Yannaras and Theological Ethics*

1.   K. T. Ware, 'Introduction', in C. Yannaras, *The Freedom of Morality* (Et Crestwood, NY 1984), p. 10.
2.   However, one should not overlook in Yannaras a certain indebtedness to traditional metaphysics: for instance, in his acceptance of a physico-logical account of God's existence and attributes based on the idea of the First Cause. Thus, see C. Yannaras, *Elements of Faith. An Introduction to Orthodox Theology* (Et Edinburgh 1991), pp. 6–7. See also, C. Yannaras, *The Freedom of Morality* (Et Crestwood, NY., 1984), pp. 14–15.
3.   Gregory Palamas, *In Defence of the Holy Hesychasts* III, pp. 2–12.
4.   C. Yannaras, *The Freedom of Morality* (Et Crestwood, NY., 1984), p. 19. On the personalism to be found in Yannaras, see R. D. Williams, 'The Theology of Personhood', *Sobornost* VI, 6 (1972), pp. 415–30.
5.   C. Yannaras, *The Freedom of Morality* (Et Crestwood, NY., 1984), p. 25.
6.   Ibid., pp. 25–6.
7.   Ibid., p. 29.
8.   Ibid., pp. 30–1.
9.   Ibid., p. 32.
10.   Ibid., p. 38.
11.   Ibid., p. 40.
12.   Hence the remarks Yannaras makes in *Elements of Faith* that: 'The virtue of mortal man does not interest us, but the eternity of the repentant man'. Here an 'either/or' has illicitly replaced a 'both/and'. See

C. Yannaras, *Elements of Faith. An Introduction to Orthodox Theology* (Et Edinburgh 1991), p. 147.

13. C. Yannaras, *The Freedom of Morality* (Et Crestwood, NY., 1984), p. 13.

14. Ibid., p. 52.

15. Ibid., p. 53.

16. Ibid., pp. 58–9.

17. Ibid., p. 85.

18. C. Yannaras, *Elements of Faith. An Introduction to Orthodox Theology* (Et Edinburgh 1991), p. 18.

19. C. Yannaras, *The Freedom of Morality* (Et Crestwood, NY., 1984), p. 86.

Chapter XII: *Paul Evdokimov and Eschatology*

1. O. Clément, *Orient-Occident. Deux Passeurs: Vladimir Lossky et Paul Evdokimov* (Geneva 1985), p. 106.

2. Ibid.

3. G. Vendrame, *Mistero e gloria. Introduzione al pensiero religioso di Paul Evdokimov* (Rome 1976), pp. 21–2.

4. P. Evdokimov, 'Quelques jalons sur un chemin de vie', *Le Buisson ardent* (Paris 1981).

5. Lev 19:33–4.

6. O. Clément, *Orient-Occident. Deux Passeurs: Vladimir Lossky et Paul Evdokimov* (Geneva 1985), p. 114.

7. P. Evdokimov, 'La Culture et l'eschatologie', *Le Semeur* 50 (1947), pp. 358–69.

8. P. Evdokimov, *L'Art de l'icône. Théologie de la beauté* (Paris 1970), p. 65.

9. Peter C. Dinh Phan, 'Culture and Eschatology: the Iconographical Vision of Paul Evdokimov' (S.T.D. thesis, Pontifical Salesian University, Rome, 1978), p. 2. See also, more fully, the same author's *Culture and Eschatology. The Iconographical Vision of Paul Evdokimov* (Berne, 1985). Cf. the comments of Dr George Pattison, Dean of King's College, Cambridge, on the phenomenon of inverse perspective whereby, in the art of the icon, we do not enclose the scene depicted within our 'point of view', but are ourselves 'looked at': 'It is, we may say, a manifestation of the eschatological world, the redeemed and

deified world, the divine life itself, reaching out into the world of the "spectator", transforming it and transfiguring it into the reality which is "represented" there.' See G. Pattison, *Art, Modernity and Faith. Restoring the Image* (London 1991), p. 130.

10.   P. Evdokimov, *L'Orthodoxie* (Neuchâtel-Paris 1958).

11.   P. Evdokimov, *Les âges de la Vie spirituelle. Des Pères du désert à nos jours* (Paris 1964), p. 47.

12.   Ibid., p. 95.

13.   Evdokimov's concern with 'radical monasticism', going into the desert to 'vomit up the interior phantom', had a profound impact on the spiritual theology of Thomas Merton, the American Cistercian. See T. Merton, *The Climate of Monastic Prayer* (Shannon 1969), p. 37–8. Merton's emphasis on compunction and dread, whereby the false and illusory persona created by one's betrayal of the image of God is frontally encountered, shows this influence particularly clearly: 'The option of absolute despair is turned into perfect hope by the pure and humble supplication of monastic prayer. The monk faces the worst, and discovers in it the hope of the best. From the darkness comes light. From death, life. From the abyss there comes, unaccountably, the mysterious gift of the Spirit sent by God to make all things new, to transform the created and redeemed world and to re-establish all things in Christ. This is the creative and healing work of the monk, accomplished in silence, in nakedness of spirit, in emptiness, in humility. It is a participation in the saving death and resurrection of Christ. Therefore every Christian may, if he so desires, enter into communion with this silence of the praying and meditating Church which is the Church of the Desert.'

The relationship between Evdokimov and Merton was explored by Bishop Rowan Williams in a paper originally presented at Oxford in 1973 and later published as an article in a collection of essays supplementary to *Sobornost*. See R. D. Williams, 'Bread in the Wilderness. The Monastic Ideal in Thomas Merton and Paul Evdokimov' in *Theology and Prayer. Essays on Monastic Themes Presented at the Orthodox-Cistercian Conference, Oxford, 1973, Sobornost* (Supplementary Papers) 3 (London 1975), pp. 78–96.

Further Reading

This list is restricted to studies in English, or English translation, of the general subject of this book.

Benz, E. (1963) *The Eastern Orthodox Church, its Thought and Life* (Et Chicago, Ill.).

Bratsiotis, P. (1968) *The Greek Orthodox Church* (Et Notre Dame, Ind.).

Bulgakov, S. B. (1935) *The Orthodox Church* (Et London).

Chrysostomos [Archbishop] (1982) *Contemporary Eastern Orthodox Thought* (Belmont, Mass.).

Fahey, M. A. (1978) 'Orthodox Ecumenism and Theology, 1970–1978',*Theological Studies* 39, pp. 446–85.

— (1983) 'Orthodox Ecumenism and Theology, 1978–1983', *Theological Studies* 44, pp. 625–92.

Gavin, F. (1962) *Some Aspects of Contemporary Greek Orthodox Thought* (New York 1962; originally published London 1923).

Johansen, A. (1961) *Theological Study in the Rumanian Orthodox Church under Communist Rule* (London).

— (1963) *Theological Study in the Russian and Bulgarian Orthodox Churches under Communist Rule* (London).

Koumantos, A. (1974) 'An Outline of the Present Theological Situation in Greece', *Sobornost* 6, 9, pp. 663–70.

Lossky, V. (1974) *Orthodox Theology: An Introduction* (Et Crestwood, NY.).

Maloney, G. A. (1976) *A History of Orthodox Theology since 1453* (Belmont, Mass.).

Meyendorff, J. (1962) *The Orthodox Church: Its Past and its Role in the World Today* (Et London).

— (1978) *Living Tradition: Orthodox Witness in the Contemporary World* (Crestwood, NY.).

Nichols, A. (1992) *Rome and the Eastern Churches. A Study in Schism* (Edinburgh 1992).

Papadopoulos, G. (1981) *Orthodoxy: Faith and Life. Christ and the Life of the Church* (Brookline, Mass.).

Schmemann, A. (1963) *The Historical Road of Eastern Orthodoxy* (Et London).

— (1969) *Russian Theology 1920–1965* (Union Theological Seminary, Va.).

Waddams, H. (1964) *Meeting the Orthodox Churches* (London).

Ware, [K.], T. (1993) *The Orthodox Church* (Harmondsworth; originally published Harmondsworth 1963).

Williams, R. D. (1989) 'Eastern Orthodox Theology', in D. Ford (ed.), *The Modern Theologians* (Oxford), II, pp. 152–70.

Yannaras, G. (1972) 'Theology in Present–Day Greece', *St Vladimir's Theological Quarterly* 16, 4, pp. 172–214.

Zernov, N. (1963) *The Russian Religious Renaissance of the Twentieth Century* (London).

Index

Abraham 103
Adam 176, 177, 178
Afanas'ev, N. 114–28, 144, 147, 164
Amphitryon 130
Andronikof, C. 71–3, 75
Apollinaris 92–3
Arius 83
Athanasius 37, 38, 53, 59, 87, 105, 173
Augustine 59, 60, 61, 77, 78, 79, 80, 82, 85, 89, 102, 103, 111, 133

Balthasar, H. U. von 180
Barth, K. 198
Basil 87
Basly, D. de 110–11
Batiffol, P. 158
Baumstark, A. 160
Bea, A. 98, 101
Belavin, T. 61
Benedict VIII 76
Berdyaev, N. 29, 96, 195
Bogolepov, A. A. 7
Botte, B. 163
Bouyer, L. 59, 60, 147, 164, 198
Bulgakov, M. 16
Bulgakov, S. B. 14, 15, 16, 17, 22, 23, 57–73, 96, 122, 123, 125, 132, 146, 195, 196
Bultmann, R. 198

Calvin, J. 112
Casel, O. 157
Cassian 111, 167
Cassiodorus 75
Ceaucescu, N. 17
Clement of Alexandria 38, 173
Clément, O. 24, 194, 197
Constantine 162
Cross, F. L. 25
Cullmann, O. 198
Cyprian 114
Cyril of Alexandria 75, 92, 106, 107, 108, 109, 110
Cyril of Jerusalem 138, 167
Cyril of Scythopolis 92

Damasus 111
Daniélou, J. 147, 160, 198
David 103
Dawson, C. 131
Denys, see Pseudo-Denys
Diepen, H. 111
Dimitrievsky, A. A. 151
Dix, G. 154, 158, 163
Dostoevsky, F. 187, 195, 196, 202
Duchesne, L. 158
Dugmore, C. W. 158, 166
Dumont, P. 98, 101
Duns Scotus 55, 111, 178
Duprey, P. 83

Eckhart, Meister　22, 25
Epiphanius　75
Eunomius　38
Eusebius　112
Evdokimov, P.　194–204

Fahey, M.　18
Festugière, A.-J.　203
Fichte, J. G.　131
Florensky, P.　59, 60, 65, 67, 96,
　134
Florovsky, G.　16, 67, 97, 128–
　45, 148, 175
Freeman, P.　158

Galtier, P.　110
Garrigues, J.-M.　52, 53
Gaudel, P.　110
Gennadios Scholarios　55
Georgievsky, E.　65
Gilson, E.　21, 37, 183, 184
Gorbachev, M.　19
Grabar, A.　162
Gregory of Cyprus　54
Gregory of Nyssa　24, 33, 172,
　173, 198
Gregory Palamas　17, 41, 43, 44–
　56, 176, 177, 183
Guichardan, S.　54

Hagenbach, R. K.　12
Halleux, A. de　52, 53
Hamilton, B.　vii
Hegel, G. W. F.　30, 58, 59, 97,
　131
Heidegger, M.　12
Henry II　76
Hildegard of Bingen　73
Hippolytus　160

Houdret, J.-P.　53
Husserl, E.　136

Ignatius of Antioch　127
Inge, W. R.　142
Irenaeus　173, 178
Ivanka, E. von　52

John, evangelist　189, 191
John the Baptist　61, 68, 103
John Paul II　180
John Chrysostom　112, 196
John Damascene　43, 102, 107,
　136, 176
John the Grammarian　92
John Maxentius　92
Joseph　32
Jugie, M.　47–8, 52, 54
Justin Martyr　163
Justinian　42

Kabasilas, N.　170, 171, 177
Kant, I.　182
Karsavin, L. P.　2, 21
Kasper, W.　38, 94, 111
Kern, C.　147, 151
Khomiakov, A. S.　31, 115–22,
　123, 124
Khrapovitsky, A.　65
Kierkegaard, S.　105
Kovalesky, E.　25
Krasnoseltsev, N. F.　151

Le Guillou, M.-J.　52
Lenin, V. I.　57
Leo the Great　92, 95, 111
Leontius of Byzantium　92, 109
Leontius of Jerusalem　92

Lossky, V. 15, 21–40, 41, 55, 67, 88, 97, 137

Marchesi, G. 90
Margarie, B. de 52, 74, 90
Maritain, J. 183, 184
Mark of Ephesus 147
Martensen, H. L. 105
Mary, Blessed Virgin 32, 61, 68
Maximus Confessor 16–17, 24, 37, 38, 42, 53, 95, 107, 134, 171, 177, 198
Mersch, E. 114
Meyendorff, Baron 40
Meyendorff, J. 3, 18, 40, 41–56, 95, 128, 147, 148
Mogila, P. 96
Möhler, J. A. 12, 114
Moses 103, 190
Mouroux, J. 29
McNulty, P. vii

Nellas, P. 170–80
Nestorius 108–9
Newman, B. 71, 73
Newman, J. H. 30, 112, 114
Nikodimos 176
Nietzsche, F. 135, 175, 187
Noah 103

O'Leary, P. 117
Oosterzee, van 101
Origen 107, 160, 173
Osorguine, J. 146
Ott, L. 11

Paul 22, 103, 108, 157, 172, 173, 179, 186
Paulinus of Aquileia 76

Pavlov, I. P. 130
Pétain, H. 196
Peter, apostle 50
Peter the Fuller 42
Peter the Great 9
Phan, P. 200
Philips, G. 53
Photius 76, 83
Pius IX 170
Pius X 28
Pius XII 111, 114
Plato 38, 102
Plotinus 38
Proclus 38
Prokopovič, F. 96
Protagoras 102
Pseudo-Denys 22, 25, 33–4, 37, 38
Pseudo-Macarius 45

Rinvolucri, M. 2
Romanides, J. 74–90
Rousseau, O. 152
Rupert of Deutz 178

Sartre, J.-P. 187
Scheeben, M. J. 12
Schelling, F. W. J. von 31, 58, 59, 111
Schmemann, A. 2, 18, 146–70
Schulz, H.-J. 127
Severus of Antioch 93
Shaw, (F.) L. 129, 133, 134, 144–5
Simansky, A. 148
Skaballanovič, M. 167
Solov'ev, V. 29, 58, 59, 60, 61, 67, 96, 130, 131
Spengler, O. 131, 132

Stalin, J.   23
Staniloae, D.   17–18
Stragorodsky, S.   65
Symeon the New Theologian   54

Tertullian   160
Teilhard de Chardin, P.   71
Theodore of Mopsuestia   93, 174
Theodoret   93
Thomas   22, 28, 37, 52, 54, 95,
   97, 108, 110
Tikhonitsky, V.   147
Tixeront, J.   12
Tolkien, J. R. R.   199
Trembelas, P.   11–12, 13, 91–
   113, 173

Trethowan, I.   54
Trotsky, L.   21

Vendrame, G.   195
Vigilius   94

Ware, K. T.   3, 54, 91, 170, 171,
   181
Welleçz, E.   166
Whitehead, A. N.   70
Willian of St Thierry   vii
Williams, R. D.   23, 24, 26, 37,
   54, 55

Yannaras, C.   13–14, 56, 170,
   181–93

Zander, L.   72